Academic
Learning
Series

Designing a
Microsoft®
Windows® 2000
Directory Services Infrastructure

Microsoft®

PUBLISHED BY
Microsoft Press
A Division of Microsoft Corporation
One Microsoft Way
Redmond, Washington 98052-6399

Copyright © 2001 by Microsoft Corporation

Library of Congress Cataloging-in-Publication Data
MCSE Training Kit : Designing a Microsoft Windows 2000 Directory Services
Infrastructure / Microsoft Corporation.
        p. cm.
   Includes index.
   ISBN 0-7356-1132-7
   ISBN 0-7356-1267-6 (Academic Learning Series)
      1. Electronic data processing personnel--Certification. 2. Microsoft
software--Examinations--Study guides. 3. Directory services (Computer network
technology) I. Title: Designing a Microsoft Windows 2000 Directory Services
Infrastructure.

   QA76.3 .M334514   2001
   005.4'4769--dc21   00-066828

Printed and bound in the United States of America.

2 3 4 5 6 7 8 9   QWT   6 5 4 3 2 1

Distributed in Canada by Penguin Books Canada Limited.

A CIP catalogue record for this book is available from the British Library.

Microsoft Press books are available through booksellers and distributors worldwide. For further information about international editions, contact your local Microsoft Corporation office or contact Microsoft Press International directly at fax (425) 706-7329. Visit our Web site at www.microsoft.com/mspress. Send comments to *tkinput@microsoft.com*.

Acquisitions Editor: Thomas Pohlmann
Project Editor: Michael Bolinger
Technical Editor: Marzena Makuta

Author: Jill Spealman

SubAssy Part No. 097-0003416
Body Part No. X08-17829

Contents

About This Book

Welcome to the *MCSE Training Kit—Designing a Microsoft Windows 2000 Directory Services Infrastructure*. This kit prepares you to analyze an organization's business and technical requirements and design a Windows 2000 directory services infrastructure.

You will learn and practice the four-stage Active Directory infrastructure design process, which includes creating a forest plan, a domain plan, an organizational unit (OU) plan, and a site topology plan. You will also learn how to create an Active Directory implementation plan, which includes planning a migration from Windows NT 4 directory services to Active Directory and planning directory service synchronization with Active Directory.

This course supports the Microsoft Certified Systems Engineer program.

Note For more information on becoming a Microsoft Certified Systems Engineer, see the section titled "The Microsoft Certified Professional Program" later in this chapter.

Each chapter in this book is divided into lessons, activities, labs, and reviews. Lessons include discussions of the key design objectives and then provide evaluations of possible decisions to be made within each design objective, and each lesson ends with a lesson summary. The activities and labs are designed to allow you to practice or demonstrate your understanding of the design objectives discussed within a chapter. Each chapter ends with a set of review questions to test your knowledge of the chapter material.

The "Getting Started" section of this introduction provides important setup instructions that describe the hardware and software requirements to use the evaluation software included in this kit.

Intended Audience

The target reader for this book is the information technology (IT) professional involved in network design (network architect, senior support professional, or consultant) who has a minimum of one year of experience implementing, administering, and configuring network operating systems, including Novell NetWare, UNIX, or Macintosh networks. The network designer has gained his or her experience in environments that have the following characteristics:

- The number of supported users ranges from 200 to more than 25,000.
- The number of physical locations ranges from 5 to more than 150.
- Typical network services and applications include file and print, database, messaging, proxy server or firewall, dial-in server, desktop management, and Web hosting.
- Connectivity needs include connecting individual offices and users at remote locations to the corporate network and connecting corporate networks to the Internet.

This book was developed for information technology (IT) professionals who need to design, plan, implement, and support Microsoft Windows 2000 Active Directory or who plan to take the related Microsoft Certified Professional exam 70-219, *Designing a Microsoft Windows 2000 Directory Services Infrastructure*.

Prerequisites

This course requires that students meet the following prerequisites:

- A working knowledge of current networking technology
- A minimum of one year of experience implementing, administering, and configuring network operating systems
- Successful completion of the Microsoft Windows 2000 MCSE Exam 70-217: *Implementing and Administering a Microsoft Windows 2000 Directory Services Infrastructure*
- Successful completion of the following core exams for the Microsoft Windows 2000 MCSE track is recommended: Exam 70-210: *Installing, Configuring, and Administering Microsoft Windows 2000 Professional*; Exam 70-215: *Installing, Configuring, and Administering Microsoft Windows 2000 Server*; Exam 70-216: *Implementing and Administering a Microsoft Windows 2000 Network Infrastructure*

Reference Materials

You might find the following reference materials useful:

- Microsoft Corporation. *Microsoft Windows 2000 Server Resource Kit.* Redmond, Washington: Microsoft Press, 2000.

- Microsoft Corporation. *MCSE Training Kit—Microsoft Windows 2000 Active Directory Services.* Redmond, Washington: Microsoft Press, 2000.

- Iseminger, David. *Active Directory Services for Microsoft Windows 2000 Technical Reference.* Redmond, Washington: Microsoft Press, 2000.

- Microsoft Corporation. *Building Enterprise Active Directory Services, Notes from the Field.* Redmond, Washington: Microsoft Press, 2000.

- Cone, Eric, *Planning for Windows 2000.* Indianapolis, Indiana: New Riders Publishing, 1999.

- Lowe-Norris, Alistair G. *Windows 2000 Active Directory Services.* Sebastopol, California: O'Reilly & Associates, 2000.

- Windows 2000 white papers and case studies, available online at *http://www.microsoft.com/windows/server/*

About the Supplemental Course Materials CD-ROM

The Supplemental Course Materials compact disc contains a variety of informational aids that may be used throughout this book. The files on the CD include interviews with Microsoft Consulting Services consultants and program managers, Windows 2000 white papers, blank copies of worksheets used for analyzing an organization's business and technical environment, online seminars, and an online version of this book. These files can be used directly from the CD-ROM or copied onto your hard disk. For more information regarding the contents of this CD-ROM, see the section titled "Getting Started" later in this introduction.

The materials on the CD supplement some of the key concepts covered in the book. You should view these materials when suggested, and then use them as a review tool while you work through the training. An online version of this book is also included on the CD with a variety of viewing options available. For information about using the online book, see the section "The Online Book" later in this introduction. (The other CD-ROM contains an evaluation edition of Windows 2000 Advanced Server.)

Features of This Book

Each chapter opens with a "Before You Begin" section, which prepares you for completing the chapter.

The chapters are then divided into lessons. Most of the chapters contain activities and labs that give you an opportunity to use and explore the design skills presented.

The "Review" section at the end of the chapter allows you to test what you have learned in the chapter's lessons.

Appendix A, "Questions and Answers," contains all of the book's questions and corresponding answers.

Notes

Several types of Notes appear throughout the lessons.

- Notes marked **Tip** contain explanations of possible results or alternative methods.
- Notes marked **Important** contain information that is essential to completing a task.
- Notes marked **Note** contain supplemental information.
- Notes marked **Caution** contain warnings about possible loss of data.
- Notes marked **More Info** contain cross-references to other critical reference material.
- Notes marked **Real World** contain references to documentation from MCS consultants, program managers, or other subject matter experts.

Conventions

The following conventions are used throughout this book.

Notational Conventions

- Characters or commands that you type appear in **bold lowercase** type.

- *Italic* in syntax statements indicates placeholders for variable information. *Italic* is also used for book titles.

- Names of files and folders appear in Title Caps, except when you are to type them directly. Unless otherwise indicated, you can use all lowercase letters when you type a filename in a dialog box or at a command prompt.

- Filename extensions appear in all lowercase.

- Acronyms appear in all uppercase.

- Monospace type represents code samples, examples of screen text, or entries that you might type at a command prompt or in initialization files.

- Square brackets [ ] are used in syntax statements to enclose optional items. For example, [*filename*] in command syntax indicates that you can choose to type a filename with the command. Type only the information within the brackets, not the brackets themselves.

- Braces { } are used in syntax statements to enclose required items. Type only the information within the braces, not the braces themselves.

- Icons represent specific sections in the book as follows:

Icon	Represents
	Supplemental course material. This material includes interviews with Microsoft Consulting Services consultants and program managers, Windows 2000 white papers, blank copies of worksheets used for analyzing an organization's business and technical environment, and online seminars. You will find these files on the book's Supplemental Course Materials CD-ROM.
	An activity or lab. You should perform the activity or lab to give yourself an opportunity to use the design skills presented in the lesson.
	Chapter review questions. These questions at the end of each chapter allow you to test what you have learned in the lessons. You will find the answers to the review questions in Appendix A, "Questions and Answers."

Fictitious Name Conventions

The content of this training kit requires the use of fictitious company and domain names in fictitious scenarios. Every effort has been made to avoid using domain names that represent live Web sites. To accomplish this, domain names for fictitious companies are represented by the first letter of the company name appended by "-100times." For example, for the fictitious company Parnell Aerospace, the main domain name will be "p-100times.com." In reality, domain names should indicate an organization's identity.

Chapter and Appendix Overview

This self-paced training course combines notes, hands-on activities and labs, professional interviews and worksheets, and review questions to teach you how to design a Windows 2000 directory services infrastructure. It is designed to be completed from beginning to end, but you can choose a customized track and complete only the sections that interest you. (See the next section, "Finding the Best Starting Point for You," for more information.) If you choose the customized track option, see the "Before You Begin" section in each chapter. Complete any preliminary work required before you begin the chapter.

The book is divided into the following chapters:

- The "About This Book" section contains a self-paced training overview and introduces the components of the training. Read this section thoroughly to get the greatest educational value from this self-paced training and to plan which lessons you will complete.

- Chapter 1, "Introduction to Active Directory," introduces you to Active Directory components, including objects, schema, domains, organizational units (OUs), trees, forests, sites, domain controllers, and the global catalog. It also introduces you to Active Directory concepts, including replication, trust relationships, group policy, DNS namespaces, and naming conventions.

- Chapter 2, "Introduction to Designing a Directory Services Infrastructure," introduces you to the tasks you need to complete before attempting to design your Active Directory infrastructure. These tasks include assembling a design team, conducting an analysis of your business environment, conducting an analysis of your technical environment, and setting up a test environment. This chapter also introduces the Active Directory infrastructure design process, which consists of creating a forest plan, creating a domain plan, creating an organizational unit (OU) plan, and creating a site topology plan.

- Chapter 3, "Creating a Forest Plan," covers how to create a forest plan, which includes designing a forest model and designing a schema modification plan. You learn how to assess an organization's forest needs and determine the number of forests it requires. You also learn how to create a schema modification policy, assess an organization's schema needs, and determine whether to modify the schema.

- Chapter 4, "Creating a Domain Plan," shows you how to create a domain plan by defining domains, defining the forest root domain, defining a domain hierarchy, naming domains, and planning DNS server deployment.

- Chapter 5, "Creating an Organizational Unit Plan," describes how to create an OU plan by defining an OU structure and then planning user accounts and groups.

- Chapter 6, "Creating a Site Topology Plan," shows you how to create a site topology plan by defining sites, placing domain controllers, defining a replication strategy, and placing global catalog servers and operations masters within a forest.

- Chapter 7, "Creating an Active Directory Implementation Plan," discusses the directory service migration and synchronization issues involved in moving from an organization's current directory service to Active Directory.

- Appendix A, "Questions and Answers," lists all of the review questions from the book showing the page number where the question appears and the suggested answer.

- Appendix B, "Base Schema Class Objects," contains a list of the basic set of schema class objects shipped with Windows 2000 Server, which can be used to determine whether you need to change the base schema and whom the changes will impact.

- Appendix C, "Base Schema Attribute Objects," contains a list of the basic set of schema attribute objects shipped with Windows 2000 Server, which can be used to determine whether you need to change the base schema and whom the changes will impact.

- The Glossary lists and defines the terms associated with your study of Windows 2000 directory services infrastructure design.

Finding the Best Starting Point for You

Because this book is self-paced, you can skip some lessons and revisit them later. Use the following table to find the best starting point for you:

If you	Follow this learning path
Are preparing to take the Microsoft Certified Professional exam 70-219, *Designing a Microsoft Windows 2000 Directory Services Infrastructure*	Read the "Getting Started" section. Then work through Chapters 1 through 7, in order.
Want to review information about specific topics from the exam	Use the "Where to Find Specific Skills in This Book" section that follows this table.

Where to Find Specific Skills in This Book

The following tables provide a list of the skills measured on certification exam 70-219, *Designing a Microsoft Windows 2000 Directory Services Infrastructure.* The tables provide the skill and where in this book you will find the lesson relating to that skill.

Note Exam skills are subject to change without prior notice and at the sole discretion of Microsoft.

Analyzing Business Requirements

Skill being measured	Location in book
Analyze the existing and planned business models	
Analyze the company model and geographical scope	Chapter 2, Lesson 2
Analyze company processes	Chapter 2, Lesson 2
Analyze the existing and planned organizational structures	
Analyze the management model	Chapter 2, Lesson 2
Analyze the company organization	Chapter 2, Lesson 2
Analyze the vendor, partner, and customer relationships	Chapter 2, Lesson 2
Analyze the acquisition plans	Chapter 2, Lesson 2

Skill being measured	Location in book
Analyze the factors that influence company strategies	
Identify company priorities	Chapter 2, Lesson 2
Identify the projected growth and growth strategy	Chapter 2, Lesson 2
Identify relevant laws and regulations	Chapter 2, Lesson 2
Identify the company's tolerance for risk	Chapter 2, Lesson 2
Identify the total cost of operations	Chapter 2, Lesson 2
Analyze the structure of IT management	
Analyze the type of administration, such as centralized or decentralized	Chapter 2, Lesson 2
Analyze the funding model	Chapter 2, Lesson 2
Analyze the use of outsourcing	Chapter 2, Lesson 2
Analyze the decision-making process	Chapter 2, Lesson 2
Analyze the change management process	Chapter 2, Lesson 2

Analyzing Technical Requirements

Skill being measured	Location in book
Evaluate the company's existing and planned technical environment	
Analyze company size and user and resource distribution	Chapter 2, Lesson 3
Assess the available connectivity between geographically remote sites	Chapter 2, Lesson 3
Assess the net available bandwidth	Chapter 2, Lesson 3
Analyze performance requirements	Chapter 2, Lesson 3
Analyze data and system access patterns	Chapter 2, Lesson 3
Analyze network roles and responsibilities	Chapter 2, Lesson 3
Analyze security considerations	Chapter 2, Lesson 3

continued

Skill being measured	Location in book
Analyze the impact of Active Directory on the existing and planned technical environment	
Assess existing systems and applications	Chapter 2, Lesson 3
Identify existing and planned upgrades and rollouts	Chapter 2, Lesson 3
Analyze technical support structure	Chapter 2, Lesson 3
Analyze existing and planned network and systems management	Chapter 2, Lesson 3
Analyze the business requirements for client computer desktop management	
Analyze end-user work needs	Chapter 2, Lesson 3
Identify technical support needs for end-users	Chapter 2, Lesson 3
Establish the required client computer environment	Chapter 2, Lesson 3

Designing a Directory Service Architecture

Skill being measured	Location in book
Design an Active Directory forest and domain structure	
Design a forest and schema structure	Chapter 3, Lessons 1 and 2
Design a domain structure	Chapter 4, Lessons 1, 2, and 3
Analyze and optimize trust relationships	Chapter 4, Lesson 3
Design an Active Directory naming strategy	
Establish the scope of Active Directory	Chapter 4, Lesson 4
Design the namespace	Chapter 4, Lesson 4
Plan DNS strategy	Chapter 4, Lesson 5
Design and plan the structure of organizational units (OUs)	
Develop an OU delegation plan	Chapter 5, Lesson 1
Plan group policy object management	Chapter 5, Lesson 1
Plan policy management for client computers	Chapter 5, Lessons 1 and 2

Skill being measured	Location in book
Plan for the coexistence of Active Directory and other directory services	
Plan directory service synchronization with Active Directory	Chapter 7, Lesson 2
Design an Active Directory site topology	
Design a replication strategy	Chapter 6, Lesson 3
Define site boundaries	Chapter 6, Lesson 1
Design a schema modification policy	
Create a schema modification policy that outlines who has control of the schema and how modifications are administered.	Chapter 3, Lesson 2
Design an Active Directory implementation plan	
Create an implementation plan that considers the directory service migration and synchronization issues involved in moving from the current directory service to Active Directory.	Chapter 7, Lessons 1 and 2

Designing Service Locations

Skill being measured	Location in book
Design the placement of operations masters	
Place operations masters, taking into account performance, fault tolerance, functionality, and manageability	Chapter 6, Lesson 4
Design the placement of global catalog servers	
Place global catalog servers, taking into account performance, fault tolerance, functionality, and manageability	Chapter 6, Lesson 4
Design the placement of domain controllers	
Place domain controllers, taking into account performance, fault tolerance, functionality, and manageability	Chapter 6, Lesson 2

continued

Skill being measured	Location in book
Design the placement of DNS servers	
Place DNS servers, taking into account performance, fault tolerance, functionality, and manageability	Chapter 4, Lesson 5
Plan for the interoperability with the existing DNS	Chapter 4, Lesson 5

Getting Started

This self-paced training course contains activities and labs to help you learn how to design a Windows 2000 directory services infrastructure. To complete all of the activities and labs, you must have one computer running Windows 2000 Advanced Server.

It is recommended that you set up the server on its own network specifically for this self-paced training because, in the event of an inadvertent change to the server, you can avoid the possibility of undesirable results if you are connected to a larger network.

Hardware Requirements

To successfully run the evaluation edition of Windows 2000 Advanced Server, all hardware should be on the Microsoft Windows 2000 Hardware Compatibility List (HCL). The latest version of the HCL can be downloaded from the Hardware Compatibility List Web page at *http://www.microsoft.com/hwtest/hcl/*. Each computer must have the following minimum configuration:

- 133 MHz or higher Pentium-compatible CPU
- 256 MB of RAM recommended minimum (128 MB minimum supported; 8 GB maximum).
- 2 GB hard disk with a minimum of 1.0 GB free space. (Additional free hard disk space is required if you are installing over a network.)
- 12X or faster CD-ROM drive
- SVGA monitor capable of 800 x 600 resolution (1024 x 768 recommended)
- High-density 3.5-inch disk drive, unless your CD-ROM is bootable and supports starting the Setup program from a CD-ROM
- Microsoft Mouse or compatible pointing device

Software Requirements

A copy of the 120-day Evaluation Edition of Windows 2000 Advanced Server is required to complete all of the activities and labs in this course.

Caution The 120-day Evaluation Edition of Windows 2000 Advanced Server provided with this training is not the full retail product and is provided only for training purposes. Microsoft Technical Support does not support evaluation editions. For additional support information regarding this book and the CD-ROMs (including answers to commonly asked questions about installation and use), visit the Microsoft Press Technical Support Web site at *http://mspress.microsoft.com/ support/*. You can also email TKINPUT@MICROSOFT.COM, or send a letter to Microsoft Press, Attn: Microsoft Press Technical Support, One Microsoft Way, Redmond, WA 98502-6399.

Setup Instructions

The following information is a checklist of the tasks that you need to perform to prepare your computer for the lessons in this book. If you do not have experience installing Windows 2000 or another network operating system, you may need help from an experienced network administrator. As you complete a task, mark it off in the check box. Step-by-step instructions for each task follow.

☐ Create Windows 2000 Advanced Server Setup diskettes.

☐ Run the Windows 2000 Advanced Server Pre-Copy and Text Mode Setup Routine.

☐ Run the GUI mode and gathering information phase of Windows 2000 Advanced Server Setup.

☐ Complete the Installing Windows Networking Components phase of Windows 2000 Advanced Server Setup.

☐ Complete the hardware installation phase of Windows 2000 Advanced Server Setup.

Note The installation information provided will help you prepare a computer for use with this book. It is not intended to teach you installation.

Installing Windows 2000 Advanced Server

To complete the exercises in this course, you should install Windows 2000 Advanced Server on a computer with no formatted partitions. During installation, you can use the Windows 2000 Advanced Server Setup program to create a partition on your hard disk, on which you install Windows 2000 Advanced Server as a stand-alone server in a workgroup.

▶ **To create Windows 2000 Advanced Server Setup Diskettes**

Complete this procedure on a computer running MS-DOS or any version of Windows with access to the Bootdisk directory on the Windows 2000 Advanced Server installation CD-ROM. If your computer is configured with a bootable CD-ROM drive, you can install Windows 2000 without using the Setup disks. To complete this procedure as outlined, bootable CD-ROM support must be disabled in the BIOS.

Important This procedure requires four formatted 1.44-MB disks. If you use diskettes that contain data, the data will be overwritten without warning.

---

1. Label the four blank, formatted 1.44-MB diskettes as follows:
   - Windows 2000 Advanced Server Setup Disk #1
   - Windows 2000 Advanced Server Setup Disk #2
   - Windows 2000 Advanced Server Setup Disk #3
   - Windows 2000 Advanced Server Setup Disk #4
2. Insert the Microsoft Windows 2000 Advanced Server CD-ROM into the CD-ROM drive.
3. If a Windows 2000 CD-ROM dialog box appears to prompt you to install or upgrade to Windows 2000, click No.
4. Open a command prompt.
5. At the command prompt, change to your CD-ROM drive. For example, if your CD-ROM drive name is E, type **e:** and press Enter.
6. At the command prompt, change to the Bootdisk directory by typing **cd bootdisk** and pressing Enter.

7. If you are creating the Setup boot diskettes from a computer running MS-DOS or a Windows 16-bit operating system, type **makeboot a:** (where A: is the name of your floppy disk drive) and press Enter. If you are creating the Setup boot diskettes from a computer running Windows NT or Windows 2000, type **makebt32 a:** (where A is the name of your floppy disk drive) and then press Enter. Windows 2000 displays a message indicating that this program creates the four Setup disks for installing Windows 2000. It also indicates that four blank, formatted, high-density floppy disks are required.

8. Press any key to continue. Windows 2000 displays a message prompting you to insert the disk that will become the Windows 2000 Setup Boot Disk.

9. Insert the blank formatted diskette labeled Windows 2000 Advanced Server Setup Disk #1 into the floppy disk drive and press any key to continue. After Windows 2000 creates the disk image, it displays a message prompting you to insert the diskette labeled Windows 2000 Setup Disk #2.

10. Remove Disk #1, insert the blank formatted diskette labeled Windows 2000 Advanced Server Setup Disk #2 into the floppy disk drive, and press any key to continue. After Windows 2000 creates the disk image, it displays a message prompting you to insert the diskette labeled Windows 2000 Setup Disk #3.

11. Remove Disk #2, insert the blank formatted diskette labeled Windows 2000 Advanced Server Setup Disk #3 into the floppy disk drive, and press any key to continue. After Windows 2000 creates the disk image, it displays a message prompting you to insert the diskette labeled Windows 2000 Setup Disk #4.

12. Remove Disk #3, insert the blank formatted diskette labeled Windows 2000 Advanced Server Setup Disk #4 into the floppy disk drive, and press any key to continue. After Windows 2000 creates the disk image, it displays a message indicating that the imaging process is done.

13. At the command prompt, type **exit** and then press Enter.

14. Remove the disk from the floppy disk drive and the CD-ROM from the CD-ROM drive.

▶ **Running the Windows 2000 Advanced Server Pre-Copy and Text Mode Setup Routine**

It is assumed for this procedure that your computer has no operating system installed, the disk is not partitioned, and bootable CD-ROM support, if available, is disabled.

1. Insert the disk labeled Windows 2000 Advanced Server Setup Disk #1 into the floppy disk drive, insert the Windows 2000 Advanced Server CD-ROM into the CD-ROM drive, and restart your computer.

   After the computer starts, Windows 2000 Setup displays a brief message that your system configuration is being checked, and then the Windows 2000 Setup screen appears.

   Notice that the gray bar at the bottom of the screen indicates that the computer is being inspected and that the Windows 2000 Executive is loading, which is a minimal version of the Windows 2000 kernel.

2. When prompted, insert Setup Disk #2 into the floppy disk drive and press Enter.

   Notice that Setup indicates that it is loading the HAL, fonts, local specific data, bus drivers, and other software components to support your computer's motherboard, bus, and other hardware. Setup also loads the Windows 2000 Setup program files.

3. When prompted, insert Setup Disk #3 into the floppy disk drive and press Enter.

   Notice that Setup indicates that it is loading disk drive controller drivers. After the drive controllers load, the Setup program initializes drivers appropriate to support access to your disk drives. Setup might pause several times during this process.

4. When prompted, insert Setup Disk #4 into the floppy disk drive and press Enter.

   Setup loads peripheral support drivers, like the floppy disk driver and file systems, and then it initializes the Windows 2000 Executive and loads the rest of the Windows 2000 Setup program.

   If you are installing the Evaluation Edition of Windows 2000, a Setup notification screen appears, informing you that you are about to install an evaluation version of Windows 2000.

5. Read the Setup Notification message and press Enter to continue.

   Setup displays the Welcome To Setup screen. Notice that, in addition to the initial installation of Windows 2000, you can use Windows 2000 Setup to repair or recover a damaged Windows 2000 installation.

6. Read the Welcome To Setup message and press Enter to begin the installation phase of Windows 2000 Setup. Setup displays the License Agreement screen.

7. Read the license agreement, pressing Page Down to scroll down to the bottom of the screen.

8. Select I Accept the Agreement by pressing F8.

   Setup displays the Windows 2000 Server Setup screen, prompting you to select an area of free space or an existing partition on which to install Windows 2000. This stage of Setup provides a way for you to create and delete partitions on your hard disk.

   If your computer does not contain any disk partitions (as required for this exercise), you will notice that the hard disk listed on the screen contains an existing unformatted partition.

9. Make sure that the Unpartitioned space partition is highlighted and then type **c**.

   Setup displays the Windows 2000 Setup screen, confirming that you've chosen to create a new partition in the unpartitioned space and informing you of the minimum and maximum sizes of the partition you might create.

10. Specify the size of the partition you want to create (at least 2 GB) and press Enter to continue.

    Setup displays the Windows 2000 Setup screen, showing the new partition as C: New (Unformatted).

Note Although you can create additional partitions from the remaining unpartitioned space during Setup, it is recommended that you perform additional partitioning tasks after you install Windows 2000. To partition hard disks after installation, use the Disk Management console.

---

11. Make sure the new partition is highlighted and press Enter.

    You are prompted to select a file system for the partition.

12. Use the arrow keys to select Format The Partition Using The NTFS File System and press Enter.

The Setup program formats the partition with NTFS. After it formats the partition, Setup examines the hard disk for physical errors that might cause Setup to fail and then copies files to the hard disk. This process will take several minutes.

Eventually, Setup displays the Windows 2000 Advanced Server Setup screen. A red status bar counts down for 15 seconds before Setup restarts the computer.

13. Remove the Setup disk from the floppy disk drive.

Important If your computer supports booting from the CD-ROM drive and this feature was not disabled in the BIOS, the computer will boot from the Windows 2000 Advanced Server installation CD-ROM after Windows 2000 Setup restarts. This will cause Setup to start again from the beginning. If this happens, remove the CD-ROM and then restart the computer.

---

14. Setup copies additional files and then restarts your machine and loads the Windows 2000 Setup Wizard.

▶ **Running the GUI mode and gathering information phase of Windows 2000 Advanced Server Setup**

This procedure begins the graphical portion of Setup on your computer.

1. On the Welcome To The Windows 2000 Setup Wizard page, click Next to begin gathering information about your computer.

   Setup configures NTFS folder and file permissions for the operating system files, detects the hardware devices in the computer, and then installs and configures device drivers to support the detected hardware. This process takes several minutes.

2. On the Regional Settings page, make sure that the system locale, user locale, and keyboard layout are correct for your language and location and then click Next.

Note You can modify regional settings after you install Windows 2000 by using Regional Options in Control Panel.

Setup displays the Personalize Your Software page, prompting you for your name and organization name. Setup uses your organization name to generate the default computer name. Many applications that you install later will use this information for product registration and document identification.

3. In the Name field, type your name; in the Organization field, type the name of an organization; and then click Next.

Note If the Your Product Key screen appears, enter the product key, located on the sticker attached to the Windows 2000 Advanced Server, Evaluation Edition, CD sleeve bound into the back of this book.

Setup displays the Licensing Modes page, prompting you to select a licensing mode. By default, the Per Server licensing mode is selected. Setup prompts you to enter the number of licenses you have purchased for this server.

4. Select the Per Server Number of concurrent connections button, type **5** for the number of concurrent connections, and then click Next.

Important Per Server Number of concurrent connections and 5 concurrent connections are suggested values to be used to complete your self-study. You should use a legal number of concurrent connections based on the actual licenses that you own. You can also choose to use Per Seat instead of Per Server.

Setup displays the Computer Name And Administrator Password page.

Notice that Setup uses your organization name to generate a suggested name for the computer.

5. In the Computer Name field, type **server1**.

Windows 2000 displays the computer name in all capital letters regardless of how it is entered.

Warning If your computer is on a network, check with the network administrator before assigning a name to your computer.

---

6. In the Administrator Password field and the Confirm Password field, type **password** (all lowercase) and click Next. Passwords are case sensitive, so make sure you type **password** in all lowercase letters.

For the labs in this self-paced training kit, you will use a password for the Administrator account. In a production environment, you should always use a complex password for the Administrator account (one that others cannot easily guess). Microsoft recommends mixing uppercase and lowercase letters, numbers, and symbols (for example, Lp6*g9).

Setup displays the Windows 2000 Components page, indicating which Windows 2000 system components Setup will install.

7. On the Windows 2000 Components page, click Next.

   You can install additional components after you install Windows 2000 by using Add/Remove Programs in Control Panel. Make sure to install only the components selected by default during Setup. Later in your training, you will be installing additional components.

   If a modem is detected in the computer during Setup, Setup displays the Modem Dialing Information page.

8. If the Modem Dialing Information page appears, enter an area code or city code and click Next.

   The Date And Time Settings page appears.

Important Windows 2000 services perform many tasks whose successful completion depends on the computer's time and date settings. Be sure to select the correct time zone for your location to avoid problems in later labs.

---

9. Enter the correct Date and Time and Time Zone settings, and then click Next.

   The Network Settings page appears, and Setup installs networking components.

▶ **Completing the Installing Windows Networking Components phase of Windows 2000 Advanced Server Setup**

Networking is an integral part of Windows 2000 Advanced Server. Many selections and configurations are available. In this procedure, basic networking is configured. In a later exercise, you will install additional network components.

1. On the Networking Settings page, make sure that Typical Settings is selected, and then click Next to begin installing Windows networking components.

   This setting installs networking components that are used to gain access to and share resources on a network and configures Transmission Control Protocol/Internet Protocol (TCP/IP) to automatically obtain an IP address from a DHCP server on the network.

Setup displays the Workgroup Or Computer Domain page, prompting you to join either a workgroup or a domain.

2. On the Workgroup Or Computer Domain page, make sure that the button No, This Computer Is Not On A Network Or Is On A Network Without A Domain is selected, and that the workgroup name is WORKGROUP, and then click Next.

Setup displays the Installing Components page, which updates to keep you informed of the installation progress as Setup installs and configures the remaining operating system components according to the options you specified. This procedure will take several minutes.

Setup then displays the Performing Final Tasks page, which shows the process's status as Setup finishes copying files, making and saving configuration changes, and deleting temporary files. Computers that do not exceed the minimum hardware requirements might take 30 minutes or more to complete this phase of installation.

Setup then displays the Completing The Windows 2000 Setup Wizard page.

3. Remove the Windows 2000 Advanced Server CD-ROM from the CD-ROM drive, and then click Finish.

Important If your computer supports booting from the CD-ROM drive and this feature was not disabled in the BIOS, the computer will boot from the Windows 2000 Advanced Server installation CD-ROM after Windows 2000 Setup restarts. This will cause Setup to start again from the beginning. If this happens, remove the CD-ROM and then restart the computer.

Windows 2000 restarts and runs the newly installed version of Windows 2000 Advanced Server.

▶ **Completing the hardware installation phase of Windows 2000 Advanced Server Setup**

During this final phase of installation, any Plug and Play hardware not detected in the previous phases of Setup will be detected.

1. At the completion of the startup phase, log on by pressing Ctrl+Alt+Delete.

2. In the Enter Password dialog box, type **administrator** in the User Name field and type **password** in the Password field.

3. Click OK.

If Windows 2000 detects hardware that was not detected during Setup, the Found New Hardware Wizard screen displays, indicating that Windows 2000 is installing the appropriate drivers.

4. If the Found New Hardware Wizard screen appears, verify that the Restart The Computer When I Click Finish check box is cleared and click Finish to complete the Found New Hardware Wizard.

   Windows 2000 displays the Microsoft Windows 2000 Configure Your Server dialog box. From this dialog box, you can configure a variety of advanced options and services.

5. Select I Will Configure This Server Later, and then click Next.

6. On the next screen that appears, clear the Show This Screen At Startup check box.

7. Close the Configure Your Server screen.

   You have now completed the Windows 2000 Advanced Server installation and are logged on as Administrator.

Note To properly shut down Windows 2000 Advanced Server, click Start, choose Shut Down, and then follow the directions that appear.

Caution If your computers are part of a larger network, you *must* verify with your network administrator that the computer names, domain name, and other information used in setting up Windows 2000 Advanced Server as described in this section do not conflict with network operations. If they do conflict, ask your network administrator to provide alternative values and use those values throughout all of the exercise in this book.

The Online Seminars

The Supplemental Course Materials CD-ROM contains online seminars that you can view by running the file from the CD-ROM. You will find a prompt within the book indicating when the demonstration should be run. You must have installed Media Player and an Internet browser on your computer to view this file. (Internet Explorer and Media Player are included on this CD for this purpose. To install either of these software products, see the installation instructions in the Readme.txt files on the CD.)

▶ **To view the online seminars**

1. Insert the Supplemental Course Materials CD-ROM into your CD-ROM drive.

2. Open the appropriate filename as indicated in the table below:

To view the online seminar	Click the file
Designing the Active Directory Structure	\chapt06\OnlineSeminars\Designing\ Portal_ActiveDirectory Structure
Comparative Active Directory Designs	\chapt06\OnlineSeminars\Comparative\ Portal_ActiveDirectory Designs
How to Migrate Your Windows NT 4 Directory Services to Windows 2000 Active Directory	\chapt07\Migration\Portal_Migration

This will run the selected online seminar in your Internet browser.

The Online Book

The CD-ROM also includes an online version of the book that you can view on the screen using Microsoft Internet Explorer 4.01 or later.

▶ **To use the online version of this book**

1. Insert the Supplemental Course Materials CD-ROM into your CD-ROM drive.

2. Select Run from the Start menu on your desktop, and type **D:\Ebook\Setup.exe** (where D is the name of your CD-ROM disk drive).

   This will install an icon for the online book on your Start menu.

3. Click OK to exit the installation wizard.

Note You must have the Supplemental Course Materials CD-ROM inserted in your CD-ROM drive to run the online book.

Sample Readiness Review Questions

With this training kit we provide 180 days of unlimited access to 25 practice test questions for the exam 70-219. The exam preparation questions are a subset of practice test questions offered in the *MCSE Readiness Review—Exam 70-219: Designing a Microsoft Windows 2000 Directory Services Infrastructure* (ISBN 0-7356-1364-8) book developed by Microsoft and MeasureUp, a Microsoft Certified Practice Test Provider.

To use these questions, create a free user account at *http://mspress.measureup.com* and register the key provided on the sticker attached to the Supplemental Course Materials CD-ROM sleeve in the back of this book. If you encounter any problems accessing the questions, please call MeasureUp's customer service at (678) 356-5050.

The Microsoft Certified Professional Program

The Microsoft Certified Professional (MCP) program provides the best method to prove your command of current Microsoft products and technologies. Microsoft, an industry leader in certification, is on the forefront of testing methodology. Our exams and corresponding certifications are developed to validate your mastery of critical competencies as you design and develop, or implement and support, solutions with Microsoft products and technologies. Computer professionals who become Microsoft certified are recognized as experts and are sought after industry-wide.

The Microsoft Certified Professional program offers eight certifications, based on specific areas of technical expertise:

- *Microsoft Certified Professional (MCP).* Demonstrated in-depth knowledge of at least one Microsoft operating system. Candidates may pass additional Microsoft certification exams to further qualify their skills with Microsoft BackOffice products, development tools, or desktop programs.

- *Microsoft Certified Professional + Internet.* MCPs with a specialty in the Internet are qualified to plan security, install and configure server products, manage server resources, extend servers to run scripts, monitor and analyze performance, and troubleshoot problems.

- *Microsoft Certified Professional + Site Building.* Demonstrated what it takes to plan, build, maintain, and manage Web sites using Microsoft technologies and products.

- *Microsoft Certified Systems Engineer (MCSE).* Qualified to effectively plan, implement, maintain, and support information systems in a wide range of computing environments with Microsoft Windows NT Server and the Microsoft BackOffice integrated family of server software.

- *Microsoft Certified Systems Engineer + Internet.* MCSEs with an advanced qualification to enhance, deploy, and manage sophisticated intranet and Internet solutions that include a browser, proxy server, host servers, database, and messaging and commerce components. In addition, an MCSE+Internet–certified professional is able to manage and analyze Web sites.

- *Microsoft Certified Database Administrator (MCDBA).* Individuals who derive physical database designs, develop logical data models, create physical databases, create data services by using Transact-SQL, manage and maintain databases, configure and manage security, monitor and optimize databases, and install and configure Microsoft SQL Server.

- *Microsoft Certified Solution Developer (MCSD).* Qualified to design and develop custom business solutions with Microsoft development tools, technologies, and platforms, including Microsoft Office and Microsoft BackOffice.

- *Microsoft Certified Trainer (MCT).* Instructionally and technically qualified to deliver Microsoft Official Curriculum through a Microsoft Certified Technical Education Center (CTEC).

Microsoft Certification Benefits

Microsoft certification, one of the most comprehensive certification programs available for assessing and maintaining software-related skills, is a valuable measure of an individual's knowledge and expertise. Microsoft certification is awarded to individuals who have successfully demonstrated their ability to perform specific tasks and implement solutions with Microsoft products. Not only does this provide an objective measure for employers to consider, it also provides guidance for what an individual should know to be proficient. And as with any skills-assessment measure or benchmark, certification brings a variety of benefits: to the individual, and to employers and organizations.

Microsoft Certification Benefits for Individuals

As a Microsoft Certified Professional, you receive many benefits:

- Industry recognition of your knowledge and proficiency with Microsoft products and technologies.

- Access to technical and product information directly from Microsoft through a secured area of the MCP Web Site.

- MSDN Online Certified Membership that helps you tap into the best technical resources, connect to the MCP community, and gain access to valuable resources and services. (Some MSDN Online benefits may be available in English only or may not be available in all countries.) See the MSDN Web site for a growing list of certified member benefits.

- Logos to enable you to identify your Microsoft Certified Professional status to colleagues or clients.

- Invitations to Microsoft conferences, technical training sessions, and special events.
- A Microsoft Certified Professional certificate.
- Subscription to *Microsoft Certified Professional* magazine (North America only), a career and professional development magazine.

Additional benefits, depending on your certification and geography, include:

- A complimentary one-year subscription to the Microsoft TechNet Technical Plus, providing valuable information on monthly CD-ROMs.
- A one-year subscription to the Microsoft Beta Evaluation program. This benefit provides you with up to 12 free monthly CD-ROMs containing beta software (English only) for many of Microsoft's newest software products.

Microsoft Certification Benefits for Employers and Organizations

Through certification, computer professionals can maximize the return on investment in Microsoft technology. Research shows that Microsoft certification provides organizations with the following:

- Excellent return on training and certification investments by providing a standard method of determining training needs and measuring results.
- Increased customer satisfaction and decreased support costs through improved service, increased productivity, and greater technical self-sufficiency.
- Reliable benchmark for hiring, promoting, and career planning.
- Recognition and rewards for productive employees by validating their expertise.
- Retraining options for existing employees so they can work effectively with new technologies.
- Assurance of quality when outsourcing computer services.

To learn more about how certification can help your company, see the backgrounders, white papers, and case studies available at *http://www.microsoft.com/mcp/mktg/bus_bene.htm*:

- Financial Benefits to Supporters of Microsoft Professional Certification, IDC white paper (1998wpidc.doc 1,608K)
- Prudential Case Study (prudentl.exe 70K self-extracting file)

- The Microsoft Certified Professional Program Corporate Backgrounder (mcpback.exe 50K)
- A white paper (mcsdwp.doc 158K) that evaluates the Microsoft Certified Solution Developer certification
- A white paper (mcsestud.doc 161K) that evaluates the Microsoft Certified Systems Engineer certification
- Jackson Hole High School Case Study (jhhs.doc 180K)
- Lyondel Case Study (lyondel.doc 21K)
- Stellcom Case Study (stellcom.doc 132K)

Requirements for Becoming a Microsoft Certified Professional

The certification requirements differ for each certification and are specific to the products and job functions addressed by the certification.

To become a Microsoft Certified Professional, you must pass rigorous certification exams that provide a valid and reliable measure of technical proficiency and expertise. These exams are designed to test your expertise and ability to perform a role or task with a product, and are developed with the input of professionals in the industry. Questions in the exams reflect how Microsoft products are used in actual organizations, giving them "real-world" relevance.

Microsoft Certified Product Specialists are required to pass one operating system exam. Candidate may pass additional Microsoft certification exams to further qualify their skills with Microsoft BackOffice products, development tools, or desktop applications.

Microsoft Certified Professional + Internet specialists are required to pass the prescribed Microsoft Windows NT Server 4, TCP/IP, and Microsoft Internet Information System exam series.

Microsoft Certified Professionals with a specialty in site building are required to pass two exams covering Microsoft FrontPage, Microsoft Site Server, and Microsoft Visual InterDev technologies to provide a valid and reliable measure of technical proficiency and expertise.

Microsoft Certified Systems Engineers are required to pass a series of core Microsoft Windows operating system and networking exams and BackOffice technology elective exams.

Microsoft Certified Systems Engineers + Internet specialists are required to pass seven operating system exams and two elective exams that provide a valid and reliable measure of technical proficiency and expertise.

Microsoft Certified Database Administrators are required to pass three core exams and one elective exam that provide a valid and reliable measure of technical proficiency and expertise.

Microsoft Certified Solution Developers are required to pass two core Microsoft Windows operating system technology exams and two BackOffice technology elective exams.

Microsoft Certified Trainers are required to meet instructional and technical requirements specific to each Microsoft Official Curriculum course they are certified to deliver. In the United States and Canada, call Microsoft at (800) 636-7544 for more information on becoming a Microsoft Certified Trainer or visit *http://www.microsoft.com/train_cert/mct/*. Outside the United States and Canada, contact your local Microsoft subsidiary.

Technical Training for Computer Professionals

Technical training is available in a variety of ways, with instructor-led classes, online instruction, or self-paced training available at thousands of locations worldwide.

Self-Paced Training

For motivated learners who are ready for the challenge, self-paced instruction is the most flexible, cost-effective way to increase your knowledge and skills.

A full line of self-paced print and computer-based training materials is available direct from the source—Microsoft Press. Microsoft Official Curriculum courseware kits from Microsoft Press, designed for advanced computer system professionals, are available from Microsoft Press and the Microsoft Developer Division. Self-paced training kits from Microsoft Press feature print-based instructional materials, along with CD-ROM–based product software, multimedia presentations, lab exercises, and practice files. The Mastering Series provides in-depth, interactive training on CD-ROM for experienced developers. They're both great ways to prepare for Microsoft Certified Professional (MCP) exams.

Online Training

For a more flexible alternative to instructor-led classes, turn to online instruction. It's as near as the Internet, and it's ready whenever you are. Learn at your own pace and on your own schedule in a virtual classroom, often with easy access to an online instructor. Without ever leaving your desk, you can gain the expertise you need. Online instruction covers a variety of Microsoft products and technologies. It includes options ranging from Microsoft Official Curriculum to choices available nowhere else. It's training on demand, with access to learning resources 24 hours a day. Online training is available through Microsoft Certified Technical Education Centers.

Microsoft Certified Technical Education Centers

Microsoft Certified Technical Education Centers (CTECs) are the best source for instructor-led training that can help you prepare to become a Microsoft Certified Professional. The Microsoft CTEC program is a worldwide network of qualified technical training organizations that provide authorized delivery of Microsoft Official Curriculum courses by Microsoft Certified Trainers to computer professionals.

For a listing of CTEC locations in the United States and Canada, visit *http://www.microsoft.com/CTEC/default.htm*.

Technical Support

Every effort has been made to ensure the accuracy of this book and the contents of the companion disc. If you have comments, questions, or ideas regarding this book or the companion disc, please send them to Microsoft Press using either of the following methods:

E-Mail:
TKINPUT@MICROSOFT.COM

Postal Mail:
Microsoft Press
Attn: MCSE Training Kit—Designing a Microsoft Windows 2000 Directory Services Infrastructure Editor
One Microsoft Way
Redmond, WA 98052-6399

Microsoft Press provides corrections for books through the World Wide Web at the following address:

http://mspress.microsoft.com/support/

Please note that product support is not offered through the above mail addresses. For further information regarding Microsoft software support options, please connect to *http://www.microsoft.com/support/* or call Microsoft Support Network Sales at (800) 936-3500.

Evaluation Edition Software Support

The Evaluation Edition of Microsoft Windows 2000 Advanced Server included with this book is unsupported by both Microsoft and Microsoft Press and should not be used on a primary work computer. For online support information relating to the full version of Microsoft Windows 2000 Advanced Server that might also apply to the Evaluation Edition, you can connect to

http://support.microsoft.com/

For information about ordering the full version of any Microsoft software, please call Microsoft Sales at (800) 426-9400 or visit *www.microsoft.com*. Information about any issues relating to the use of the Evaluation Edition with this training kit is posted to the Support section of the Microsoft Press Web site (*http://mspress.microsoft.com/support/*).

C H A P T E R   1

Introduction to Active Directory

About This Chapter

You use a directory service to uniquely identify users and resources on a network. Active Directory directory services in Microsoft Windows 2000 is a significant enhancement over the directory services provided in previous versions of Windows. Active Directory provides a single point of network resource management, allowing you to add, remove, and relocate users and resources easily. This chapter introduces you to Active Directory. As you read through the lessons in this chapter, keep in mind that the concepts introduced here will be examined in greater detail in later chapters as you learn how to design a directory services infrastructure.

Before You Begin

To complete this chapter, you must be familiar with basic administration and design concepts in Windows NT or Windows 2000.

Lesson 1: Active Directory Overview

Active Directory provides a method for designing a directory structure that meets the needs of your organization. This lesson introduces the use of objects in Active Directory and the function of each of its components.

After this lesson, you will be able to

- Explain the purpose of Active Directory
- Explain the purpose of object attributes and the schema in Active Directory
- Identify the components of Active Directory
- Describe the function of Active Directory components
- Explain the purpose of the global catalog in Active Directory

Estimated lesson time: 30 minutes

Windows 2000 Active Directory

A directory stores information related to the network resources to facilitate locating and managing these resources. A *directory service* is a network service that identifies all resources on a network and makes them accessible to users and applications. A directory service differs from a directory in that it is both the source of the information and the service making the information available to users.

Active Directory is the directory service included in Windows 2000 Server. Active Directory includes the directory, which stores information about network resources, as well as all the services that make the information available and useful. The information about user data, printers, servers, databases, groups, computers, and security policies stored in the directory, is organized into objects.

Active Directory Objects

An *object* is a distinct named set of attributes that represents a network resource. Object *attributes* are characteristics of objects in the directory. For example, the attributes of a user account might include the user's first name, last name, and logon name, while the attributes of a computer account may include the computer name and description (see Figure 1.1).

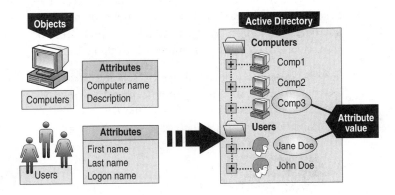

Figure 1.1   Active Directory objects and attributes

Some objects, known as *containers*, can contain other objects. For example, a domain is a container object that can contain users, computers, and other objects. In Figure 1.1, the Users folder is a container that contains users.

Active Directory Schema

The Active Directory schema defines objects that can be stored in Active Directory. The schema is a list of definitions that determines the kinds of objects and the types of information about those objects that can be stored in Active Directory. Because the schema definitions are themselves stored as objects, they can be administered in the same manner as the rest of the objects in Active Directory.

The schema contains two types of definition objects: schema class objects and schema attribute objects. As shown in Figure 1.2, class objects and attribute objects are defined in separate lists within the schema. Schema class and attribute objects are also referred to as *schema objects* or *metadata*.

Schema class objects describe the possible Active Directory objects that can be created. A schema class object functions as a template for creating new Active Directory objects. Each schema class is a collection of schema attribute objects. When you create a schema class, the schema attributes store the information that describes the object. The User class, for example, is composed of many schema attributes, including Network Address, Home Directory, and so on. Every object in Active Directory is an instance of a schema class object.

Schema attribute objects define the schema class objects with which they are associated. Each schema attribute is defined only once and can be used in multiple schema classes. For example, the Description attribute is used in many schema classes but is defined only once in the schema, ensuring consistency.

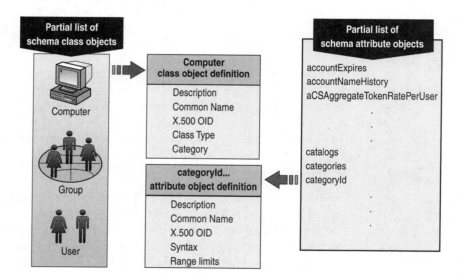

Figure 1.2   Schema class and attribute objects

A set of basic schema classes and attributes is shipped with Windows 2000 Server. Experienced developers and network administrators may dynamically extend the schema by defining new classes and attributes for existing classes. For example, if you need to provide information about users not currently defined in the schema, you must extend the schema for the User class. However, extending the schema is an advanced operation with possibly serious consequences. Because schemas cannot be deleted, but only deactivated, and a schema is automatically replicated, you must plan and prepare carefully before extending the schema. Schema extension is discussed in Chapter 3, "Creating a Forest Plan."

Active Directory Components

Active Directory uses components to build a directory structure that meets the needs of your organization. The logical structures of your organization are represented by the following Active Directory components: domains, organizational units, trees, and forests. The physical structure of your organization is represented by the following Active Directory components: sites (physical subnets) and domain controllers. Active Directory completely separates the logical structure from the physical structure.

In addition to the components that represent the logical and physical structures of your organization, Active Directory automatically builds the global catalog on the first domain controller in a forest. The global catalog serves as the central repository of selected information about objects in a tree or forest.

Logical Structures

In Active Directory, you organize resources in a logical structure that mirrors the logical structure of your organization. Grouping resources logically allows you to find a resource by its name rather than by its physical location. Because you group resources logically, Active Directory makes the network's physical structure transparent to users. Figure 1.3 illustrates the relationships of the Active Directory components.

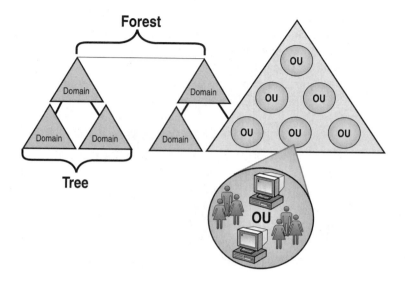

Figure 1.3   Resources organized in a logical structure

Domains

The core unit of logical structure in Active Directory is the *domain*, which can store millions of objects. Objects stored in a domain are those vital to the network. These vital objects are items the networked community needs to do its job: printers, documents, e-mail addresses, databases, users, distributed components, and other resources. All network objects exist within a domain, and each domain stores information only about the objects it contains. Active Directory is made up of one or more domains. A domain can span more than one physical location. Domains share these characteristics:

- All network objects exist within a domain, and each domain stores information only about the objects that it contains. Theoretically, a domain directory can contain up to 10 million objects, but 1 million objects per domain is a more practical number.

- A domain is a security boundary. Access control lists (ACLs) control access to domain objects. ACLs contain the permissions associated with objects that control which users can gain access to an object and what type of access users can gain to the objects. In Windows 2000, objects include files, folders, shares, printers, and other Active Directory objects. None of the security policies and settings—such as administrative rights, security policies, and ACLs—can cross from one domain to another. The domain administrator has absolute rights to set policies only within that domain.

Grouping objects into one or more domains allows your network to reflect your company's organization. See Chapter 4, "Creating a Domain Plan," to read about domain design.

Organizational Units

An *organizational unit* (OU) is a container used to organize objects within a domain into a logical administrative group. This organization typically mirrors your organization's functional or business structure. An OU can contain objects such as user accounts, groups, computers, printers, applications, file shares, and other OUs from the same domain. The OU hierarchy within a domain is independent of the OU hierarchy structure of other domains—each domain can implement its own OU hierarchy. By adding OUs to other OUs, or *nesting*, you can provide administrative control in a hierarchical fashion. See Chapter 5, "Creating an Organizational Unit Plan," to read about OU design.

OUs provide a means for handling administrative tasks, such as the administration of users and resources, as they are the smallest scope to which you can delegate administrative authority. See Chapter 5, "Creating an Organizational Unit Plan," to read about planning for delegation.

In Figure 1.4, the microsoft.com domain mirrors the organization of a shipping company and contains three OUs: US, Orders, and Disp, where the last two are nested within the US OU. In the summer months, the number of orders taken for shipping increases and management has requested the addition of a subadministrator for the Orders department. The subadministrator must have permission only to create user accounts and provide users with access to Orders department files and shared printers. Rather than creating another domain, the request can be met by assigning the subadministrator the appropriate permissions within the Orders OU.

If the subadministrator was later required to create user accounts in the US, Orders, and Disp OUs, you could grant the administrator the appropriate permissions separately within each OU. However, because the Orders and Disp OUs are nested in the US OU, a more efficient method is to assign permissions once in the US OU and allow them to be inherited by the Orders and Disp OUs. By default, all child objects (the Orders and Disp OUs) within Active Directory inherit permissions from their parents (the US OU). Granting permissions at a higher level and using inheritance capabilities can reduce administrative tasks.

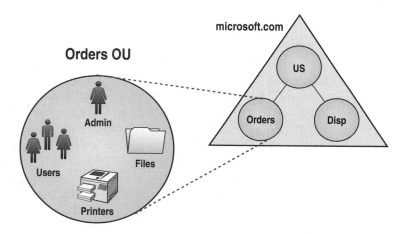

Figure 1.4   Using an organizational unit to handle administrative tasks

Trees

A *tree* is a grouping or hierarchical arrangement of one or more Windows 2000 domains that you create by adding one or more child domains to an existing parent domain. Domains in a tree share a contiguous namespace and a hierarchical naming structure. Namespaces are covered in detail in the next lesson. Trees share these characteristics:

- Following Domain Name System (DNS) standards, the domain name of a child domain is the relative name of that child domain appended with the name of the parent domain. In Figure 1.5, microsoft.com is the parent domain and us.microsoft.com and uk.microsoft.com are its child domains. The child domain of uk.microsoft.com is sls.uk.microsoft.com.

- All domains within a single tree share a common schema, which is a formal definition of all object types that you can store in an Active Directory deployment.

- All domains within a single tree share a common global catalog, which is the central repository of information about objects in a tree.

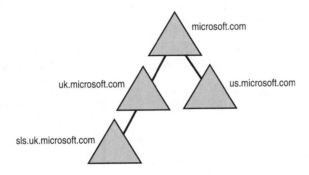

Figure 1.5   A domain tree

By creating a hierarchy of domains in a tree, you can retain security and allow for administration within an OU or within a single domain of a tree. The tree structure easily accommodates organizational changes. Chapter 3, "Creating a Forest Plan," discusses tree design.

Forests

A *forest* is a grouping or hierarchical arrangement of one or more separate, completely independent domain trees. As such, forests have the following characteristics:

- All trees in a forest share a common schema.

- Trees in a forest have different naming structures, according to their domains.

- All domains in a forest share a common global catalog.

- Domains in a forest operate independently, but the forest enables communication across the entire organization.
- Implicit two-way transitive trusts exist between domains and domain trees.

In Figure 1.6, microsoft.com and msn.com form a forest. The namespace is contiguous only within each tree.

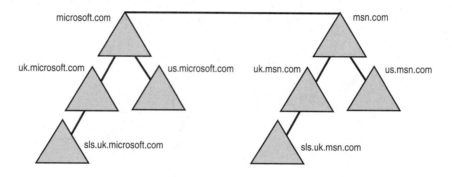

Figure 1.6   A forest of trees

Forest design is discussed in detail in Chapter 3, "Creating a Forest Plan."

Physical Structure

The physical components of Active Directory are sites and domain controllers. You will use these components to develop a directory structure that mirrors the physical structure of your organization.

Sites

A *site* is a combination of one or more Internet Protocol (IP) subnets connected by a highly reliable and fast link to localize as much network traffic as possible. Typically, a site has the same boundaries as a local area network (LAN). When you group subnets on your network, you should combine only subnets that have fast, cheap, and reliable network connections with one another. "Fast" network connections are at least 512 kilobits per second (Kbps). An available bandwidth of 128 Kbps and higher is sufficient.

With Active Directory, sites are not part of the namespace. When you browse the logical namespace, you see computers and users grouped into domains and OUs, not sites. Sites contain only computer objects and connection objects used to configure replication between sites. A single domain can span one or multiple geographical sites, and a single site can include user accounts and computers belonging to multiple domains. See Chapter 6, "Creating a Site Topology Plan," to read about site design.

Domain Controllers

A *domain controller* is a computer running Windows 2000 Server that stores a replica of the domain directory (local domain database). Because a domain can contain one or more domain controllers, each domain controller in a domain has a complete replica of the domain's portion of the directory.

The following list describes the functions of domain controllers:

- Each domain controller stores a complete copy of all Active Directory information for that domain, manages changes to that information, and replicates those changes to other domain controllers in the same domain.

- Domain controllers in a domain automatically replicate all objects in the domain to each other. When you perform an action that causes an update to Active Directory, you are actually making the change at one of the domain controllers. That domain controller then replicates the change to all other domain controllers within the domain. You can control replication of traffic between domain controllers in the network by specifying how often replication occurs and the amount of data that Windows 2000 replicates at one time.

- Domain controllers immediately replicate certain important updates, such as the disabling of a user account.

- Active Directory uses multimaster replication, in which no one domain controller is the master domain controller. Instead, all domain controllers within a domain are peers, and each domain controller contains a copy of the directory database that can be written to. Domain controllers may hold different information for short periods of time until all domain controllers have synchronized changes to Active Directory.

- Domain controllers detect collisions, which can occur when an attribute is modified on a domain controller before a change to the same attribute on another domain controller is completely propagated. Collisions are detected by comparing each attribute's property version number, a number specific to an attribute that is initialized upon creation of the attribute. Active Directory resolves the collision by replicating the changed attribute with the higher property version number.

- Having more than one domain controller in a domain provides fault tolerance. If one domain controller is offline, another domain controller can provide all required functions, such as recording changes to Active Directory.

- Domain controllers manage all aspects of users' domain interaction, such as locating Active Directory objects and validating user logon attempts.

There are two domain modes: mixed mode and native mode. Mixed mode allows a Windows 2000 domain controller to interact with any domain controllers in the domain that are running previous versions of Windows NT. Native mode does not allow any domain controllers in the domain to run previous versions of Windows NT.

In general, there should be one domain controller for each domain in each site for authentication purposes. However, authentication requirements for your organization determine the number of domain controllers and their location. Chapter 6, "Creating a Site Topology Plan," discusses the placement of domain controllers.

Catalog Services—The Global Catalog

Active Directory allows users and administrators to find objects, such as files, printers, or users, in their own domain. However, finding objects outside of the domain and across the enterprise requires a mechanism that allows the domains to act as one entity. A *catalog service* contains selected information about every object in all domains in the directory, which is useful in performing searches across an enterprise. The catalog service provided by Active Directory services is called the global catalog.

The *global catalog* is the central repository of information about objects in a tree or forest. By default, a global catalog is created automatically on the initial domain controller in the first domain in the forest, known as the *global catalog server.* Using Active Directory services multimaster replication, the global catalog information is replicated between global catalog servers in other domains. It stores a full replica of all object attributes in the directory for its host domain and a partial replica of all object attributes contained in the directory for every domain in the forest. The partial replica stores attributes most frequently used in search operations (such as a user's first and last names, logon name, and so on). Attributes are marked or unmarked for replication in the global catalog when they are defined in the Active Directory schema. Object attributes replicated to the global catalog inherit the same permissions as in source domains, ensuring that data in the global catalog is secure.

Global Catalog Roles

The global catalog performs two key directory roles:

- It enables network logon by providing universal group membership information to a domain controller when a logon process is initiated.

- It enables finding directory information regardless of which domain in the forest actually contains the data.

When a user logs on to the network, the global catalog provides universal group membership information for the account to the domain controller processing the user logon information. If there is only one domain controller in a domain, the domain controller holds the global catalog. If there are multiple domain controllers in the network, one domain controller is configured to hold the global catalog. If a global catalog is not available when a user initiates a network logon process, the user is able to log on only to the local computer.

Important If a user is a member of the Domain Admins group, he or she is able to log on to the network even when the global catalog is not available.

The global catalog is designed to respond to user and programmatic queries about objects anywhere in the domain tree or forest with maximum speed and minimum network traffic. Because a single global catalog contains information about all objects in all domains in the forest, a query about an object that is not contained in the local domain can be resolved by a global catalog server in the domain in which the query is initiated. Thus, finding information in the directory does not produce unnecessary query traffic across domain boundaries.

The Query Process

A *query* is a specific request made by a user to the global catalog in order to retrieve, modify, or delete Active Directory data. The following steps, illustrated in Figure 1.7, describe the query process:

1. The client queries its DNS server for the location of the global catalog server.
2. The DNS server searches for the global catalog server location and returns the IP address of the domain controller designated as the global catalog server.
3. The client queries the IP address of the domain controller designated as the global catalog server. The query is sent to port 3268 on the domain controller; standard Active Directory queries are sent to port 389.
4. The global catalog server processes the query. If the global catalog contains the attribute of the object being searched for, the global catalog server provides a response to the client. If the global catalog does not contain the attribute of the object being searched for, the query is referred to Active Directory.

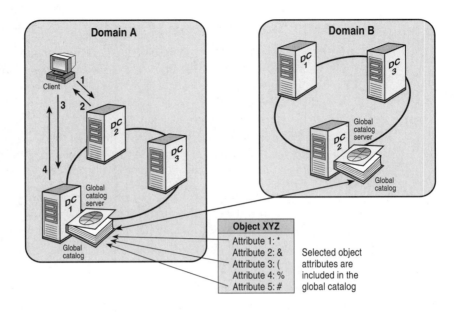

Figure 1.7   The query process

You can configure any domain controller or designate additional domain controllers as global catalog servers. When considering which domain controllers to designate as global catalog servers, base your decision on the ability of your network structure to handle replication and query traffic. The availability of additional servers can provide quicker responses to user inquiries, as well as redundancy. Therefore, it is recommended that every major site in your enterprise have at least one global catalog server. See Chapter 6, "Creating a Site Topology Plan," to read about placing global catalog servers.

Lesson Summary

In this lesson you learned that an object is a distinct named set of attributes that represents a network resource in Active Directory. Object attributes are characteristics of objects in the directory. The Active Directory schema is a list of definitions that determines the kinds of objects and the types of information about those objects that can be stored in an Active Directory forest. Because the schema definitions are stored as objects, they can be administered in the same manner as the rest of the objects in Active Directory. There are two types of definition objects in the schema: schema class objects and schema attribute objects.

You also learned that Active Directory offers you a method for designing a directory structure to reflect your organization's business structure and operations. Active Directory completely separates the logical structure of the domain hierarchy from the physical structure.

In Active Directory, grouping resources logically enables you to find a resource by its name rather than by its physical location. The core unit of logical structure in Active Directory is the domain, which stores information only about the objects that it contains. An OU is a container used to organize objects within a domain into logical administrative groups. A tree is a grouping or hierarchical arrangement of one or more Windows 2000 domains, and a forest is a grouping or hierarchical arrangement of one or more trees.

The physical structure of Active Directory is based on sites and domain controllers. A site is a combination of one or more IP subnets connected by a high-speed link. A domain controller is a computer running Windows 2000 Server that stores a replica of the domain directory.

Finally, you learned that the global catalog is a service and a physical storage location that contains a replica of selected attributes for every object in Active Directory. You can use the global catalog to locate objects anywhere in the network without replication of all domain information between domain controllers.

Lesson 2: Understanding Active Directory Concepts

In Windows 2000 and Active Directory services there are several new concepts and some changes to the concepts used in Windows NT. These concepts include replication, trust relationships, group policies, DNS namespaces, and naming conventions. It is important that you understand the meaning of these concepts as applied to Active Directory.

After this lesson, you will be able to

- Explain Active Directory replication
- Explain the security relationships between domains in a tree (trusts)
- Explain the purpose and function of group policy
- Describe the DNS namespace used by Active Directory
- Describe the naming conventions used by Active Directory

Estimated lesson time: 20 minutes

Replication

Users and services should be able to access directory information at any time from any computer in the domain tree or forest. *Replication* ensures that changes to a domain controller are reflected in all domain controllers within a domain. Directory information is replicated to domain controllers both within and among sites.

What Information Is Replicated

The information stored in the directory is partitioned into three categories. Each of these information categories is referred to as a *directory partition*. These directory partitions are the units of replication. The following information is contained in each directory:

- Schema information, which defines the objects that can be created in the directory and the attributes those objects can have. This information is common to all domains in the domain tree or forest.
- Configuration information, which describes the logical structure of the deployment, including information such as domain structure or replication topology. This information is common to all domains in the domain tree or forest.

- Domain data, which describes all of the objects in a domain. This data is domain-specific and is not distributed to any other domains. For the purpose of finding information throughout the domain tree or forest, selected attributes for all objects in all domains are stored in the global catalog.

Schema and configuration information is replicated to all domain controllers in the domain tree or forest. All of the domain data for a particular domain is replicated to every domain controller in that domain. All of the objects in every domain, and selected attributes for all objects in a forest, are replicated to the global catalog.

A domain controller stores and replicates

- The schema information for the domain tree or forest
- The configuration information for all domains in the domain tree or forest
- All directory objects and properties for its domain (this data is replicated to any additional domain controllers in the domain; for the purpose of finding information, a subset of the properties of all objects in the domain is replicated to the global catalog)

A global catalog stores and replicates

- The schema information for a forest
- The configuration information for all domains in a forest
- Selected attributes for all directory objects in the forest (replicated between global catalog servers only)
- All directory objects and all their properties for the domain in which the global catalog is located

Caution Extensions to schemas in a global catalog should be approached with caution. Schema extensions can have disastrous effects on large networks because the extensions cannot be deleted (only disabled) and because of the large amount of network traffic generated as the extensions are synchronized throughout the forest.

How Replication Works

Active Directory replicates information in two ways: *intrasite* (within a site) and *intersite* (between sites). The need for up-to-date directory information is balanced with the limitations imposed by available network bandwidth.

Intrasite Replication

Within a site, a Windows 2000 service known as the Knowledge Consistency Checker (KCC) automatically generates a topology for replication among domain controllers in the same domain using a ring structure. The topology defines the path for directory updates to flow from one domain controller to another until all domain controllers in the site receive the directory updates.

The ring structure ensures that there are at least two replication paths from one domain controller to another; if one domain controller is down temporarily, replication still continues to all other domain controllers, as shown in Figure 1.8.

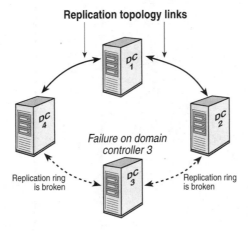

Figure 1.8   Intrasite replication topology

The KCC analyzes the replication topology within a site every 15 minutes to ensure that it still works and is efficient. If you add or remove a domain controller from the network or a site, the KCC reconfigures the topology to reflect the change.

Intersite Replication

To ensure replication between sites, you must manually connect them by creating *site links*. Site links represent network connections and allow replication to occur. Active Directory uses the network connection information to generate connection objects that provide efficient replication and fault tolerance, as shown in Figure 1.9.

You provide information about the replication transport used, cost of a site link, times when the link is available for use, and how often the link should be used. Active Directory uses this information to determine which site link will be used to replicate information. Customizing replication schedules so replication occurs during specific times, such as when network traffic is light, will make replication more efficient. Replication and site link configuration are discussed in Chapter 6, "Creating a Site Topology Plan."

Note When operating in native mode, Windows 2000 domain controllers do not replicate with pre–Windows 2000 domain controllers.

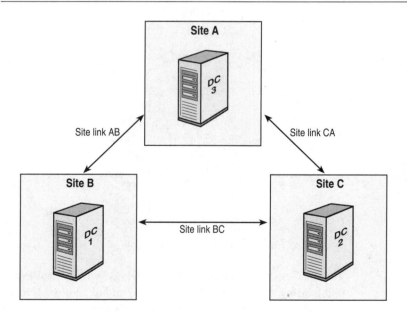

Figure 1.9   Intersite replication topology

Trust Relationships

A *trust relationship* is a link between two domains in which the trusting domain honors the logon authentication of the trusted domain. Active Directory supports two forms of trust relationships:

- Implicit two-way transitive trust. A relationship between parent and child domains within a tree and between the top-level domains in a forest. This is the default; trust relationships among domains in a tree are established and maintained implicitly (automatically). Transitive trust is a feature of the Kerberos authentication protocol, which provides the distributed authentication and authorization in Windows 2000.

  For example, in Figure 1.10 a Kerberos transitive trust simply means that if Domain A trusts Domain B, and Domain B trusts Domain C, then Domain A trusts Domain C. As a result, a domain joining a tree immediately has trust relationships established with every domain in the tree. These trust relationships make all objects in the domains of the tree available to all other domains in the tree.

  Transitive trust between domains eliminates the management of interdomain trust accounts. Domains that are members of the same tree automatically participate in a transitive, bidirectional trust relationship with the parent domain. As a result users in one domain can access resources to which they have been granted permission in all other domains in a tree.

- Explicit one-way nontransitive trust. A relationship between domains that are not part of the same tree. A nontransitive trust is bounded by the two domains in the trust relationship and does not flow to any other domains in the forest. In most cases, you must explicitly (manually) create nontransitive trusts. For example, in Figure 1.10, a one-way, nontransitive trust is shown where Domain C trusts Domain 1, so users in Domain 1 can access resources in Domain C.

Explicit one-way nontransitive trusts are the only form of trust possible between

- A Windows 2000 domain and a Windows NT domain
- A Windows 2000 domain in one forest and a Windows 2000 domain in another forest
- A Windows 2000 domain and an MIT Kerberos V5 realm, allowing a client in a Kerberos realm to authenticate to an Active Directory domain to access network resources in that domain

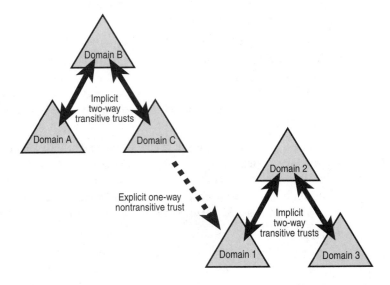

Figure 1.10   Active Directory supports two types of trust relationships

Group Policy

Group policies are collections of user and computer configuration settings that can be linked to computers, sites, domains, and OUs to specify the behavior of users' desktops. For example, using group policies, you can determine the programs that are available to users, the programs that appear on the user's desktop, and Start menu options.

To create a specific desktop configuration for a particular group of users, you create group policy objects (GPOs). GPOs are collections of group policy settings. Each Windows 2000 computer has one local GPO and may, in addition, be subject to any number of nonlocal (Active Directory–based) GPOs. Local GPOs are overridden by nonlocal GPOs. Nonlocal GPOs are linked to Active Directory objects (sites, domains, or OUs) and can be applied to either users or computers. Following the inheritance properties of Active Directory, nonlocal GPOs are applied hierarchically from the least restrictive group (site) to the most restrictive group (OU) and are cumulative.

How Group Policy Is Applied

Because nonlocal GPOs are applied hierarchically, the user or computer's configuration is a result of the GPOs applied to its site, domain, and OU. Group policy settings are applied in the following order:

1. Local GPO. Each Windows 2000 computer has exactly one GPO stored locally.
2. Site GPOs. Any GPOs that have been linked to the site are applied next. GPO application is synchronous; the administrator specifies the order of GPOs linked to a site.
3. Domain GPOs. Multiple domain-linked GPOs are applied synchronously; the administrator specifies the order of GPOs linked to a domain.
4. OU GPOs. GPOs linked to the OU highest in the Active Directory hierarchy are applied first, followed by GPOs linked to its child OU, and so on. Finally, the GPOs linked to the OU that contains the user or computer are applied. At the level of each OU in the Active Directory hierarchy, one, many, or no

GPOs can be linked. If several group policies are linked to an OU, then they are applied synchronously in an order specified by the administrator.

Figure 1.11 shows how group policy is applied for the example Marketing and Servers OUs.

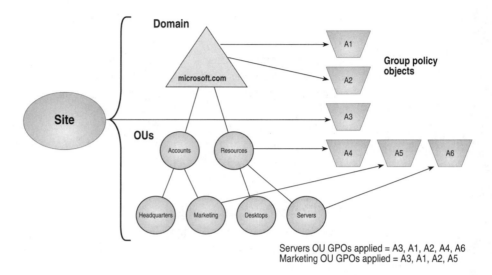

Servers OU GPOs applied = A3, A1, A2, A4, A6
Marketing OU GPOs applied = A3, A1, A2, A5

Figure 1.11   How group policy is applied

The default order for the application of group policy settings is subject to the following exceptions:

- A computer that is a member of a workgroup processes only the local GPO.
- No Override. Any GPO linked to a site, domain, or OU (not the local GPO) can be set to No Override with respect to that site, domain, or OU, so that none of its policy settings can be overwritten. When more than one GPO has been set to No Override, the one highest in the Active Directory hierarchy (or higher in the hierarchy specified by the administrator at each fixed level in Active Directory) takes precedence. No Override is applied to the GPO link.

- Block Policy Inheritance. At any site, domain, or OU, group policy inheritance can be selectively marked as Block Policy Inheritance. However, GPO links set to No Override are always applied and cannot be blocked. Block Policy Inheritance is applied directly to the site, domain, or OU. It is not applied to GPOs, nor is it applied to GPO links. Thus, Block Policy Inheritance deflects *all* group policy settings that reach the site, domain, or OU from above (by way of linkage to parents in the Active Directory hierarchy) no matter what GPOs those settings originate from.

- Loopback setting. Loopback is an advanced group policy setting that is useful on computers in certain closely managed environments such as kiosks, laboratories, classrooms, and reception areas. Loopback provides alternatives to the default method of obtaining the ordered list of GPOs whose user configuration settings affect a user. By default, a user's settings come from a GPO list that depends on the user's location in Active Directory. The ordered list goes from site-linked to domain-linked to OU-linked GPOs, with inheritance determined by the location of the user in Active Directory and in an order specified by the administrator at each level. Loopback can be Not Configured, Enabled, or Disabled as can any other group policy setting. In the Enabled state, loopback can be set to Replace or Merge mode.

  - Replace. In this case, the GPO list for the user is replaced in its entirety by the GPO list already obtained for the local computer at startup. The computer's GPOs replace the user GPOs normally applied to the user.

  - Merge. In this case, the GPO list is concatenated. The GPO list obtained for the local computer at startup is appended to the GPO list obtained for the user at logon. Because the GPO list obtained for the computer is applied later, it has precedence if it conflicts with settings in the user's list.

You should plan your GPO settings and the Active Directory objects to which they will be applied to provide the most efficient group policy management for your organization. Chapter 5, "Creating an Organizational Unit Plan," discusses planning for group policy.

DNS Namespace

Active Directory, like all directory services, is primarily a namespace. A *namespace* is any bounded area in which a name can be resolved. *Name resolution* is the process of translating a name into some object or information that the name represents. The Active Directory namespace is based on the DNS naming scheme, which allows for interoperability with Internet technologies. Private networks use DNS extensively to resolve computer names and to locate computers within their local networks and the Internet. DNS provides the following benefits:

- DNS names are user friendly, which means they are easier to remember than IP addresses.

- DNS names remain more constant than IP addresses. An IP address for a server can change, but the server name remains the same.

- DNS allows users to connect to local servers using the same naming convention as the Internet.

Note To read more about DNS, open your Web browser and use an Internet search engine to run a search on "RFC 1034" and "RFC 1035". RFCs (Request for Comments) are the official documents of the Internet Engineering Task Force (IETF) that specify the details for new Internet specifications or protocols. RFC 1034 is entitled "Domain Names—Concepts and Facilities" and RFC 1035 is entitled "Domain Names—Implementation and Specification."

Because Active Directory uses DNS as its domain naming and location service, Windows 2000 domain names are also DNS names. Windows 2000 Server uses dynamic DNS, which enables clients with dynamically assigned addresses to register directly with a server running the DNS service and update the DNS table dynamically. Dynamic DNS eliminates the need for other Internet naming services, such as Windows Internet Naming Service (WINS), in a homogeneous environment.

Note To read more about dynamic DNS, open your Web browser and use an Internet search engine to run a search on "RFC 2136". RFC 2136 is entitled "Dynamic Updates in the Domain Name System (DNS Update)."

Important For Active Directory and associated client software to function correctly, you must have installed and configured the DNS service.

Domain Namespace

The *domain namespace* is the naming scheme that provides the hierarchical structure for the DNS database. Each node represents a partition of the DNS database. These nodes are referred to as *domains*.

The DNS database is indexed by name; therefore, each domain must have a name. As you add domains to the hierarchy, the name of the parent domain is appended to its child domain (called a *subdomain*). Consequently, a domain's name identifies its position in the hierarchy. For example, in Figure 1.12, the domain name *sales.microsoft.com* identifies the sales domain as a subdomain of the *microsoft.com* domain and *microsoft* as a subdomain of the *com* domain.

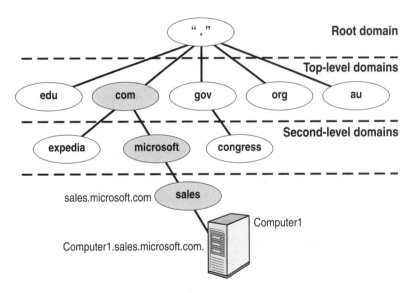

Figure 1.12   Hierarchical structure of a domain namespace

The hierarchical structure of the domain namespace consists of a root domain, top-level domains, second-level domains, and host names.

There are two types of namespaces:

- Contiguous namespace. The name of the child object in an object hierarchy always contains the name of the parent domain. A tree is a contiguous namespace.
- Disjointed namespace. The names of a parent object and a child of the same parent object are not directly related to one another. A forest is a disjointed namespace. For example, consider the domain names
  - www.microsoft.com
  - msdn.microsoft.com
  - www.msn.com

The first two domain names create a contiguous namespace within microsoft.com, but the third domain is part of disjointed namespace.

Note The term *domain*, in the context of DNS, is not related to *domain* as used in Windows 2000 directory services. A Windows 2000 domain is a group of computers and devices that are administered as a unit.

The DNS naming scheme is discussed in Chapter 4, "Creating a Domain Plan."

Root Domain

The *root domain* is at the top of the hierarchy and is represented as a period (.). The Internet root domain is managed by several organizations, including Network Solutions, Inc.

Top-Level Domains

Top-level domains are arranged by organization type or geographic location. Table 1.1 provides some examples of top-level domain names.

Table 1.1   Examples of Top-Level Domains

Top-level domain	Description
gov	Government organizations
com	Commercial organizations
edu	Educational institutions
org	Noncommercial organizations
net	Commercial sites or networks

Note Individual country names may also be a part of top-level domains. Examples of country domain names are "au" for Australia or "fr" for France.

Top-level domains can contain second-level domains and host names.

Second-Level Domains

Organizations, such as Network Solutions, Inc., and others, assign and register *second-level domains* to individuals and organizations for the Internet. A second-level name has two name parts: a top-level name and a unique second-level name. Table 1.2 provides some examples of second-level domains.

Table 1.2   Examples of Second-Level Domains

Second-level domain	Description
ed.gov	United States Department of Education
microsoft.com	Microsoft Corporation
stanford.edu	Stanford University
w3.org	World Wide Web Consortium
pm.gov.au	Prime Minister of Australia

Note In the case of country names, "gov.au", "edu.au", and "com.au" are top-level domains. If the name is structured as "company.au", however (and in this case only), ".au" is top-level.

Host Names

Host names refer to specific computers on the Internet or a private network. For example, in Figure 1.12, Computer1 is a host name. A host name is the leftmost portion of a *fully qualified domain name* (FQDN), which describes the exact position of a host within the domain hierarchy. In Figure 1.12, Computer1.sales.microsoft.com. (including the end period, which represents the root domain) is an FQDN.

Note The host name does not have to be the same as the computer name, NetBIOS, or any other naming protocol.

Zones

A *zone* is a database containing resource records for a portion of a DNS namespace. Zones provide a way to partition the domain namespace into manageable sections.

Multiple zones in a domain namespace are used to distribute administrative tasks to different groups. For example, Figure 1.13 depicts the microsoft.com domain namespace divided into two zones. The two zones allow one administrator to manage the microsoft and sales domains and another administrator to manage the development domain.

A zone must encompass a contiguous domain namespace. For example, in Figure 1.13, you could not create a zone that consists of only the sales.microsoft.com and development.microsoft.com domains because the sales and development domains are not contiguous.

The name-to-IP-address mappings for a zone are stored in the zone database file. Each zone is anchored to a specific domain, referred to as the zone's *root domain*. The zone database file does not necessarily contain information for all subdomains of the zone's root domain, only those subdomains within the zone.

In Figure 1.13, the root domain for Zone1 is microsoft.com, and its zone file contains the name-to-IP-address mappings for the microsoft and sales domains.

The root domain for Zone2 is development, and its zone file contains the name-to-IP-address mappings for the development domain only. The zone file for Zone1 does not contain the name-to-IP-address mappings for the development domain, although development is a subdomain of the microsoft domain.

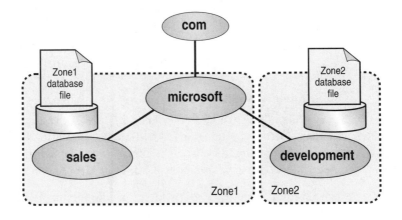

Figure 1.13   Domain namespace divided into zones

Name Servers

A DNS name server stores the zone database file. DNS name servers use the zone database files to handle the DNS name resolution process. Name servers can store data for one zone or multiple zones. A name server is said to have authority for the domain namespace that the zone encompasses. When a DNS name server receives a DNS query, it responds in one of three ways: by returning the requested name or IP-resolution information, by returning a pointer to another DNS name server, or by indicating that the information is not available. There are three main types of DNS name servers: primary, secondary, and master.

A *primary name server* gets data from the local zone and is the authoritative server (performs administrative tasks) for the zone. A *secondary name server* is a backup DNS server and receives data from another name server. A zone can have multiple secondary name servers and should have at least one to perform zone transfers, provide redundancy, improve access speed, and reduce the load on the primary name server. A *master name server* is a primary or secondary name server for a zone that is designated to provided updated DNS information to a secondary server.

Naming Conventions

Every object in Active Directory is identified by a name. Active Directory uses a variety of naming conventions: distinguished names, relative distinguished names, globally unique identifiers, and user principal names.

Distinguished Name

Every object in Active Directory has a *distinguished name* (DN) that uniquely identifies the object and contains sufficient information for a client to retrieve the object from the directory. The DN includes the name of the domain that holds the object, as well as the complete path through the container hierarchy to the object.

For example, the following DN identifies the Firstname Lastname user object in the microsoft.com domain (where *Firstname* and *Lastname* represent the actual first and last name of a user account):

```
/DC=COM/DC=microsoft/OU=dev/CN=Users/CN=Firstname  Lastname
```

Table 1.3 describes the attributes in the example.

Table 1.3   Distinguished Name Attributes

Attribute	Description
DC	Domain component name
OU	Organizational unit name
CN	Common name

DNs must be unique. Active Directory does not allow duplicate DNs.

Note To read more about distinguished names, search on the Internet for "RFC 1779". RFC 1779 is entitled "A String Representation of Distinguished Names."

Relative Distinguished Name

Active Directory supports querying by attributes, so you can locate an object even if the exact DN is unknown or has changed. The *relative distinguished name* (RDN) of an object is the part of the name that is an attribute of the object itself. In the preceding example, the RDN of the Firstname Lastname user object is Firstname Lastname. The RDN of the parent object is Users.

You can have duplicate RDNs for Active Directory objects, but you cannot have two objects with the same RDN in the same OU. For example, if a user account is named Jane Doe, you cannot have another user account called Jane Doe in the same OU. However, objects with duplicate RDN names can exist in separate OUs because they have different DNs (see Figure 1.14).

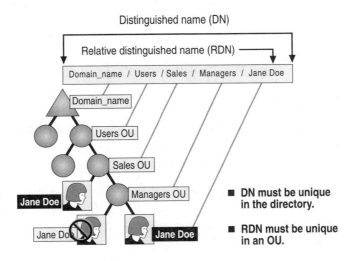

Figure 1.14   Distinguished names and relative distinguished names

Globally Unique Identifier

A *globally unique identifier* (GUID) is a 128-bit number that is guaranteed to be unique within the enterprise. GUIDs are assigned to objects when the objects are created. The GUID never changes, even if you move or rename the object. Applications can store the GUID of an object and use the GUID to retrieve that object regardless of its current DN.

In earlier versions of Windows NT, each domain resource was associated with a security identifier (SID) that was generated within the domain. This meant that the SID was guaranteed to be unique only within the domain. A GUID is unique across all domains, meaning that you can move objects from domain to domain and they will still have a unique identifier.

User Principal Name

Each user account has a "friendly" name, the *user principal name* (UPN). The UPN is composed of a shorthand name for the user account and the DNS name of the tree where the user account object resides. For example, *Firstname Lastname* (substitute the first and last names of the actual user) in the microsoft.com tree might have a UPN of FirstnameL@microsoft.com (using the full first name and the first letter of the last name).

Lesson Summary

In this lesson you learned about several new concepts introduced with Active Directory, including replication, trust relationships, group policies, DNS namespaces, and naming conventions.

You learned that Active Directory includes replication to ensure that changes to a domain controller are reflected in all domain controllers within a domain. Within a site, the KCC automatically generates a ring topology for replication among domain controllers in the same domain. Between sites, you must specify how your sites are connected by using site links.

A trust relationship is a link between two domains in which the trusting domain honors the logon authentication of the trusted domain. Active Directory supports two forms of trust relationships: implicit two-way transitive trusts and explicit one-way nontransitive trusts.

You also learned that group policies are collections of user and computer configuration settings that can be linked to computers, sites, domains, and OUs to specify the behavior of users' desktops. To create a specific desktop configuration for a particular group of users, you create group policy objects (GPOs), collections of group policy settings. Each Windows 2000 computer has one local GPO and may, in addition, be subject to any number of nonlocal (Active Directory–based) GPOs. Local GPOs are overridden by nonlocal GPOs. Nonlocal GPOs are linked to Active Directory objects (sites, domains, or OUs) and can be applied to either users or computers. Following the inheritance properties of Active Directory, nonlocal GPOs are applied hierarchically from the least restrictive group (site) to the most restrictive group (OU) and are cumulative.

In this lesson you also learned that Active Directory uses DNS as its domain naming and location service; therefore Windows 2000 domain names are also DNS names. Windows 2000 Server uses dynamic DNS, so clients with dynamically assigned addresses can register directly with a server running the DNS service and dynamically update the DNS table. There are contiguous namespaces and disjointed namespaces.

Finally, you learned about the naming conventions employed by Active Directory: DNs, RDNs, GUIDs, and UPNs.

Review

The following questions are intended to reinforce key information presented in the chapter. If you are unable to answer a question, review the appropriate lesson and then try the question again. Answers to the questions can be found in Appendix A, "Questions and Answers."

1. Your organization would like to include the languages in which each staff member is proficient in the Active Directory database. What action must you take to accomplish this and why?

2. How would you arrange two OUs, Orders and Deliveries, so that the Orders OU has administrative control of the Deliveries OU but the Deliveries OU does not have administrative control of the Orders OU?

3. You are considering adding global catalog servers to your network. What are the advantages of such an action? Disadvantages?

4. Your client requires all Windows computers in his organization to display the company logo as the background wallpaper. What action should you take?

5. Your network has a parent domain named stateuniversity.microsoft.com. You want to add a child domain named stateuniversity.expedia.com to form a tree. Can you arrange these domains in a tree? Why or why not?

C H A P T E R 2

Introduction to Designing a Directory Services Infrastructure

About This Chapter

This chapter introduces you to the tasks you need to complete before attempting to design your Active Directory directory services infrastructure. Before you can begin your design you must assemble a design team, conduct an analysis of your business environment, conduct an analysis of your technical environment, and set up a test environment. This chapter also introduces the Active Directory infrastructure design process.

Before You Begin

To complete the lessons in this chapter, you must have the basic knowledge of the Active Directory components and concepts covered in Chapter 1, "Introduction to Active Directory."

Lesson 1: Design Overview

This lesson introduces you to the Active Directory infrastructure design. It also explains the tools you need to create an infrastructure design and provides an overview of the design process.

After this lesson, you will be able to

- State the function of an Active Directory infrastructure design
- Explain the benefits of creating an Active Directory infrastructure design
- Describe the resources necessary to create an Active Directory infrastructure design
- Describe the Active Directory infrastructure design process
- Recall the design guiding principles

Estimated lesson time: 10 minutes

What Is an Active Directory Infrastructure Design?

Before you implement Active Directory in your organization, you need to devise some type of plan. An *Active Directory infrastructure design* is a plan you create that represents your organization's network infrastructure. You use this plan to determine how you will configure Active Directory to store information about objects on your network and make the information available to users and network administrators. This self-paced training kit provides a framework for developing your Active Directory infrastructure design.

Because your Active Directory infrastructure design is key to the success of your Windows 2000 deployment, you must thoroughly gather information for, develop, and test your design before deployment. A significant amount of rethinking, redevelopment, and retesting may also be necessary at various points during the design process to ensure that your design meets the needs of your organization. An effective infrastructure design helps you provide a cost-effective deployment, eliminating the need to spend time and money reworking your infrastructure.

Design Tools

To develop an effective Active Directory infrastructure design, you must assemble the following tools:

- Design team
- Business and technical analyses
- Test environment

Assembling a Design Team

Before you begin designing your Active Directory infrastructure, you must identify the people in your organization who should be involved in the design process and assemble them into a *design team*. The obvious candidates for the design team are the system and network administrators. However, because your infrastructure design must encompass enterprise-wide business requirements, the team must also include input from staff and management who represent a cross section of your organization. To ensure that all aspects of your organization are addressed in your Active Directory implementation, you may want to employ a multilevel team design consisting of three panels:

- Infrastructure designers
- Staff representatives
- Management representatives

The *infrastructure designers* panel consists of the key personnel involved in designing your Active Directory infrastructure. To avoid slowdowns that naturally occur when a number of people are involved in making decisions, the infrastructure designers have authority and are the driving force behind the infrastructure design process. Although the number of members may vary depending on the size of the organization, the infrastructure designers panel should contain system administrators, network administrators, and members of the information technology management organization. During the design process, infrastructure designers function as consultants, performing the following tasks:

- Interviewing staff and management representatives to understand their business and their customers

- Interviewing staff and management representatives to determine system needs
- Interpreting system needs and incorporating them into infrastructure design decisions
- Facilitating collaborative design decisions between business units

The skills set for infrastructure designers must include both Windows 2000 technical skills and soft skills. *Soft skills* are the abilities to "read" people and to communicate and collaborate with them in a diplomatic fashion. Though it's imperative for members of this panel to maintain a high level of Windows 2000 and Active Directory knowledge, it is also extremely important for the members to be proficient in interviewing people, understanding business needs, and facilitating a collaborative environment between people and business units in an organization. Almost three-fourths of the time spent developing an infrastructure design may be spent working with people to determine organizational needs. Infrastructure designers who lack soft skills may require additional training to ensure the success of their Active Directory infrastructure design.

Note This self-paced training kit assumes that you are an infrastructure designer or one of the key personnel involved in designing the Active Directory infrastructure for your organization.

The *staff representatives* panel consists of personnel throughout the organization who are responsible for carrying out daily operations. The panel should contain an exemplary staff member from each business unit or department within the organization. During the design process, staff representatives function as advisors, performing the following tasks:

- Communicating information about business functions and customers to infrastructure designers
- Communicating business needs to infrastructure designers
- Communicating and collaborating with staff representatives from other business units in the enterprise to make infrastructure design decisions
- Reviewing design decisions made by infrastructure designers

The skills set for staff representatives must include the ability to understand and openly communicate business needs for the business unit they represent and an interest in taking part in infrastructure design. It is not necessary for staff representatives to maintain high levels of Windows 2000 technical knowledge.

The *management representatives* panel consists of management level personnel who are responsible for approving business decisions within the organization. The panel should contain a selected group of upper-level business unit managers. Management representatives must have the authority and ability to approve and support design decisions made by infrastructure designers at *each stage* of the design development process. Requiring management approval at each stage of development invites scrutiny throughout the design process and encourages managerial support for the finished design. During the design process, management representatives function as advisors and gatekeepers, performing the following tasks:

- Communicating information about business functions and customers to infrastructure designers
- Communicating business needs to infrastructure designers
- Communicating and collaborating with management representatives from other business units in the enterprise to make infrastructure design decisions
- Reviewing and approving design decisions made by infrastructure designers

The skills set for management representatives must include the ability to understand and openly communicate business needs within the business unit they represent and an interest in taking part in infrastructure design. It is not necessary for management representatives to maintain high levels of Windows 2000 technical knowledge.

Figure 2.1 shows the design team assembled by Hiabuv Toys, a fictitious toy company. Note that communication and information flows between the staff and management representatives while it ultimately flows up to the infrastructure designers.

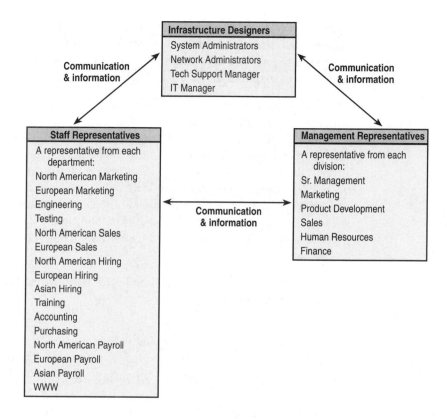

Figure 2.1   Multilevel team design for Hiabuv Toys

The design team members selected for each panel must be willing and be permitted to commit their time and talents throughout the design process to ensure that the infrastructure design effectively meets the requirements of their organization.

Analyzing Business and Technical Environments

After you've assembled a design team, the next design tools you need to assemble are analyses of your organization's business and technical environments. Most often, your organization will have a business infrastructure or network already in place; it's up to you as an infrastructure designer to call on members of the design team to help you assemble documentation about these environments. You will learn how to analyze your business and technical environments in Lessons 2 and 3.

Real World Read the "Designing in the Real World: Pre-Design Processes" interview with Dave Trulli, Program Manager, Microsoft Corporation, for a real-world perspective on some pre-design processes, including assembling a design team, gathering information for business and technical environment analyses, and distributing information to members of the design team. You can find the interview on the Supplemental Course Materials CD-ROM (\chapt02\Interview).

Testing Environment

After you complete your infrastructure design, you should be prepared to test it in a test environment. A *test environment* is a simulation of your production environment that allows you to test parts of your Windows 2000 deployment, such as your Active Directory infrastructure design, without risk to your organization's network. To ensure the success of your organization's Windows 2000 deployment, your organization should establish a test environment.

Important Building a Windows 2000 test lab and the planning and conducting of tests in the lab are beyond the scope of this course. For more information on the lab development and testing processes, refer to the *Microsoft Windows 2000 Server Deployment Planning Guide* volume of the *Microsoft Windows 2000 Server Resource Kit.*

By setting up your infrastructure design in a test environment, you will be able to see how the design actually works and determine whether any changes are necessary for improvement. Setting up your design in a test environment is an invaluable tool in the development of an effective design.

The Design Process

After you've assembled your design team, gathered business and network analyses, and established a test environment, you're ready to begin planning your infrastructure design. As illustrated in Figure 2.2, the Active Directory infrastructure design process consists of four stages:

1. Creating a Forest Plan
2. Creating a Domain Plan
3. Creating an Organizational Unit Plan
4. Creating a Site Topology Plan

1. Create a Forest Plan

2. Create a Domain Plan

3. Create an Organizational Unit Plan

4. Create a Site Topology Plan

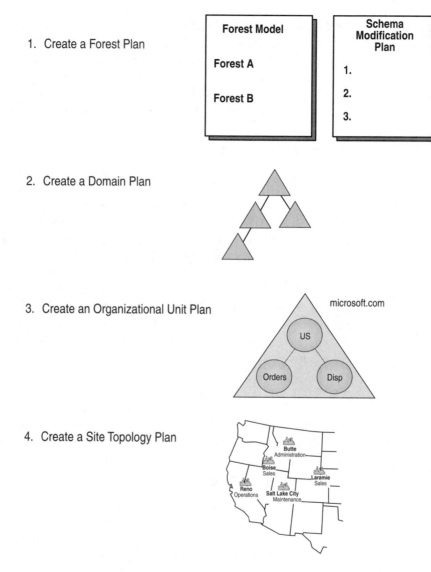

Figure 2.2   Stages of the Active Directory infrastructure design process

You should be aware that designing your Active Directory infrastructure is an iterative process—you will be revisiting each stage of the process several times before your design is ready for implementation.

Stage One—Creating a Forest Plan

During this stage, you consult your business and technical analysis documents and assess the forest structure your organization requires. You also assess any changes currently planned to address growth and flexibility needs and changes that would help meet the ideal design specifications of the organization. From these assessments you design a forest model.

In this stage you also create a schema modification policy, a plan that outlines who has control of the schema and how modifications that affect the entire forest are administered. You assess an organization's schema needs and, adhering to the schema modification policy, you determine whether to modify the schema. If it is necessary to modify the schema you design a schema modification plan.

Stage Two—Creating a Domain Plan

When you create a domain plan, you consult your business and technical analysis documents and assess the domain structure your organization requires. You also assess any changes currently planned to address growth and flexibility needs and changes that would help meet the ideal design specifications of the organization. From these assessments, you define domains, define the forest root domain, and define a domain hierarchy. Then you assess domain naming needs and choose names for each domain in the organization. Finally, you plan DNS server deployment by assessing the organization's current DNS server environment and determining the placement of DNS servers. To determine the placement of DNS servers, you plan additional zones, determine the existing DNS services employed on DNS servers, and determine the zone replication method to use. The end result of a domain plan is a domain hierarchy diagram that includes domain names and planned zones.

Stage Three—Creating an Organizational Unit Plan

During this stage, you consult your business and technical analysis documents and assess the organizational unit (OU), user, and group structure your organization requires. You also assess any changes currently planned to address growth and flexibility needs and changes that would help meet the ideal design specifications of the organization. From these assessments you define an OU structure and then plan user accounts and groups. The end result of an OU plan is a diagram of OU structures for each domain, a list of users in each OU, and a list of groups in each domain.

Stage Four—Creating a Site Topology Plan

During the final phase of the design process, you consult your business and technical analysis documents and assess the site topology your organization requires. You also assess any changes currently planned to address growth and flexibility needs and changes that would help meet the ideal design specifications of the organization. From these assessments, you design a logical representation of an organization's physical network. Creating a site topology plan includes defining sites, placing domain controllers, defining a replication strategy, and placing global catalog servers and operations masters within a forest. The end result of a site topology plan is a site diagram that includes domain controllers, operations masters roles, site links, and a site link table that provides details about site link configurations. Depending on the needs of the organization, a site topology plan may also include a site link bridge table and a preferred bridgehead server table.

Design Guiding Principles

As you design your Active Directory infrastructure, you should keep the following design guiding principles in mind:

- Design for simplicity. Simple infrastructures are easier to explain, maintain, and debug. However, more complex structures can add value that cannot be attained through simpler designs. Your design team must be prepared to analyze the effects of added complexity to determine whether such a structure is justified.

- Design to accommodate change. Change will affect your organization. Your design team should consider how changes can affect your Active Directory infrastructure and plan a design that can accommodate them.

- Design to meet ideal design specifications. Construct the first pass of your design to meet your organization's ideal infrastructure design specifications. Your design team can then consider the cost of such a design and whether it is feasible. The design can then be refined to meet the resources allocated.

- Consider alternatives. Create more than one design. Your design team can compare designs and combine ideas into a new design that best meets your organization's needs.

More Info Read the white paper "Windows 2000: Designing and Deploying Active Directory Service for the Microsoft Internal Corpnet," for a discussion of the internal design and deployment activities associated with the successful upgrade of the Microsoft enterprise network to Windows 2000. You can find the white paper on the Supplemental Course Materials CD-ROM (\chapt02\Corpnet). You may want to refer to this document as you study each stage of the Active Directory infrastructure design process.

Lesson Summary

In this lesson you learned that an Active Directory infrastructure design is a plan that represents your organization's network infrastructure. This plan is used to determine how you will configure Active Directory. You learned that the purpose of creating an Active Directory infrastructure design before actually implementing Active Directory is to test and refine your infrastructure in an off-network environment, eliminating the need to spend time and money reworking your actual network infrastructure.

You also learned that to develop an effective Active Directory infrastructure design, you must assemble a design team, business and technical environment analyses, and a test environment. You walked through the four stages of the design process: creating a forest plan, creating a domain plan, creating an organizational unit plan, and creating a site topology plan. Finally, you were introduced to the design guiding principles.

Lesson 2: Analyzing the Current Business Environment

For the purposes of this training kit, an organization's *business environment* defines how it organizes and manages its nontechnical resources. Before you can begin planning your Active Directory infrastructure you must analyze the current state of your business environment. This lesson covers the items you need to consider when analyzing your business environment.

After this lesson, you will be able to

- Analyze your organization's products and customers
- Analyze your organization's business structure
- Analyze your organization's business processes
- Analyze the factors that influence your organization's business strategy
- Analyze your organization's information technology (IT) management organization

Estimated lesson time: 40 minutes

Analyzing the Current Business Environment

Your organization's business environment has a direct effect on your Active Directory infrastructure. To analyze the current business environment, you will need to analyze the following components of your organization:

- Products and customers
- Business structure
- Business processes
- Factors that influence company strategies
- Information technology (IT) management organization

To analyze each component thoroughly, you'll need to use your interviewing skills to gather information from various members of your design team. One of the best ways to gather information is to develop a worksheet that outlines what you need to know about each component and then use the worksheet to interview your team members.

Note The Supplemental Course Materials CD-ROM that accompanies this book contains blank copies of interview worksheets (\chapt02\worksheets) that you can use to conduct your own business environment analysis. The worksheets are only a starting point; you should modify them to meet your own analysis needs.

The result of your interviews and the completed worksheets will be a *business environment analysis document* that describes the current state of each business environment component. When complete, this document can be distributed to each member of the design team, providing a starting point for discussion and assessment of future needs. In this lesson, you will examine the completed worksheets that constitute the business environment analysis document for Hiabuv Toys, a fictitious toy company whose design team we viewed in the previous lesson.

You will use your business environment analysis document in conjunction with your business environment needs assessment to determine the location and function of components in your Active Directory infrastructure plan. You will learn to conduct needs assessments for your business environment as you learn and practice each stage of the infrastructure design process in Chapters 3–6.

Analyzing Products and Customers

Understanding your organization's products and customers is a starting point for analyzing your business environment. Products are sets of tangible or intangible attributes assembled to provide benefits to a customer and can include goods, services, places, persons, and ideas. Customers are the entities that purchase products. The completed Products and Customers Worksheet for Hiabuv Toys analyzes the organization's products and customers.

Hiabuv Toys Products and Customers Worksheet

Use this worksheet as a guide for gathering data about your organization's products and customers.

1. List and briefly describe the products or services provided by your organization.

   Molded plastic action figures, molded plastic toys, molded plastic yard ornaments, plastic model vehicles, plastic plant and animal models.

2. Describe how new products or services are developed in your organization.

   Potential new products are brought through the concept stage by members of senior management in the Marketing departments. The Engineering department develops a product prototype. The Testing department tests the prototype for market potential, safety, and durability. If the product is satisfactory, it is manufactured, distributed, and sold in the retail marketplace.

3. Identify and briefly describe the current stage of each product or service in its life cycle (introduction, growth, maturity, or decline). Note the current age (in years) of each product or service.

   Molded plastic action figures and plastic model vehicles have been manufactured by Hiabuv Toys for only five years; these products are in the growth stage of their life cycle. Hiabuv Toys is known for the lifelike detail it uses to portray action figures. Its model vehicle line is regarded as a premium line and includes models of rare and one-of-a kind vehicles.

   Various molded plastic toys and yard ornaments have been manufactured by Hiabuv Toys for more than 20 years; these products are in the maturity stage of their life cycle. The designs and colors for toys and ornaments are changed periodically to keep up with current trends.

   Plastic plant and animal models have been manufactured by Hiabuv Toys for 20 years; these products are in the decline stage of their life cycle. At this time, computer technology is a more popular method for teaching students about plant and animal structures.

4. Describe how your organization's products or services are packaged.

   Molded plastic action figures are blister-packed; molded plastic toys and yard ornaments are sold loose from a display carton; plastic model vehicles and plastic plant and animal models are sold in individual cartons.

5. Describe how your organization's products or services are priced.

Molded plastic action figures are priced at $5; molded plastic toys and yard ornaments range from $4 to $10; plastic model vehicles range from $30 to $100; plastic plant and animal models range from $20 to $200.

6. Describe how your organization's products or services are manufactured or created.

All Hiabuv Toys products are created at its molded plastic manufacturing plant in Taipei, Taiwan.

7. Describe how your organization's products or services are distributed.

Hiabuv Toys products sold in North America are distributed to retail outlets through the Seattle distribution center. Hiabuv Toys products sold in Europe are distributed to retail outlets through the London distribution center.

8. Describe how your organization's products or services are promoted.

Molded plastic action figures and plastic model vehicles are advertised on television, in children's magazines, and on the Internet. Molded plastic toys and yard ornaments are not promoted. Plastic plant and animal models are advertised in publications that target educational institutions and teachers.

9. Describe the customers served by your organization's products or services.

Retail toy and discount stores purchase action figures, molded plastic toys, and yard ornaments for resale to children and adults in their outlets. High-end toy and hobby stores purchase the plastic model vehicles for resale to model vehicle enthusiasts in their outlets. Educational institutions and teachers purchase plant and animal models for use as presentation aids in elementary and secondary school classes.

10. Describe how customer interactions are handled by your organization.

Interactions with retail customers for all products are handled by the Sales department, typically by the retailer's sales representative. Interactions with end customers for molded plastic action figures, plastic model vehicles, and plastic plant and animal models are handled through a toll-free hotline. Safety issues concerning all products are expedited to Product Development management.

continued

> **Hiabuv Toys Products and Customers Worksheet,** *continued*
>
> ---
>
> 11. Describe how customers use your organization's products or services.
>
>   **Molded plastic action figures and molded plastic toys are used for amusement by young children. Molded plastic yard ornaments and plastic model vehicles are used for decorative or display purposes by older children and adults. Plastic plant and animal models are used for educational purposes by schools and teachers.**
>
> 12. Where are your customers located?
>
>   **Both retail customers and end customers are located in North America and Europe. A new Hiabuv Toys Web site is generating limited sales to customers outside of these areas.**

Note A blank copy of this worksheet is located on the Supplemental Course Materials CD-ROM (\chapt02\worksheets\Products&Customers).

Analyzing Current Business Structure

A *business structure* represents the daily operating structure of your organization. To determine the current business structure of your organization, you must under stand how your company conducts daily operations both administratively and geographically.

An organization's *administrative structure* represents the functions, divisions, departments, or positions within an organization and how they are related, including the organization's hierarchy and authority structure. The administrative structure reflects how your company is managed and how it conducts administrative operations. Special operations, such as the relationships an organization may have set up with vendors, partners, customers, or proposed acquisition entities may also be represented in the administrative structure. Such special operations may require representation in your Active Directory infrastructure.

An organization's *geographical structure* represents the physical locations of the functions, divisions, departments, or positions within an organization. It reflects how your company is organized geographically, whether regionally, nationally, or internationally.

The completed Business Structures Worksheet for Hiabuv Toys shows the organization's administrative and geographical structures.

Hiabuv Toys Business Structures Worksheet

Use this worksheet as a guide for gathering data about business structures in your organization.

1. Diagram the administrative structure of your organization.

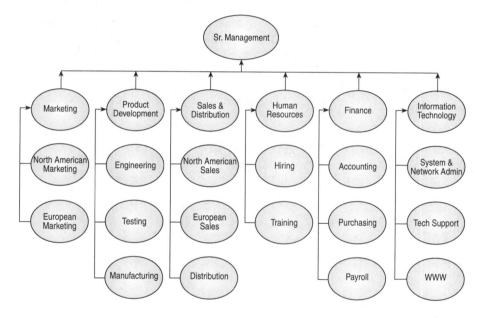

2. List and briefly describe the purpose of each division or department in the administrative structure. To whom do these divisions report?

   Senior Management division contains the management personnel for each division; it is the decision-making center for the entire organization. Marketing division contains North American and European Marketing departments. Product Development division contains the product Engineering, Testing, and Manufacturing departments. Sales and Distribution division contains North American and

continued

Hiabuv Toys Business Structures Worksheet, *continued*

European Sales departments, also the Distribution department. Human Resources division contains the Hiring and Training departments. Finance division contains the Accounting, Purchasing, and Payroll departments. Information Technology division contains the System & Network Administration, Technical Support, and World Wide Web departments. All divisions report to Senior Management.

3. Indicate the number of network users in each division of the administrative structure and the total number of network users in the organization.

   Approximate number of users by division: Senior Management (60); Marketing (200); Product Development (360); Sales & Distribution (600); Human Resources (130); Finance (200); Information Technology (200). Approximate total number of network users: 1,750. Approximate total number of employees: 2,385.

4. Diagram the geographical structure of your organization.

5. List each administrative division and describe where it is located in the geographical structure.

   Administrative division locations

   Senior Management: Chicago. Marketing: North American Marketing—Chicago; European Marketing—London. Product Development: Engineering and Testing—Chicago; Manufacturing—Taipei. Sales: North American Sales—Chicago; North American Distribution—Seattle; European Sales and Distribution—London. Human Resources: North American Hiring—Chicago; European Hiring—London; Asian Hiring—Taipei; Training: Chicago. Finance: Accounting, Purchasing, North American Payroll—Chicago; European Payroll—London; Asian payroll—Taipei. Information Technology: North American System & Network Administration—Chicago; European System & Network Administration—London; Asian System & Network Administration—Taipei.

6. List the number of network users in each location.

   Approximate number of users in each location: Taipei (240); Seattle (100); Chicago (1,030); London (380). Approximate total number of network users: 1,750. Approximate total number of employees: 2,385.

7. Describe how the network users in each department currently use the network.

   Marketing: Users access the network using workstations assigned to them and their home PCs. About 15 laptops are available for remote access while traveling.

   Product Development: Users in Engineering, Testing, and management personnel in the Manufacturing department access the network using workstations assigned to them and their home PCs. About 20 laptops are available for remote access while traveling.

   Sales & Distribution: Users in North American and European Sales access the network using laptops through remote access and their home PCs. Management personnel in the Distribution department access the network using workstations assigned to them.

   Human Resources: Users in the North American, European, and Asian Hiring departments access the network using workstations assigned to them and their home PCs. Personnel in the Training department access the network using laptops through remote access and their home PCs.

continued

Hiabuv Toys Business Structures Worksheet, *continued*

Finance: Users access the network using workstations assigned to them and their home PCs. About 25 laptops are available for remote access while traveling.

Information Technology: Users access the network using workstations or servers assigned to them and their home PCs. About 20 laptops are available for remote access while traveling.

8. Add any special operations to your administrative structure diagram.

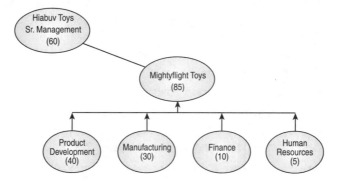

Hiabuv Toys has recently acquired Mightyflight Toys, a small designer and manufacturer of nylon kites located in Miami. Mightyflight Toys is a small company, with only 135 employees and 85 users. In the partnership agreement, Mightyflight Toys can use resources in the Marketing, Sales, Distribution, and Information Technology departments at Hiabuv Toys. The rest of the Mightyflight Toys organization has been left intact to retain its quality products.

Note A blank copy of this worksheet is located on the Supplemental Course Materials CD-ROM (\chapt02\worksheets\BusinessStructures).

Analyzing Current Business Processes

A *business process* is a series of steps that must be taken to achieve a desired result within the organization. To determine the current business processes active in your organization, you must analyze your organization's

- Information flow
- Communication flow
- Decision-making processes

The business processes employed by your organization have a direct effect on your Active Directory infrastructure.

Information Flow

Information flow refers to the process by which data arrives at its destination. The completed Information Flow Worksheet analyzes the information flow in the Engineering department of Hiabuv Toys.

Engineering Department, Hiabuv Toys, Information Flow Worksheet

Use this worksheet as a guide for gathering data about information flow in each department in your organization.

1. List the information that your department currently stores and maintains on the network and note the location of this information.

    The Engineering department currently stores the following items on the network: proposed, current, and retired product designs; product development documen-tation; end-user product documentation (for model vehicles and plant and animal models); a knowledge base; and administrative information for supervisory personnel. Designs are stored in the Design folder in the ProductDevel\ Engineering folder. Documentation is stored in the Docs folder in the ProductDevel\ Engineering folder. The knowledge base is stored in the Knowledge folder in the ProductDevel\ Engineering folder. Supervisory personnel store administrative information in the Admin folder in the ProductDevel\ Engineering folder.

continued

Engineering Department, Hiabuv Toys, Information Flow Worksheet, *continued*

2. List the users or groups of users who need access to the information that your department stores on the network. Briefly note the reason why the users need access to this information.

   There are five groups of engineers: MPEngineers (molded products), AFEngineers (action figures), MVEngineers (model vehicles), PAEngineers (plant and animal models), and SupvEngineers (supervisory engineers). Within the Design folder in the ProductDevel\Engineering folder, each group needs access to only the folder that contains the product designs for their group, MoldedProducts, ActionFigures, ModelVehicles, or PAModels. Supervisory engineers need access to all of the design folders and the Admin folder in the ProductDevel\Engineering folder.

3. Note how the users currently access this information and whether there are any restrictions in place for accessing it.

   Engineering department users currently access information from their work-stations. If they are traveling they must be able to have the same access remotely from a laptop computer. There are no time restrictions on the Engineering department for accessing information.

4. List other information on the network that is used by each department but stored and maintained by another department. Include the name of the department that is responsible for storing and maintaining the information and note the location of this information.

   The Engineering department uses source documents prepared by the North American and European Marketing departments in the SourceDocs folder in the Marketing\Specs folder.

5. List the users or groups of users who need access to information used by each department but stored and maintained by another department. Briefly note the reason why the users need access to this information.

   All of the engineering groups need access to the Marketing\Specs\SourceDocs folder in order to view the most current requirements and specifications for new products they are designing.

6. Note how the users currently access this information and whether there are any restrictions in place for accessing it.

   Engineering department users currently access marketing source documents from their workstations. If they are traveling they must be able to access these documents remotely from a laptop computer. There are no time restrictions on the Engineering department for accessing the marketing documents.

7. Specify entities responsible for administering information flow for your department.

   The System & Network Administration department administers information flow for the Engineering department.

8. Note any known difficulties or problems encountered with the current flow of information in your department.

   The ProductDevel\Engineering\Design folder does not always contain the most up-to-date designs. Also, when logging on remotely, users have access to designs produced by other engineering groups, which they should not have.

Note A blank copy of this worksheet is located on the Supplemental Course Materials CD-ROM (\chapt02\worksheets\InformationFlow).

Communication Flow

Communication flow refers to the process by which ideas, messages, or information arrive at their destination. The completed Communication Flow Worksheet analyzes the communication flow in the Engineering department of Hiabuv Toys.

Engineering Department, Hiabuv Toys, Communication Flow Worksheet

Use this worksheet as a guide for gathering data about communication flow in each department in your organization.

1. List the methods of communication currently used by your department that are maintained on the network.

   E-mail, Microsoft NetMeeting

continued

Engineering Department, Hiabuv Toys, Communication Flow Worksheet, *continued*

2. Note how these communication methods are accessed.

   Engineering department users currently access e-mail and NetMeeting from their workstations. If they are traveling they must be able to access these services remotely from a laptop computer.

3. List the users or groups of users who use the methods of communication that are maintained on the network. Briefly note the reasons why the users need to use each method of communication.

   MPEngineers (molded products), AFEngineers (action figures), MVEngineers (model vehicles), PAEngineers (plant and animal models), and SupvEngineers (supervisory engineers) need access to e-mail to send messages and files. These groups also need access to NetMeeting to participate in meetings with the European Marketing and Manufacturing departments, to collaborate in files, and to share information over the Internet or intranet.

4. Note any time restrictions currently in place for accessing each communication method.

   The Engineering department has no time restrictions for accessing e-mail or NetMeeting.

5. Specify entities responsible for administering communication methods for your department.

   The System & Network Administration department administers e-mail and NetMeeting for the Engineering department.

6. Note any known difficulties or problems encountered by your department with the current communication methods.

   Users in the Engineering department cannot consistently access e-mail when logging on remotely from a laptop computer.

Note A blank copy of this worksheet is located on the Supplemental Course Materials CD-ROM (\chapt02\worksheets\CommunicationFlow).

Decision-Making Processes

Decision making is the process of identifying options and then selecting an action to solve a specified problem. How options are identified and actions are selected in your organization affects the business environment. Similarly the options identified by your design team and the actions taken by the infrastructure designers are the foundation of your Active Directory infrastructure design. It's important to learn about the decision-making processes used in your organization so that you can anticipate decisions that may affect the business environment and so that you can develop a decision-making process for your design team.

To identify your options, you must gather information about the problem and analyze it. For decisions that require you to choose one action from only two choices, you can list the pros and cons of each choice or even weight the pros and cons of each choice. For decisions that require you to choose a solution from more than two choices, you can set up a decision matrix. A *decision matrix* is a comparison of the criteria used to make a decision with the available options. First, research, define, and weight the criteria you'll use to make the decision. Then score each choice as to how well it meets the criteria. Table 2.1 is an example of a decision matrix Hiabuv Toys may have used to decide on the location of their manufacturing plant. The first number represents the weighted score. The number in parentheses represents the unweighted score.

Table 2.1.   A Sample Decision Matrix

Criterion	Weight (1-low to 5-high)	Taipei	Tokyo	Sydney
Property Cost	2	3 (6)	1 (2)	3 (6)
Taxes	4	3 (12)	1 (4)	3 (12)
Wage Cost	5	3 (15)	1 (5)	2 (10)
Heating Costs	4	5 (20)	3 (12)	4 (16)
AC Costs	4	2 (8)	4 (16)	3 (12)
Access to Shipping Routes	3	5 (15)	5 (15)	4 (12)
Shipping Time	3	5 (15)	4 (12)	2 (6)
Total: Weighted (Unweighted)	Maximum: 25 (125)	26 (91)	19 (66)	21 (74)

After you've determined your options, the next step is to choose an action or make the decision that solves the problem. In an organization, there are five basic ways to choose an action, either by command, consultation, delegation, consensus, or voting. *Command decisions* are decisions made by one person. While one person can make the decision swiftly, the quality of a command decision can be low, since it is limited to the considerations of only one person. *Consultative decisions* are still made by one person, but only after that person gathers facts, ideas, and opinions from other people. This process involves a variety of people but still hinges on the analysis and judgment of one person. *Delegated decisions* are simply decisions that have been pushed down an organization's chain of command. The delegate must still choose a way to make the decision. *Consensus decisions* involve getting agreement from the entire group affected by the decision. Because the decision is not made until the entire group agrees, this method is the most time consuming and still does not guarantee that an effective decision will be made. Decisions made by *voting* are determined by the majority of the group affected by the decision. Voting is not an effective method of reaching a decision because no support is required from the group.

A good practice is to determine how infrastructure planning decisions will be made and let all design team members know. It's important that the team members understand whether they are making infrastructure design decisions or providing the recommendations for decisions. The completed Decision Making Worksheet analyzes the decision-making processes used at Hiabuv Toys.

Hiabuv Toys Decision Making Worksheet

Use this worksheet as a guide for gathering data about your organization's decision-making processes.

1. What decisions are made at the division level in your organization?

    Decisions made at the division level must adhere to the company's business strategy and affect the direction of the company. For example, the Senior Management division may decide that it needs to gather information to decide whether it would be more efficient to make the Manufacturing department a separate division.

2. What decisions are made at the departmental level in your organization?

Decisions made at the departmental level must adhere to the company's business strategy and affect the direction of each particular department. For example, the Training department may need to gather information and decide whether it is feasible to offer online training for employees.

3. What decisions are made by staff members?

Decisions made by staff members must adhere to the company's business strategy and affect the direction of that individual's work or projects within his or her department. For example, a salesperson may need to gather information and decide whether a retailer serviced by a competitor may be a potential sales prospect.

4. What decision-making process will the Active Directory infrastructure design team use?

Within the design team, the infrastructure designers will make decisions that affect the infrastructure design. The decisions will be made by consensus, only after assembling all of the necessary information. If there are problems during this decision-making process, the causes of the problems will be determined and corrected. Decisions will be communicated to the staff and management representatives, who will have the opportunity to provide feedback.

5. Note any known difficulties or problems encountered with the decision-making processes in your organization.

The amount of time needed to make business decisions is often longer than necessary.

Note A blank copy of this worksheet is located on the Supplemental Course Materials CD-ROM (\chapt02\worksheets\DecisionMaking).

Analyzing Business Strategy Influences

A *business strategy* is the long-range plan for defining and achieving the objectives set up by an organization. Factors related to an organization's objectives, environment, and resources can influence its business strategies.

- Organizational objectives that may affect business strategy include company priorities, projected growth and growth strategy, and risk tolerance.

- Environmental factors that may affect business strategy include the state of the local, regional, national, and international economy; changing technology; social and cultural factors; laws and regulations; competitors; customers; suppliers; and government agencies.

- Resource factors that may affect business strategy include financial resources, including the total cost of operations; human resources; and technological resources.

The factors that influence your business strategy can have a direct effect on your Active Directory infrastructure. The completed Business Strategy Influences Worksheet analyzes the factors that may influence the business strategy of Hiabuv Toys.

Hiabuv Toys Business Strategy Influences Worksheet

Use this worksheet as a guide for analyzing the factors that may influence your organization's business strategies.

1. Identify the priorities of your organization.

   Three priorities for Hiabuv Toys are creating new products, retaining employees, and cost-effective manufacturing.

2. What is the projected growth of your organization? Describe your organization's growth strategy.

   Hiabuv Toys is projected to grow by 20 percent in the next three years. Several new products are in concept stage and projected to increase revenues. Hiabuv Toys sees growth in new products and concentrates its efforts in the Marketing and Product Development divisions. Because the plastic plant and animal models are in the declining stage of their life cycle, resources previously devoted to this product line will be gradually reallocated to new products.

3. Describe your organization's tolerance for risk.

   Hiabuv Toys has a low tolerance for risk; all new policies, processes, and systems are implemented in stages and only with complete assurances that a return to the previous state is possible if problems are encountered.

4. What events in the local, regional, national, and international economy are relevant to your organization?

   Political, economic, and trade events that affect Asia, and more specifically Taiwan, North America, and more specifically the United States, the European Union, and more specifically the United Kingdom are relevant to Hiabuv Toys.

5. What technologies are relevant to each division in your organization?

   Marketing: communications technologies and Internet marketing capabilities. Product Development: plastic manufacturing and plastic recycling technologies, environmentally friendly packaging, computer-assisted design and manufacturing, and robotics. Sales: communications technologies, Internet sales capabilities, order tracking. Human Resources: Internet hiring, intranet-based training. Finance: communications technologies, Internet purchasing. Information Technology: company-wide operating system, applications used throughout the company, computer-assisted support, Internet technologies used throughout the company.

6. What social and cultural factors are relevant to your organization?

   (1) Business norms in Taiwan, North America, and the European Union must be tolerated and observed. (2) The fact that a majority of Hiabuv Toys products are geared toward children and the assumption that the number of children in the target countries is declining is kept in mind when planning new products.

7. What government agencies, laws, and regulations are relevant to your organization?

   Hiabuv Toys is subject to the government agencies and laws in its operations in Taiwan, the United States, and the United Kingdom. Hiabuv Toys is subject to the trade rules established for the United States and the United Kingdom. Therefore, products may not be shipped to countries under embargo, and so on. Hiabuv Toys products must meet safety regulations established in countries in North America and the European Union.

8. Who are your organization's competitors?

   Hiabuv Toys has two main competitors in the action figure and model vehicle product line. One competitor is twice the size of Hiabuv Toys with international distribution and the second competitor is smaller with distribution only in Australia. There is one competitor in the plant and animal model product line, about the same size as Hiabuv Toys but also offering simulated rocks, minerals, and gemstones. There is one competitor in molded products, a larger company with international distribution that also produces children's outdoor play equipment.

continued

Hiabuv Toys Business Strategy Influences Worksheet, *continued*

9. What is the total cost of operations for each product? (Compute the sum of your fixed costs, such as rent, salaries, and property taxes, and your variable costs, such as labor and materials, for a specific amount of products or services produced.)

   The total cost of operations for each product line is as follows: Molded plastic action figures are $1.11 each; molded plastic toys and molded plastic yard ornaments range from $1.22 to $5.02 each; plastic model vehicles range from $13.40 to $55.66 each; plastic plant and animal models range from $11.50 to $102.00 each.

10. What human resources are available to your organization?

   Due to a tight labor market, the professional labor currently available for departments in the Chicago area is extremely limited. Plastics engineers are especially scarce, as well as World Wide Web programmers. Labor for manufacturing in Taiwan is available at present but shows signs of tightening as the workforce shifts its skills to computer-based jobs. Labor for distribution in Seattle also shows signs of tightening. A moderate labor market in the London area provides adequate professional and distribution personnel. Retaining the current personnel worldwide is a major priority for Hiabuv Toys.

Note A blank copy of this worksheet is located on the Supplemental Course Materials CD-ROM (\chapt02\worksheets\BusinessStrategy).

Analyzing the Information Technology Management Organization

Information technology (IT) is the application of technology to the management and processing of information. In an organization, IT management refers to the management of the computing environment, usually performed by the IT, IS (information services) or MIS (management information services) departments. The IT management organization and the processes it employs can affect your Active Directory infrastructure.

To analyze your current IT management organization, you must gather information about its administrative structure, either centralized, decentralized, or some combination of both. In *centralized* administration structures, one team provides service and network administration. In *decentralized* structures, a number of teams, often divided by location or business function, provide services. Some structures provide both centralized and decentralized services depending on business needs. It is also helpful to recognize how your IT management organization is funded and how it handles decision making and changes in the organization. The completed IT Management Organization Worksheet analyzes the IT division at Hiabuv Toys.

Hiabuv Toys IT Management Organization Worksheet

Use this worksheet as a guide for gathering data about your company's information technology management organization.

1. Diagram the administrative structure of your IT organization.

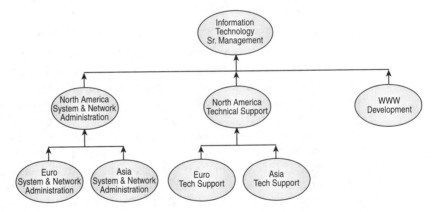

2. Is the administrative structure centralized, decentralized, or a combination of both?

   Because IT services are provided by a number of teams based on business function and location, the IT management organization at Hiabuv Toys provides a decentralized administrative structure.

continued

Hiabuv Toys IT Management Organization Worksheet, *continued*

3. Who is responsible for constructing the budget? Who approves the budget?

   The North America System & Network Administration, North America Technical Support, and WWW department managers construct the departmental budget. The Information Technology senior managers approve the departmental budget.

4. In what month is the budget established? When does your organization's fiscal year begin?

   The information technology division establishes its budget for the next fiscal year in July. The fiscal year begins on September 1.

5. What budget issues will affect your Active Directory infrastructure planning?

   Resources for new server hardware will be scarce; a limited amount of resources will be available for improved network links.

6. List each IT service that is outsourced and the vendors who perform the service.

   Some minimal software development is performed by the A. Datum Corporation. Cabling services are provided by ProElectron, Inc. Equipment moving services are provided by Costoso, Ltd.

7. Describe how decisions are made in your IT management organization.

   Decisions made by IT senior managers that affect the direction of the company are made after consulting with others in the organization. For example, IT senior managers may decide to upgrade the company-wide operating system or change the e-mail system used company-wide. Decisions made by department managers affect the individual departments and are made by consensus of department members. For example, the System & Network Administration department may decide to physically move a server for the convenience of its users. Decisions made by staff members in the IT organization affect the direction of that individual's work or projects within the department. For example, a member of the Tech Support department may design a list of FAQs to be distributed throughout the organization to address typical support issues.

8. How are IT changes handled by the IT management organization?

   First, the department must recognize when an IT-related change is necessary by monitoring how IT functions are meeting the needs of the organization. If needs are not being met, and a change is required, the department gathers data for possible

solutions and selects a solution. An implementation plan for the change is developed. The plan is tested by implementing the change in a test environment. Modifications are made until the change is implemented satisfactorily in the test environment. When the plan and the change are satisfactory, the change is implemented in a small sector of the organization. The change is monitored; if the results are satisfactory, the change is implemented in stages throughout the remainder of the organization.

9. Note any known difficulties or problems encountered in your company's IT management organization.

   It is often unclear as to who is responsible for system administration tasks in the North American System & Network Administration department. The European Tech Support department is often overwhelmed with support issues.

Note A blank copy of this worksheet is located on the Supplemental Course Materials CD-ROM (\chapt02\worksheets\ITManagement).

Lesson Summary

In this lesson you learned to analyze each component of your business environment, including the current products and customers, business structures, business processes, factors that influence company strategies, and your IT management organization. An organization's business environment defines how it organizes and manages its nontechnical resources. Your organization's business environment has a direct effect on your Active Directory infrastructure.

You also learned to create a document, the business environment analysis document, that describes the current state of each business environment component in your organization. The business environment analysis document includes the completed Products and Customers, Business Structures, Information Flow, Communication Flow, Decision Making, Business Strategy Influences, and IT Management Organization worksheets. When complete, this document can be distributed to each member of the design team, providing a starting point for discussion and needs assessment.

Lesson 3: Analyzing the Current Technical Environment

For the purposes of this training kit, an organization's *technical environment* defines how it organizes and manages its technical resources. Before you can begin planning your Active Directory infrastructure you must analyze the current state of your technical environment. This lesson covers the items you need to consider when analyzing your technical environment.

After this lesson, you will be able to

- Analyze your organization's current network architecture
- Analyze your organization's current hardware
- Analyze your organization's current software
- Analyze your organization's current technical standards
- Analyze your organization's current DNS environment
- Analyze your organization's current Windows NT domain architecture

Estimated lesson time: 40 minutes

Analyzing the Current Technical Environment

By analyzing your company's current technical environment, you can determine the technical requirements for implementing Active Directory. When you analyze your organization's current technical environment, you will need to analyze each component of the current technical environment, including

- Network architecture
- Hardware
- Software
- Technical standards
- DNS environment (if applicable)
- Windows NT domain architecture (if applicable)

To analyze each component thoroughly, you'll need to use your interviewing skills to gather information from various members of your design team. One of the best ways to gather information is to develop a worksheet that outlines what you need to know about each component and then use the worksheet to interview your team members. The Supplemental Course Materials CD-ROM that accompanies this book contains blank copies of interview worksheets that you can use to conduct your own technical environment analysis. The worksheets are only a starting point; you should modify them to meet your own analysis needs.

The result of your interviews and the completed worksheets will be a *technical environment analysis document* that describes the current state of each component of the technical environment. When complete, this document can be distributed to each member of the design team, providing a starting point for discussion and assessing future needs. In this lesson, you will examine the completed worksheets that constitute the technical environment analysis document for Hiabuv Toys, a fictitious toy company whose business environment we analyzed in the previous lesson.

You will use your technical environment analysis document in conjunction with your technical environment needs assessment to determine the location and function of components in your Active Directory infrastructure plan. You will learn to conduct needs assessments for your technical environment as you learn and practice each stage of the infrastructure design process in Chapters 3–6.

Analyzing the Current Network Architecture

By analyzing network architecture, you portray the physical environment of your organization's network, which includes the current

- Location of points on the network
- Number of users at each location
- Network type used at each location
- Location, link speed, and percentage of average available bandwidth of remote network links

---

Note Average available bandwidth is the amount of bandwidth that remains when you take the total bandwidth available for a link and subtract the amount of network traffic that occurs on the link during peak traffic.

- TCP/IP subnets at each location
- Speed of local network links
- Location of domain controllers
- List of servers at each location and the services that run on them
- Location of firewalls in the network

The completed Network Architecture Worksheet for Hiabuv Toys analyzes the organization's network architecture.

Hiabuv Toys Network Architecture Worksheet

Use this worksheet as a guide for gathering data about your organization's network architecture.

1. Diagram the network architecture of your organization by identifying the locations on the network, the number of users at each location, the links between locations, the link speed, and the percentage of average available bandwidth on each link during normal business hours. Indicate any links that are pay-by-usage, historically unreliable, or intermittently available or that can only connect using Simple Mail Transfer Protocol (SMTP).

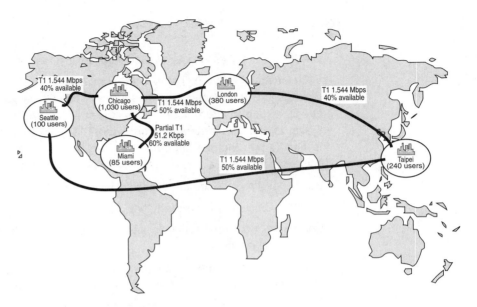

2. List the network type (Windows, Novell) used at each location.

   All servers at all locations use a Windows NT 4 network.

3. List the TCP/IP subnets at each location.

   Seattle: 140.10.*x.x.* Chicago: 141.10.*x.x.* Miami: 143.20.*x.x.* London: 144.31.*x.x.* Taipei: 150.30.*x.x.*

4. List the local network link speed at each location.

   Each location has a high-speed backbone connecting a set of 10- to 100-MB LANs.

5. List the location of domain controllers in the network.

   Seattle: 2 domain controllers. Taipei: 2 domain controllers. Chicago: 4 domain controllers. Miami: 2 domain controllers. London: 3 domain controllers.

continued

Hiabuv Toys Network Architecture Worksheet, *continued*

6. List the servers at each location, their purpose, and the services that run on them.

   Each location has an Exchange server and at least one file server. The London and Chicago locations each have SQL servers to handle the personnel, financial, client, and tech support information. The Seattle and London locations each have an SQL server to handle distribution information. The Chicago location has a CAD server to handle the Engineering department's product development information. The Taipei location has a server to handle manufacturing information.

7. List the location of all firewalls in the network.

   Only the Chicago site currently has a firewall.

8. Note any known difficulties or problems encountered with the current network architecture in your organization.

   Chicago currently has no direct link to Taipei. A direct link could free up some bandwidth between Chicago and Seattle and Chicago and London. Also, there is only one link to Miami; if outages occur, the Miami site would be isolated. The lack of firewalls at various locations presents a security risk.

Note A blank copy of this worksheet is located on the Supplemental Course Materials CD-ROM (\chapt02\worksheets\NetworkArch).

Analyzing the Current Hardware and Software

The purpose of analyzing the hardware and software currently in use on your network is to determine its compatibility with Windows 2000 Server. The first step in your analysis should be to conduct an inventory of the hardware and installed software. The second step is to compare your inventory with the list of hardware and software compatible with Windows 2000 Server, available at http://www.microsoft.com/windows2000/upgrade/compat/default.asp.

Your hardware inventory should include the name of each device and the manufacturer's name and model number. Depending on the device type, you may need to include more information about the device such as processor type, memory, or disk capacity. The types of devices you should consider for your inventory include audio or sound cards, computers, cameras or digital cameras, CD-R/RW, controller cards, DVD, input devices, modems, monitors, networking, printers, scanners, smart card readers, storage, TV tuners, uninterruptible power supply (UPS), USB/ 1394, video, and any other devices that are installed.

Your software inventory should include the name of the product, the version number, the manufacturer's name, and the language (for example, English or French) used in the software. Depending on the software, you may need to include more information about the software such as whether it's a service pack or patch release. The categories of software products you should consider for your inventory will depend on the individual needs of the company, but in general they include arts & entertainment, commerce, connectivity and communications, cross-platform tools/ integration, data processing, data warehousing, multimedia, network infrastructure, operating systems, system management, user interface enhancements and accessibility, utilities and servers, and workflow and conferencing.

The completed Hardware and Software Worksheet for Hiabuv Toys inventories the Seattle location's hardware and the Training department's installed software and notes whether each is compatible with Windows 2000 Server.

Hiabuv Toys – Hardware & Software Worksheet

Use this worksheet as a guide for inventorying and analyzing your organization's hardware and installed software.

1. List your organization's hardware devices by location. Put a * next to items that are not compatible with Windows 2000 Server.

   Hardware—Seattle location

   4 Servers: (2) Generic Pentium CPUs (64 MB RAM*), (2) Dell PowerEdge 4400 (Pentium III 2 GB ECC RAM)

   105 Workstations: (30) Generic Pentium CPUs (64 MB RAM*), (25) Dell Dimension XPS B (Pentium III, 512 MB RDRAM), (50) Dell Optiplex GX110 (Pentium III, 512 MB SDRAM)

   10 Printers: (9) HP Laserjet 7550+, (1) HP Color Laserjet 4500N

   2 Scanners: (2) UMAX Astra 1220S

   1 SCSI Storage Unit: Dell Power Vault 210S

   1 UPS Unit: APC Smart-UPS 3000RM

2. List the software used in your organization by department. Put a * next to software that is not compatible with Windows 2000 Server.

   Software—Training department (located in Chicago)

   Microsoft Windows NT Workstation 4

   Microsoft Office 2000 Professional, English

   Microsoft Internet Explorer 5.01

   Adobe Acrobat 4, English

   Adobe Photoshop 5.5, English

   Visio Professional 5, English

   McAfee VirusScan 4, English*

   WinZip 8

3. Note any known difficulties or problems encountered with the hardware or software currently installed in your organization.

   The two old Seattle servers occasionally overheat and will need to be replaced.

Note A blank copy of this worksheet is located on the Supplemental Course Materials CD-ROM (\chapt02\worksheets\Hardware&Software).

Analyzing the Current Technical Standards

Your organization's technical standards are the conventions currently in place for the technical environment. Technical standards usually include

- Standard hardware configurations for desktops, servers, and other devices
- Standard software configurations for user desktops
- Naming conventions for users, groups, devices, and domains
- Network performance standards
- Security standards

The completed Standards Worksheet for Hiabuv Toys analyzes the technical standards currently in place for the Engineering department in the organization.

Hiabuv Toys Technical Standards Worksheet

Use this worksheet as a guide for gathering data about the technical standards currently in place in your organization.

1. List the standard hardware configuration for desktops in each department in your organization.

   Engineering department: 800EB MHz Pentium III processor (128 MB RDRAM, 30-GB hard drive), 21" monitor (32-MB graphics card), DVD-ROM drive (12x max), CD-RW drive (8x/4x/32x max), digital sound card, speakers, mouse, and modem. This standard was implemented 6 months ago; hardware will continue to be updated for the next 12 months.

2. List the standard hardware configuration for servers in your organization.

   Standard server configuration for departments, including Engineering: 2 Pentium III processors at 800 MHz, 133-MHz system bus, 32-KB level 1 cache, 256-KB full speed level 2 cache, 2-GB ECC 133 MHz SDRAM memory, 36-GB hard drive, external

continued

Hiabuv Toys Network Architecture Worksheet, *continued*

storage unit, tape backup unit, 21" monitor, CD-ROM drive, 3.5" diskette drive, mouse, and modem. This standard was implemented 6 months ago; hardware will continue to be updated for the next 12 months.

3. List the standard desktop configuration for users in each department in your organization.

   All users in Engineering see the Hiabuv Toys logo during startup and a standard Hiabuv Toys screen saver. Shortcuts to software, such as the CAD program used to design products and the Microsoft Office Shortcut Bar appear on the desktop. Users are prohibited from making changes to their desktops.

4. Indicate the standard security settings that apply to the organization, which include password, account lockout, and Kerberos-related settings. Then indicate any areas within the organization that differ from this standard.

   For the entire organization, the maximum password age is 45 days, with a minimum password length of 8 characters. However, for the Engineering department, the maximum password age is 30 days, with a minimum password length of 12 characters. For the entire organization, the account lockout threshold is three invalid attempts. However, for the Engineering department, the account lockout threshold is two invalid attempts.

5. List the naming conventions for users, groups, devices, and domains in your organization.

   Users: Each user name consists of the last name of the user. If there is more than one user with the same last name, the user's first initial is used before the last name. If there is more than one user with the same first initial and last name, the first and second initials are used before the last name.

   Groups: Each group name consists of the name of the group followed by the abbreviated department name.

   Devices: Each device name consists of the name of the device followed by the abbreviated department name. Numbers are placed after the department name when duplicate devices exist in the same department.

   Domains: A domain name is descriptive of the domain.

6. List the network performance standards set by your organization.

   Hiabuv Toys has the following performance goals: 100% up time, except for time required for system maintenance, 50% available bandwidth for all site links during peak traffic periods, and changes replicated to each site every 20 minutes.

7. List objects that must be hidden from users and the users from which the objects must be hidden.

   Engineering and payroll servers and software must be hidden from users.

8. List the security standards set by your organization.

   Password standards: change password every 30 days, the last nine passwords are remembered; a password must be seven or more characters.

   Account standards: accounts are locked out for 60 minutes after three faulty logon attempts; logon hours, account expiration dates, and specific workstations are set for consultants, contractors, and temps.

   Files, folders, and shared folders: department supervisors receive relevant training to standardize permissions for each department.

9. Note any known difficulties or problems encountered with the standards currently set by your organization.

   The naming convention for groups makes group names difficult for users to remember. Departments still need help setting the appropriate permissions for files, folders, and shared folders.

Note A blank copy of this worksheet is located on the Supplemental Course Materials CD-ROM (\chapt02\worksheets\TechStandards).

Analyzing the Current DNS Environment

A Domain Name System (DNS) service is a name resolution service used to translate host names to IP addresses in Active Directory. As you learned in Chapter 1, for Active Directory and associated client software to function correctly, you must have installed and configured Windows 2000 DNS. If your organization does not currently use DNS, there is nothing to analyze at this time. However, if your organization is already using another DNS service, it's important to find out whether the service is compatible with Active Directory and how it is currently structured.

The minimum requirement for a DNS service to be compatible with Active Directory is for the service to support service resource records (SRV RRs), as described in RFC 2052, and dynamic update, as described in RFC 2136. Many established DNS environments operate on UNIX servers running the BIND (Berkeley Internet Name Domain) implementation of DNS. If your DNS environment is running BIND version 8.1.2 or later, it supports SRV RRs and dynamic update and is compatible with Active Directory DNS requirements. If your organization is currently running Windows NT 4 DNS, your DNS service is also compatible with Active Directory DNS requirements.

Note To read more about service resource records, launch an Internet search engine and run a search on "RFC 2052" and "RFC 2136." RFCs (Request for Comments) are the official documents of the Internet Engineering Task Force (IETF) that specify the details for new Internet specifications or protocols. RFC 2052 is entitled "A DNS RR for Specifying the Location of Services (DNS SRV)." RFC 2136 is entitled "Dynamic Updates in the Domain Name System (DNS Update)."

Although the DNS services described here are compatible with Active Directory, only the Windows 2000 DNS service allows you to use Active Directory as the data storage and replication engine. With some planning, you will be able to migrate from these compatible DNS services to Windows 2000 DNS.

The completed DNS Environment Worksheet for Hiabuv Toys analyzes the organization's existing DNS environment.

Hiabuv Toys DNS Environment Worksheet

Use this worksheet as a guide for gathering data about your organization's existing DNS environment.

1. Indicate the type of DNS service currently used in your organization.

2. Diagram the existing DNS namespace used in your organization. Indicate the location of domain name servers.

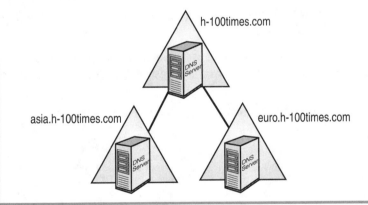

Note A blank copy of this worksheet is located on the Supplemental Course Materials CD-ROM (\chapt02\worksheets\DNSEnvironment).

Analyzing the Current Windows NT Domain Architecture

In Windows NT, you can group users and servers into domains for administrative purposes. In Windows 2000, organizational units (OUs) have been introduced to handle administration, while domains still provide administration but hold OUs and many more objects than in Windows NT. The purpose of analyzing the current Windows NT domain architecture employed in your organization is to understand the workings of the present domain structure so that you can convert each of the domains into an Active Directory domain, tree, and forest structure. If your organization does not currently use Windows NT, there is nothing to analyze at this time.

The completed Windows NT Domain Architecture Worksheet for Hiabuv Toys analyzes the organization's existing Windows NT domain architecture.

Hiabuv Toys Windows NT Domain Architecture Worksheet

Use this worksheet as a guide for gathering data about your organization's Windows NT domain architecture.

1. Use ovals to diagram the existing domains in your organization's Windows NT architecture. Include arrows to represent the direction of trusts between domains and the name of each domain.

2. Indicate the location of domain controllers in the network.

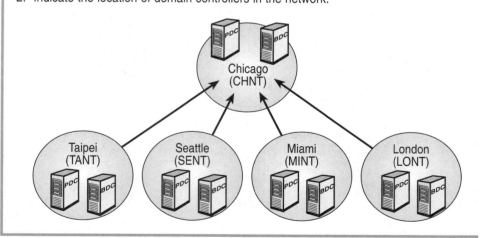

Note A blank copy of this worksheet is located on the Supplemental Course Materials CD-ROM (\chapt02\worksheets\NTDomain).

Lesson Summary

In this lesson you learned to analyze each component of your technical environment, including the current network architecture, hardware, software, technical standards, DNS environment, and Windows NT domain architecture. An organization's technical environment defines how it organizes and manages its technical resources. Your organization's technical environment has a direct effect on your Active Directory infrastructure.

You also learned to create a document, the technical environment analysis document, which describes the current state of each technical environment component in your organization. The technical environment analysis document includes the completed Network Architecture, Hardware and Software, Technical Standards, DNS Environment, and Windows NT Domain Architecture worksheets. When complete, this document can be distributed to each member of the design team, providing a starting point for discussion and assessing needs.

Lab 2.1: Analyzing Business Environment

Lab Objectives

After completing this lab, you will be able to

- Analyze the current business structure for an organization
- Diagram the administrative and geographic structures of an organization

About This Lab

In this lab, you will analyze a portion of the existing business environment at a small company.

Before You Begin

Before you begin this lab, you must have

- Knowledge of the components that constitute an organization's business environment

Exercise: Analyzing a Current Business Structure

Review the scenario and complete the Business Structures Worksheet.

Scenario

You have been selected to be an infrastructure planner on the Active Directory infrastructure design team for Vigor Airlines, a regional airline with five offices located in Montana, Idaho, Nevada, Utah, and Wyoming. You work at the company's headquarters in Butte, Montana. Your first task is to interview some of the staff representatives on the design team to find out Vigor's business structure. Using your Business Structures Worksheet, you interview Greg Chapman, who manages the IT department from his office in Butte, Montana. Greg tells you that there are about 100 employees in the Administration department at headquarters, but only 75 of those are network users. The Administration department serves as the decision-making unit of the organization and carries out administrative functions. The network users in Administration use the network for marketing, accounting, training, and IT functions. Greg explains the basics about the other departments. The Maintenance department is located at the Salt Lake City, Utah, office, which has 50 employees, of which about 40 are network users. The Operations department is located at the Reno, Nevada, office, which has 100 employees, of which all are network users. The Boise, Idaho, and Laramie, Wyoming, offices are small sales offices with a combined total of 50 network users. The Maintenance, Operations, and Sales departments all report to the Administrative department.

You contact members of the design team from the Maintenance, Operations, and Sales departments to confirm the number of users, to find out the purpose of each department, and to find out how the users use the network. The Maintenance department is responsible for maintaining the company's aircraft. The users in this department use the network to document their maintenance activities and to maintain parts inventories. The Operations department is responsible for coordinating the components that keep the aircraft flying, such as scheduling food purveyors, baggage handlers, pilots and flight attendants, and purchasing fuel. They use the network to coordinate all of these activities. The Sales department is responsible for advertising and selling seats on airline flights. The users in this department use the system for ticketing and developing advertisements. You find out from another design team member in the Laramie sales office that they will soon be moving to Colorado Springs.

Exercise Questions

Complete the Business Structures Worksheet.

Business Structures Worksheet

Use this worksheet as a guide for gathering data about business structures in your organization.

1. Diagram the administrative structure of your organization.

2. List and briefly describe the purpose of each division or department in the administrative structure. Where do these divisions report?

   _____

   _____

   _____

   _____

3. Indicate the number of network users in each division of the administrative structure and the total number of network users in the organization.

   _____

   _____

   _____

   _____

4. Diagram the geographical structure of your organization.

5. List each administrative division and describe where it is located in the geographical structure.

   _____

   _____

   _____

   _____

6. List the number of network users in each location.

   _____

   _____

   _____

   _____

7. Describe how the network users in each department currently use the network.

   _____

   _____

   _____

   _____

8. Add any special operations to your administrative structure diagram.

Review

The following questions are intended to reinforce key information presented in the chapter. If you are unable to answer a question, review the appropriate lesson and then try the question again. Answers to the questions can be found in Appendix A, "Questions and Answers."

1. You are the manager of your organization's IT department. You assemble a design team that consists of a system administrator, a network administrator, a member of your help desk team, a systems trainer from the training department, and you. What pitfalls might you encounter with your current team?

2. You are a design team member and receive a completed business environment analysis document for review. When reviewing the business structure you notice that the diagram shown below is the only diagram included in that part of the analysis. What other diagrams should be included as part of the business structure analysis?

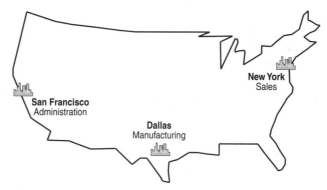

3. You have inventoried all the hardware devices used in your organization. What's the next step in conducting an analysis of hardware used in your organization?

CHAPTER 3

Creating a Forest Plan

About This Chapter

After you and your design team finish gathering information about an organization, the next stage in designing an Active Directory directory services infrastructure is to create a forest plan. Creating a forest plan includes designing a forest model and designing a schema modification plan. To design a forest model, you assess an organization's forest needs and determine the number of forests it requires. To design a schema modification plan, you create a schema modification policy, assess an organization's schema needs, and determine whether to modify the schema. This chapter shows you how to create a forest plan.

Before You Begin

To complete the lessons in this chapter, you must have

- Knowledge of Active Directory components and concepts covered in Chapter 1, "Introduction to Active Directory"
- Knowledge of business and technical environment analyses components covered in Chapter 2, "Introduction to Designing a Directory Services Infrastructure"

Lesson 1: Designing a Forest Model

The first step in creating a forest plan is to design a forest model for an organization's Active Directory infrastructure. This lesson walks you through the steps for designing a forest model, including assessing the factors in the organization's environment that impact its forest model and determining the number of forests to use.

After this lesson, you will be able to

- Assess the factors in an organization's environment that impact its forest model
- Indicate the reasons for using multiple forests in an Active Directory infrastructure
- Explain the implications of using multiple forests
- Analyze an organization's environment to design its forest model

Estimated lesson time: 20 minutes

Understanding Forests

In Active Directory, a forest is a distributed database. The database is a collection of one or more Windows 2000 domains that share a single schema, configuration container, and global catalog and are linked by implicit two-way transitive trusts. Forests help users interact with the directory and help administrators manage multiple domains.

Recall that the Active Directory *schema* is a list of definitions that determines the kinds of objects and the types of information about those objects that can be stored in Active Directory. The schema is a naming context that is replicated to every domain controller in the forest. A *naming context* is a tree of objects stored in Active Directory. The Schema Admins predefined universal group has full control of the schema.

The *configuration container* stores configuration objects that represent the structure of Active Directory, including display specifiers, extended rights, partitions, sites, domain controllers, services, well-known security principals, and other configuration objects. The configuration container is a naming context that is replicated to every domain controller in the forest. The Enterprise Admins predefined universal group has full control of the configuration container.

Recall that the *global catalog* is the central repository of information about objects in a tree or forest. It stores a full replica of all object attributes in the directory for its host domain and a partial replica for all object attributes contained in the directory of every domain in the forest. The global catalog allows users and administrators to find objects outside of the domain and across the enterprise with speed and efficiency. It also allows users to log on easily by using an abstracted (shortened) *user principal name* (UPN), rather than specifying the default (full domain path) UPN. For example, if the user Sherri has her user account in sls.uk.microsoft.com she must type sherri@sls.uk.microsoft.com to log on. By abstracting the sls.uk.microsoft.com domain name in the domain tree, the global catalog allows her to type sherri@microsoft.com when logging on.

Design Step: Designing a Forest Model

To design the forest model needed for your organization, you must complete the following tasks:

1. Assess the organization's forest needs.
2. Determine the number of forests for your organization.

Assessing Forest Needs

To design a forest model for your organization, you must first consult the following business and technical environment analysis documents compiled earlier by your design team:

- Business Structures Worksheet. Assess the current administrative structure of your organization.

- IT Management Organization Worksheet. Assess current structure and administration practices in your organization's IT management organization.

- Technical Standards Worksheet. Assess current administrative and security standards.

In addition to assessing these requirements, it is imperative that you assess any changes that may be planned for the sites or domain controller locations to address growth, flexibility, and the ideal design specifications of the organization.

Note Blank copies of the worksheets are located on the Supplemental Course Materials CD-ROM (\chapt02\worksheets). Completed examples of the worksheets are located in Chapter 2, "Introduction to Designing a Directory Services Infrastructure."

Determining the Number of Forests

Because Windows 2000 domains in a forest share a single schema, configuration container, and global catalog and are linked by two-way transitive trusts, you should strive to have only one forest for your organization. Ideally, the use of multiple forests should be temporary, and reserved for situations such as a merger, acquisition, or partnership where two or more organizations must be joined. You must realize that by defining multiple forests you will be requiring users in your organization to take a series of complex steps just to use the directory. Refer to "Implications of Using Multiple Forests," later in this lesson, for further information.

Reasons to Use Multiple Forests

Although you should strive to define only one forest for your organization, there are some situations that may warrant the use of multiple forests. You may need to consider using multiple forests if any of the following are true:

- Network administration is separated into autonomous groups that do not trust each other.
- Business units are politically separated into autonomous groups.
- Business units must be separately maintained.
- There is a need to isolate the schema, configuration container, or global catalog.
- There is a need to limit the scope of the trust relationship between domains or domain trees.

If you want to separate business units or keep specific users from accessing resources *and you cannot achieve this through your domain or OU structure*, a multiple forest model can be an effective tool for creating privacy and security.

Important Although the reasons above may indicate that you need to define multiple forests, you should always consult your design team before proceeding with a multiple forest model. Examine all options for delegating administration using domains or OUs before you define multiple forests.

Implications of Using Multiple Forests

Adding a forest increases administrative and usability costs. When determining whether to use multiple forests, keep the following administrative issues in mind:

- Schema. Each forest has its own schema. You will need to maintain the contents and administration group memberships for each schema separately even if they are similar. Refer to Lesson 2, "Designing a Schema Modification Plan," for details.

- Configuration container. Each forest has its own configuration container. You will need to maintain the contents and administration group memberships for each configuration container separately even if they are similar.

- Trusts. An explicit one-way nontransitive trust is the only trust relationship permitted between domains in different forests. You must explicitly (manually) set up and maintain a series of one-way nontransitive trusts to accommodate domains requiring interforest trust relationships. Figure 3.1 is an example of an interforest trust relationship.

- Replication. Replication of objects between forests is manual and requires the development of new administrative policies and procedures.

- Merging forests or moving domains. Forests cannot be merged in a one-step operation; you must clone security principals, migrate objects, decommission domain controllers, downgrade them to member servers, and add each to the new forest domain.

- Moving objects. Although objects can be moved between forests, you must use the ClonePrincipal tool to clone security principals in the new forest, or the LDAP Data Interchange Format (LDIFDE.EXE) command-line tool to move other objects.

- **Smart card logon.** Default UPNs must be maintained for smart cards to be able to log on across forests.

- **Additional domains.** Each forest must contain at least one domain. Additional domains increase hardware and administrative costs. Refer to Chapter 4, "Creating a Domain Plan," for further information.

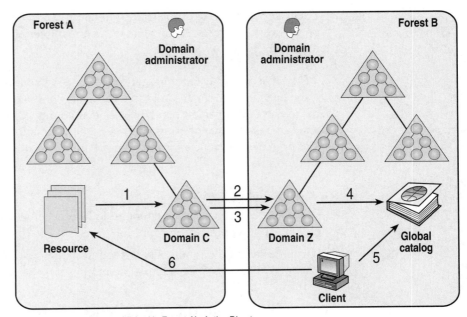

1. Resource published in Forest A's Active Directory.
2. Domain administrators in both domains configure explicit one-way nontransitive trust; Domain C trusts Domain Z, so users in Domain Z can access resources in Domain C.
3. Either domain administrator, with the correct permissions in both forests, imports resource object into forest using the LDIFDE command-line tool.
4. Object replicates to Forest B's global catalog.
5. User finds object by querying Forest B's global catalog.
6. User accesses resource in Forest A.

Figure 3.1   An interforest trust relationship

When determining whether to use multiple forests, also keep the following usability issues in mind:

- User logon. When a user logs on to a computer outside his or her own forest, he or she must specify the default UPN, which contains the full domain path for the user account, rather than just the easy-to-remember abstracted UPN. The default UPN is required because the domain controller in the forest will not be able to find the abstracted UPN in its global catalog. The user's abstracted UPN resides only in the global catalog in the user's forest.

- User queries. Users must be trained to make explicit queries across all of an organization's forests. Incomplete or incorrect queries can negatively affect users' work.

All of the reasons for using multiple forests involve administrative issues. However, the negative effects of a multiple forest scenario have the greatest impact on users. You should consider that the issues that are important to administrators are not the same issues that are important to users. Unless the use of multiple forests in your organization appears transparent to users, you should try not to create separate forests.

▶   **To design a forest model**

1. Consider the reasons for using multiple forests and determine whether your organization requires one or multiple forests.

2. If your organization requires multiple forests, temporarily label each forest (Forest A, Forest B, etc.) and list the reasons why each forest is required.

Design Step Example: Designing a Forest Model

Figure 3.2 shows a forest model for the A. Datum Corporation, an Internet service provider (ISP) that hosts Active Directory for some of its clients. The forests needed for the organization have only been identified. At this point, the forest has not been named, nor have domains within it been placed in a hierarchy.

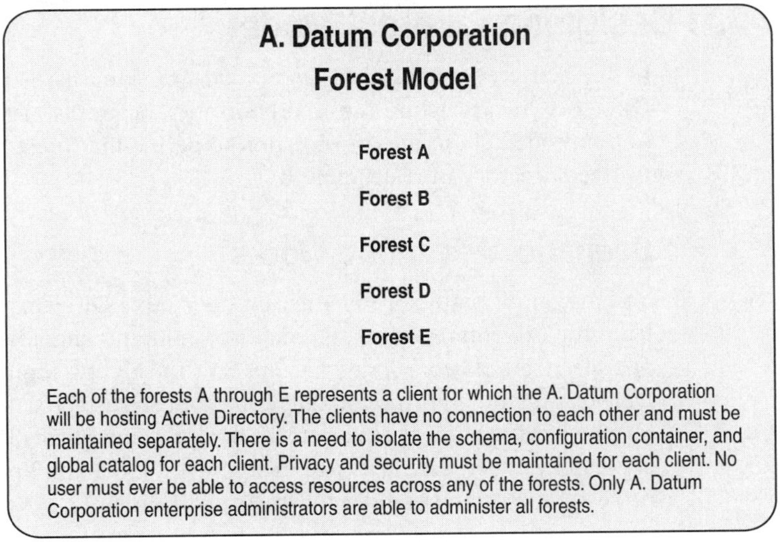

```
┌─────────────────────────────────────────────────────────────┐
│                   A. Datum Corporation                        │
│                      Forest Model                             │
│                                                               │
│                        Forest A                               │
│                                                               │
│                        Forest B                               │
│                                                               │
│                        Forest C                               │
│                                                               │
│                        Forest D                               │
│                                                               │
│                        Forest E                               │
│                                                               │
│  Each of the forests A through E represents a client for which the A. Datum Corporation │
│  will be hosting Active Directory. The clients have no connection to each other and must be │
│  maintained separately. There is a need to isolate the schema, configuration container, and │
│  global catalog for each client. Privacy and security must be maintained for each client. No │
│  user must ever be able to access resources across any of the forests. Only A. Datum │
│  Corporation enterprise administrators are able to administer all forests. │
└─────────────────────────────────────────────────────────────┘
```

Figure 3.2   Forest model for A. Datum Corporation

Lesson Summary

In this lesson you learned the steps for designing a forest model, including assessing the factors in the organization's environment that impact its forest model and determining the number of forests to use. You learned that the factors within the organization that can affect the forest model include administrative structures, IT management organization structure and administration practices, and the current administrative and security standards. In addition, changes currently planned to address growth and flexibility needs and changes that would help to meet the ideal design specifications of the organization can also affect the forest model.

You also learned that you should always strive to define only one forest for your organization. However, there are some situations that may warrant the use of multiple forests. You learned the reasons for using multiple forests and the implications of using them. Finally, you learned that you should always consult your design team before proceeding with a multiple forest model. It is important to examine all options for delegating administration using domains or OUs before you define multiple forests.

Activity 3.1: Designing a Forest Model

In this activity you will read about a design team that is planning the Active Directory infrastructure for an organization. Your task is to analyze the information provided about the organization to define the forest model needed for the Active Directory infrastructure.

Scenario: Adventure Works

You are an infrastructure planner on the Active Directory infrastructure design team for Adventure Works, a retailer of camping and adventure equipment that operates from its corporate office in Salt Lake City; regional offices in Portland, Denver, Austin, and Atlanta; and 200 retail stores across the United States. The business and technical environment analysis documents have been compiled and copies have been distributed to everyone on the team. You are now in the process of designing a forest model for the organization.

Taking a look at the current business structures and IT management organization, you make these notes: since its inception, Adventure Works has operated a separate network with a separate IT management department for the retail stores. This department is responsible for administering all of the Windows NT point-of-sale workstations and the large database servers that handle inventory at each retail store. At the corporate and regional offices, the retail store network has always been considered a separate entity. You set up a phone conference with several members of the retail IT management department and find that they are adamant about continuing their network administration role for the retail stores.

While considering the changes currently planned to address growth and flexibility needs and the changes that would help meet the ideal design specifications of the organization, you interview four members of senior management and find that one of their goals is to synch up the inventory database system in the retail network with the purchasing and distribution systems to create a single view of all products and systems. The current setup has sometimes caused product availability to vary widely in retail stores. Another goal is to cultivate and recruit employees from the retail stores for operations in the corporate office. One of the ways management envisions doing this is by providing retail employees easy access to the corporate intranet and e-mail systems and using the systems to foster a more unified company environment.

1. List the advantages of using a multiple forest model for Adventure Works.

2. List the disadvantages of using a multiple forest model for Adventure Works.

3. Which model would you choose and why?

Lesson 2: Designing a Schema Modification Plan

After you've designed a forest model for your organization, the next step in creating a forest plan is to plan any schema modifications necessary for meeting the needs of your organization. Because Active Directory provides all the directory services most organizations will ever need, you will rarely consider modifying the schema. However, there are valid reasons why your organization may need to change the schema. Modifying the schema is a complex operation that requires an understanding of how the schema functions and detailed planning. This lesson walks you through the steps necessary to plan schema modifications, including creating a schema modification policy, assessing an organization's schema needs, and determining whether to modify the schema.

After this lesson, you will be able to

- Create a schema modification policy
- Identify the factors in an organization's environment that impact its schema
- Indicate the reasons for modifying the schema
- Explain the implications of modifying the schema
- Analyze an organization's environment to design its schema modification plan

Estimated lesson time: 20 minutes

Understanding the Schema

Recall that the Active Directory schema is a list of objects that define the kinds of objects and the types of information about those objects that can be stored in Active Directory. The schema is stored in the schema table as part of the NTDS.DIT file. There are two types of objects in the schema: schema class (classSchema) objects and schema attribute (attributeSchema) objects. Schema class objects describe the possible Active Directory objects that can be created, functioning as a template for creating new Active Directory objects. Schema class objects are arranged in a hierarchy of classes, subclasses, and superclasses and consist of mandatory (mustContain) schema attributes and optional (mayContain) schema attributes. Each schema attribute is defined only once and can be used in multiple schema object classes. Schema class objects and attribute objects are defined in separate lists within the schema.

A basic set of schema classes and attributes, often called the *base schema* or base *directory information tree* (DIT), is shipped with Windows 2000 Server. There are nearly 200 schema class objects and more than 900 schema attribute objects provided in the base schema. By adding objects to a Windows 2000 deployment, you create additional instances of existing base schema classes.

If the base schema doesn't meet the needs of your organization, you must consider modifying the schema or creating additional schema class and/or attribute objects; this process is called *extending* the schema. Because schema that you add cannot be deleted, but only deactivated, and a schema is automatically replicated, you must plan and prepare carefully before extending the schema. Inconsistencies in the schema brought about by modifications can cause problems that may impair or disable Active Directory. Before it becomes necessary to extend the schema, your organization must create a schema modification policy that outlines the process for extending the schema. Having a schema modification policy in place can prevent potential problems when extending the schema.

To determine whether the base schema meets the needs of your organization, you must familiarize yourself with the base schema class and attribute objects. If you know the types of data that Active Directory will hold, you can more effectively determine whether you need to change the base schema and whom the changes will impact.

Note You can find lists of the base schema class objects in Appendix B, "Base Schema Class Objects" and base schema attribute objects in Appendix C, "Base Schema Attribute Objects."

Viewing the Base Schema

To view the base schema in Windows 2000, you must first install the Active Directory Schema snap-in, which is available only after you install all of the Windows 2000 administration tools. After installing the administration tools, you need to add the snap-in to Microsoft Management Console (MMC) by using the Add/Remove Snap-in dialog box accessible from the Console menu. You can then access the Active Directory Schema snap-in using the MMC.

Caution Because of the serious consequences of modifying the schema, the schema is set for read-only access by default. If you decide to follow along with this lesson by opening the Active Directory Schema snap-in, verify with your administrator that schema modification has not been enabled.

Viewing Schema Class Objects

After you open the Classes folder in the Active Directory Schema snap-in, you can scroll through the list of schema class objects, shown partially in Figure 3.3 and included in its entirety on the Supplemental Course Materials CD-ROM. Each class has a name, type, and description. The type—abstract, auxiliary, or structural—is used to create the hierarchical structure of the schema class objects.

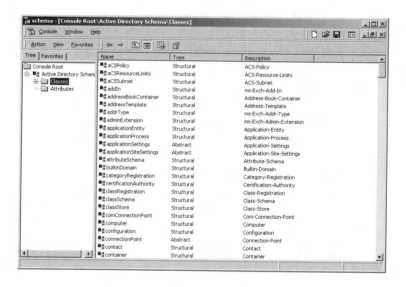

Figure 3.3   Schema class objects in Active Directory

An *abstract class* provides a basic definition of a class that can be used to form structural classes. An *auxiliary class* is used to group schema attributes that you want to apply as a group to a structural class. It can be used to extend the definition of a class that inherits from it, but cannot be used to form a class by itself. *Structural classes* use a hierarchy that begins with an object class called top. All schema class objects of structural type are descendants of top and inherit the attributes of top. The example in Figure 3.4 shows how the user class inherits sample attributes from its parent classes, organizationalPerson, person, and top. It also inherits sample attributes from its auxiliary classes, mailRecipient and securityPrincipal. You can view the parent class and auxiliary classes for a schema class object on the Relationship tab in the Properties dialog box for the class object. If you want to create a new class in the schema, the classSchema class object defines which objects are required and which are optional.

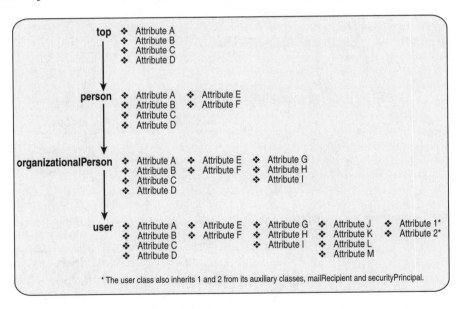

Figure 3.4   Attribute inheritance for the user class object

Viewing Schema Attribute Objects

After you open the Attributes folder in the Active Directory Schema snap-in, you can scroll through the list of schema attribute objects, as shown partially in Figure 3.5 and listed in its entirety on the Supplemental Course Materials CD-ROM. Each attribute has a name, syntax, and description. The syntax indicates the format of the attribute. If you want to create a new attribute in the schema, the attributeSchema class object defines which attributes are required and which are optional.

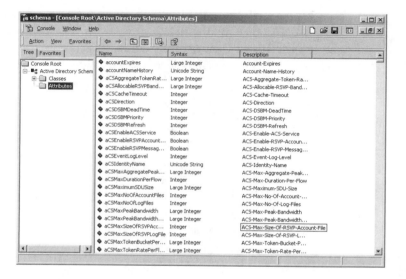

Figure 3.5   Schema attribute objects in Active Directory.

Note A detailed discussion about the Active Directory schema is beyond the scope of this training kit. For more information refer to the *Microsoft Windows 2000 Server Distributed Systems Guide* volume of the *Microsoft Windows 2000 Server Resource Kit.*

Schema Admins Group

The Schema Admins predefined universal group is the only group authorized to make changes to the Active Directory schema. However, the members of the Schema Admins group are determined by members of the Local Admins, Domain Admins, and Enterprise Admins groups in the forest root domain. To effectively control who can modify the schema, you should monitor the membership of these groups and restrict membership if necessary by using group policy.

Design Step: Designing a Schema Modification Plan

To plan schema modifications for your organization, you must complete the following tasks:

1. Create a schema modification policy.

2. Assess the organization's schema needs.

3. Determine whether to modify the schema.

Creating a Schema Modification Policy

A *schema modification policy* is a written plan you create to administer schema modifications that affect the entire forest. It outlines who has control of the schema and how modifications are administered. Because these schemas are shared between domains in a forest, changes applied to them affect the entire network and must be carefully planned and controlled. As part of your forest plan document, you should create a schema modification policy for each forest in your forest model.

▶   **To create a schema modification policy**

1. List the entity (division, department) that controls the Schema Admins predefined universal group.

2. List the members of the Schema Admins predefined universal group.

3. Appoint a schema modification approval committee. List the members.

4. List the steps required for initiating a schema modification.

5. List the steps required for testing a schema modification.

6. List the steps required for implementing a schema modification.

The Schema Modification Policy Worksheet has been created to assist you in setting up a schema modification policy for your organization. The following is an example of a completed worksheet for the fictitious A. Datum Company.

A. Datum Corporation Schema Modification Policy Worksheet

Use this worksheet as a guide for setting up a schema modification policy for your organization.

1. List the entity (division, department) that controls the Schema Admins predefined universal group.

   IT Management department

2. List the members of the Schema Admins predefined universal group.

   Fuller, Joanna

   Price, Jeff

3. Appoint a schema modification approval committee. List the members.

   Martin, Mindy

   Nash, Mike

4. List the steps required for planning a schema modification.

   Develop a schema modification request for approval by the schema modification approval committee. With your modification request, include

   - **a description of the modification**
   - **a justification for the modification**
   - **an assessment of the modification's impact on existing objects, network traffic, and the process of creating new objects.**

   If you are adding a new schema object class, specify the following:

   - **object identifiers (OIDs) for the new class (obtained from your ISO Name Registration Authority)**
   - **class type**

- the location of the class in the hierarchy
- whether the new class will pass the system's consistency and safety checks

5. List the steps required for testing a schema modification.

    1. **Test the proposed modification in an approved test environment.**

    2. **Determine whether the proposed modification meets its intended needs.**

    3. **Test and plan a recovery method.**

    4. **Obtain approval to implement the modification from the schema modification approval committee.**

6. List the steps required for implementing a schema modification.

    1. **Restrict membership of the Schema Admins group.**

    2. **Enable a write copy on the schema operations master.**

    3. **Verify that all domain controllers receive the change.**

    4. **Return the schema operations master to a read-only copy.**

Note A blank copy of the Schema Modification Policy worksheet is located on the Supplemental Course Materials CD-ROM (\chapt03\worksheets\SchemaMod).

Assessing Schema Needs

To determine whether you need to plan schema modifications for your organization, you must identify all the data that the organization needs to store in the Active Directory database. To do this, you should consult the business and technical environment analysis documents compiled earlier by your design team. In addition, you should also consider whether changes currently planned to address growth and flexibility needs and any other changes that would help meet the ideal design specifications for the organization would require schema modifications.

Determining Whether to Modify the Schema

Because the Active Directory schema contains hundreds of the most common object classes and attributes that users of a server system require, the need to change the schema is rare. However, some organizations may require object classes or attributes not anticipated in the default schema. In this case, administrators will need to plan and test schema modifications carefully because any new object class or attribute created in the schema is added permanently. Object classes or attributes can be added to the schema but they cannot be deleted, only deactivated.

The following modifications can be made to the schema:

- Create a new class
- Modify an existing class
- Deactivate classes
- Create a new attribute
- Modify an existing attribute
- Deactivate attributes

Reasons to Modify the Schema

Although you should avoid modifying the schema for your organization, there are some situations that may warrant schema modification. You may need to modify the schema if any of the following are true:

- An existing schema class object meets your needs with the addition of an attribute or attributes. Adding attributes to an existing schema class object is the easiest type of schema modification. To add attributes, you can create a new attribute and add it to the class, add new attributes directly from the list of attributes available for the class, or you can add a parent to the existing schema object class to provide the functionality your organization needs. You can also create a new subclass that is derived from another class. Add the new attributes to the subclass and it will also inherit attributes from the original class.

- An existing schema class object requires a new, unique set of attributes. To handle a new, unique set of attributes, create an auxiliary class that is connected to an existing class and add the unique set of attributes to the auxiliary class. Then, add the auxiliary class to the schema class object.

- None of the existing schema class objects meet your needs. If none of the existing schema class objects meet your needs, you must create a new schema class. Creating a new class is the most complex type of schema modification and requires the following planning activities:

  - Obtaining the object identifiers (OIDs) for your new class from your ISO Name Registration Authority

  - Choosing an appropriate class type

  - Determining the location of your class in the hierarchy

  - Determining the attributes for the class

  - Determining whether the new class will pass the system's consistency and safety checks

- An existing schema class object or attribute object is no longer relevant to your organization. If a class or attribute object is no longer relevant, you can deactivate it.

Automatic Schema Modification

The schema will be modified automatically if you choose to install a directory-enabled application. A *directory-enabled application* is software that has the capability to read Active Directory objects (and their attributes) or has the capability to create schema class or attribute objects. These capabilities allow the application to integrate directly with Active Directory, combining services and reducing the total cost of ownership and network overhead. Be sure to test directory-enabled applications that modify the schema before installing them on the network.

Implications of Modifying the Schema

Modifying the schema affects the entire forest. When determining whether to modify the schema, consider how schema modification affects the following:

- Existing object instances. By modifying the schema, you can make an existing object instance invalid. If a schema attribute object is added to or removed from a schema class object, any existing instances of the class object become invalid because they no longer match the class definition. Although Active Directory will allow you to search for an invalid attribute and remove it from existing object instances, there is no search facility to add attribute objects to existing object instances.

- Replication. By modifying the schema, you can cause temporary inconsistencies in the schema that will result in replication failure if an instance of a newly created class object is replicated to a domain controller before the newly created class. If schema replication failure occurs, Active Directory automatically replicates the schema from the schema operations master to the target domain controller, and the schema cache is updated. Then, the instance of the newly created class object is replicated to the target domain controller.

- Network traffic. By modifying the schema and then choosing to replicate attributes to the global catalog, you can negatively affect network performance during replication. Replicating attributes to the global catalog causes all global catalogs to replicate all objects, not just the modified schema attributes, and significantly increases network traffic.

▶ **To design a schema modification plan**

1. Create a schema modification policy.

2. Consider the reasons for modifying the schema and determine whether your organization needs to modify the schema.

3. If your organization needs to modify the schema, follow the steps you set up for planning a schema modification in your organization's schema modification policy.

Design Step Example: Designing a Schema Modification Plan

The following example describes planning schema modifications at the fictitious A. Datum Company.

A. Datum Company Schema Modification Plan

While gathering information for the Active Directory infrastructure plan, the design team at the A. Datum Company learns that the management of the human resources department for one of its clients (forests) would like to include the languages spoken by its users in the directory. Currently, there is no attribute in the user schema object class that can handle languages spoken, so the design team is considering planning a schema modification. To plan a schema modification, the A. Datum Corporation's schema modification policy requires the team to do the following:

- Submit schema modification requests to the schema modification approval committee. With the request are included a description of the modification; a justification for the modification; and an assessment of the modification's impact on existing objects, network traffic, and the process of creating new objects.

- If adding a new schema object class, specify the following: OIDs for the new class (obtained from the ISO Name Registration Authority), class type, the location of the class in the hierarchy, and whether the new class will pass the system's consistency and safety checks.

- Obtain approval to test the modification from the schema modification approval committee.

Here is the design team's schema modification plan:

- Modification description. The modification requires a languages spoken attribute to include languages spoken by users in the directory. Because the company's needs can be met by adding a single attribute to an existing schema class object, it's expected that the modification can be attained by adding a languagesSpoken schema attribute object to the existing user schema class object.

- Modification justification. After discussion with the human resources department it was found that a languages spoken attribute is indeed necessary to meet the A. Datum Corporation's top-priority globalization initiative.

- Assessment of impact. The new languages spoken attribute cannot be a mandatory attribute; unless it is an optional attribute for the user schema class object, all existing users will become invalid. In addition, if the languages spoken attribute is a mandatory attribute it will no longer be possible to use the Active Directory Users and Computers snap-in to add users. The addition of the languagesSpoken schema attribute should not significantly affect network traffic other than the initial replication to all domain controllers.

Lesson Summary

In this lesson you learned the steps for planning schema modifications, including creating a schema modification policy, assessing an organization's schema needs, and determining whether to modify the schema. A schema modification policy is a plan you create to administer schema modifications that affect the entire forest, outlining who has control of the schema and how modifications are administered. You learned that you must assess all the data that the organization needs to store in the Active Directory schema by consulting the business and technical environment analysis documents compiled by your design team.

You also learned that because the Active Directory schema contains hundreds of the most common object classes and attributes that users of a server system require, the need to change the schema is rare. You learned the types of modifications that can be made to the Active Directory schema and the reasons for making modifications. Finally, you learned to plan schema modifications by following the steps you set up for planning a schema modification in your organization's schema modification policy.

Lab 3.1: Creating a Forest Model and Schema Modification Plan

Lab Objectives

After completing this lab, you will be able to

- Design a forest model
- Design a schema modification plan

About This Lab

In this lab, you will analyze a portion of the existing environment at a medium-sized company to design its forest model and schema modification plan.

Before You Begin

Before you begin this lab, you must be able to

- Analyze an organization's environment to design its forest model
- Analyze an organization's environment to design its schema modification plan

Exercise 1: Designing a Forest Model

In this exercise, you will analyze the existing environment at a medium-sized company to create a forest model. Review the scenario, and then create the forest model.

Scenario

Your design team is planning the Active Directory infrastructure for LitWare, Inc., a publisher of books and online children's literature. LitWare, Inc., publishes online children's literature in French. Last year it acquired Lucerne Publishing, a major publisher of books in German. Because the businesses are so different and because multiple languages are involved, Lucerne Publishing has retained its IT management department and is run with a minimum of involvement from LitWare, Inc. LitWare, Inc., has no initiatives to change this arrangement. LitWare, Inc., has 10,000 employees in Paris; Lucerne Publishing has 3,000 employees in Berlin and 4,000 employees in Lucerne.

Exercise Questions

Answer the following questions to create a forest model.

1. List the advantages of using a multiple forest model for LitWare, Inc.

2. List the disadvantages of using a multiple forest model for LitWare, Inc.

3. Would you use a single or a multiple forest model for Lit Ware, Inc.? Why?

Exercise 2: Designing a Schema Modification Plan

In this exercise, you will continue with the LitWare, Inc., scenario and analyze the existing environment to design a schema modification plan. Review the scenario, and then design the schema modification plan.

Scenario

While gathering information for the Active Directory infrastructure plan, your design team learns that the management of the distribution department at Lucerne Publishing would like to include the title of each book published and the book's ISBN in the directory. Currently, there are no schema attributes or classes that handle book titles and ISBNs, so the design team is considering initiating a schema modification. By placing the titles and ISBNs in the directory, managers in the distribution department hope to ready themselves for the installation of a new directory-enabled inventory application.

To plan a schema modification, the schema modification policy of LitWare, Inc., requires the team to do the following:

- Submit schema modification requests to the schema modification approval committee at Lucerne Publishing. With the request are included a description of the modification; a justification for the modification; and an assessment of the modification's impact on existing objects, network traffic, and the process of creating new objects.

- For new schema object class, specify the following: OIDs for the new class (obtained from the ISO Name Registration Authority), class type, the location of the class in the hierarchy.

- Obtain approval to test the modification from the schema modification approval committee at Lucerne Publishing.

Exercise Questions

Complete each of the following questions about designing a schema modification plan.

1. What items should be included in a schema modification plan for LitWare, Inc.?

2. Should the design team design a schema modification plan? Why or why not?

Review

The following questions are intended to reinforce key information presented in the chapter. If you are unable to answer a question, review the appropriate lesson and then try the question again. Answers to the questions can be found in Appendix A, "Questions and Answers."

1. What is the number of forests you should strive for? Why?

2. Your organization is considering the implementation of four forests to handle business units that do not wish to work together. The decision makers do not realize the impact of multiple forests on users. What action should you take to assist the users?

3. Your organization has implemented two forests. A user in the Accounting domain in Forest 1 needs to access resources located in the Finance domain in Forest 2. However, you must not allow the Finance domain in Forest 2 to access the Accounting domain resources in Forest 1. What must you do to allow access to the resources?

4. Why should you avoid changing the Active Directory schema?

5. You added a schema class object and a set of schema attribute objects to your organization's schema to represent products made by one of the divisions in the organization. After one year, that organization is spun off and the attributes are no longer needed. What should you do?

6. Your organization has recently implemented Active Directory and currently has no plans to modify the schema. Why should you familiarize yourself with the base schema class and attribute objects?

C H A P T E R   4

Creating a Domain Plan

About This Chapter

After you and your design team finish creating a forest plan, the next stage in
designing an Active Directory directory services infrastructure is to create a
domain plan. To create a domain plan, you define domains, define the forest root
domain, define a domain hierarchy, name domains, and plan DNS server deployment. The end result of a domain plan is a domain hierarchy diagram. This chapter discusses the process of creating a domain plan.

Real World Read the "Designing in the Real World & Creating a Domain Plan" interview with Darron Inman, Microsoft Consulting Services, for a real-world perspective of creating a domain plan. You can find the interview on the Supplemental Course Materials CD-ROM (\chapt04\DomainPlanInterview).

Before You Begin

To complete this chapter, you must have

- Knowledge of Active Directory components and concepts covered in Chapter 1, "Introduction to Active Directory"

- Knowledge of business and technical environment analyses components covered in Chapter 2, "Introduction to Designing a Directory Services Infrastructure"

- Knowledge and skills covered in Chapter 3, "Creating a Forest Plan"

Lesson 1: Defining Domains

The first step in creating a domain plan is to define domains. When you define domains, you determine the domains needed for each forest in your organization. This lesson discusses how to define domains, which includes assessing an organization's domain needs and determining the number of domains it requires.

After this lesson, you will be able to

- Identify the factors in an organization's environment that impact its need for domains
- Indicate the reasons for using multiple domains in an Active Directory infrastructure
- Explain the implications of defining multiple domains
- Analyze an organization's environment to define its domains

Estimated lesson time: 30 minutes

Understanding Domains

In Active Directory services, a domain is a partition of a forest, or a partial database. When you define domains, data is placed where it is most relevant in small databases, resulting in a large database that is efficiently distributed over the network. Recall that in Windows 2000 and Active Directory, domains represent security boundaries. Each domain has a unique name and provides access to centralized user accounts and group accounts maintained by the domain administrator. Active Directory is made up of one or more domains, each of which can span one or more sites.

Goals for Defining Domains

There are two goals you should keep in mind when defining the domains for your organization:

- Define domains based on the organization's geographical structure
- Minimize the number of domains

Defining Domains Based on Geographical Structure

In Chapter 2, "Introduction to Designing a Directory Services Infrastructure," one of the ways you learned to represent the geographical structure of an organization was by diagramming your organization's network architecture. You should use your network architecture diagram as a guide when defining domains for your organization. You should also consider other infrastructures currently employed in the organization. For example, if your organization has already invested in a DNS structure, you should probably retain this structure. Similarly, if your organization is using a large Microsoft Exchange operation, you may want to base your domain structure on the same model. Before you change existing infrastructures, you must weigh the cost of the change against the potential benefits.

Because functional structures such as divisions, departments, or project teams are always subject to change, defining domains based on these structures in the organization is strongly discouraged. The domain structures you create in Windows 2000 are not as flexible as your business environment. Once you create a domain and place it in a hierarchy, that domain cannot be easily moved or renamed. If the domain is a forest root domain it can *never* be moved or renamed.

Minimizing the Number of Domains

One of the guiding principles for designing your Active Directory infrastructure is to design for simplicity; this includes minimizing the number of domains. Whenever possible, it's best to limit your infrastructure design to one domain that is administered through organizational units (OUs). Adding domains to the forest increases management and hardware costs.

If you are upgrading from Windows NT, it is likely that you will need to consolidate domains. The principles for defining multiple domains in Windows NT no longer apply in Windows 2000. These principles are

- Security Accounts Manager (SAM) size limitations. In Windows NT, the SAM database had a limitation of about 40,000 objects per domain. In Windows 2000, each domain can contain more than one million objects, so it is no longer necessary to define a new domain just to handle more objects.

- Primary Domain Controller (PDC) availability requirements. In Windows NT, only one computer in a domain, the PDC, could accept updates to the domain database. In Windows 2000, all domain controllers accept updates, eliminating the need to define new domains just to provide fault tolerance.

- Limited delegation of administration within domains. In Windows NT, domains were the smallest units of administrative delegation. In Windows 2000, OUs allow you to partition domains to delegate administration, eliminating the need to define domains just for delegation.

For information on designing OUs to delegate administration, see Chapter 5, "Creating an Organizational Unit Plan."

Design Step: Defining Domains

To define domains, you must complete the following tasks:

1. Assess the organization's domain needs.
2. Determine the number of domains for your organization.

Assessing Domain Needs

To define domains for your organization, you must first consult the following documents compiled earlier by your design team:

- Business Structures Worksheet. Assess current administrative and geographical structure to determine possible domain locations.

- Network Architecture Worksheet. Assess current network architecture to determine possible domain locations.

- Technical Standards Worksheet. Assess current administrative and security standards to determine need for domains.

- Hardware & Software Worksheet. Assess the hardware devices and software that are not compatible with Windows 2000.

- Windows NT Domain Architecture Worksheet. Assess current domain structure to determine ways to consolidate domains.
- Forest model. Assess the number of forests planned for the organization to determine domain locations.

Note Blank copies of the worksheets are located on the Supplemental Course Materials CD-ROM (\chapt02\worksheets). Completed examples of the worksheets are located in Chapter 2, "Introduction to Designing a Directory Services Infrastructure." The forest model is discussed in Chapter 3, "Creating a Forest Plan."

In addition to assessing the information compiled in these documents, it is imperative that you also assess changes currently planned to business structures, network architecture, technical standards, and the existing domain architecture to address growth, flexibility, and the ideal design specifications of the organization.

Determining the Number of Domains

You must determine the number of domains for each forest in your organization. While one domain may effectively represent the structure of small or medium-sized organizations, larger and more complex organizations may find that one domain is not sufficient. To determine the number of domains for your organization's Active Directory infrastructure, you must carefully consider the reasons for defining multiple domains. Before adding any domains you should be able to state the purpose of the new domain and justify it in terms of administrative and hardware costs.

Reasons to Define Multiple Domains

These are the reasons to consider using multiple domains:

- To meet security requirements
- To meet administrative requirements
- To optimize replication traffic
- To retain Windows NT domains

When you're attempting to justify a new domain, consider all of the reasons together; there may be more than one reason for defining a domain.

Tip Do not use multiple domains to accommodate polarized groups or for isolated resources that are not easily assimilated into other domains. Both the groups and the resources are usually better candidates for OUs.

Meeting Security Requirements

The settings in the Account Policies subdirectory in the Security Settings node of a group policy object can be specified only at the domain level. If the security requirements set in the Account Policies subdirectory vary throughout your organization, you will need to define separate domains to handle the different requirements. The Account Policies subdirectory contains the following policies:

- Password Policy. Contains settings for passwords, such as password history, age, length, complexity, and storage.

- Account Lockout Policy. Contains settings for account lockout, such as lockout duration, threshold, and the lockout counter.

- Kerberos Policy. Contains Kerberos-related settings, such as user logon restrictions, service and user ticket lifetimes, and enforcement.

Meeting Administrative Requirements

Some organizations may need to establish boundaries to meet special administrative requirements that cannot be accommodated by establishing OUs in one domain. Special requirements might include satisfying specific legal or privacy concerns. For example, an organization may have a privacy requirement that outside administrators not be given control over sensitive product development files. In a one-domain scenario, members of the Domain Admins predefined global group would have complete control over all objects in the domain, including the sensitive files. By establishing a new domain containing the files, the first Domain Admins group is outside of the new domain and no longer has control of the files.

Optimizing Replication Traffic

In organizations with one or more sites, you must consider whether site links can handle the replication traffic associated with a single domain. In a forest with one domain, all objects in the forest are replicated to every domain controller in the forest. If objects are replicated to locations where they are not used, bandwidth is used unnecessarily. By defining multiple small domains and replicating only those objects that are relevant to a location, you can reduce network traffic and optimize replication. However, you must weigh the savings achieved by optimizing replication against the cost of hardware and administration for the additional domains.

To determine whether you should define a domain to optimize replication traffic, you must consider

- Link capacity and availability. If a link is operating near capacity or is not available for replication traffic during specific times of the day, it may not be able to handle replication traffic, and you should consider defining another domain. However, if links are idle at specific times, replication could be scheduled to occur during these times, provided the appropriate bandwidth is available.

- Whether replication traffic will compete with other traffic. If a link carries other, more important traffic that you do not want disturbed by replication traffic, you should consider defining another domain.

- Whether link is pay-by-usage. If replication traffic will cross an expensive pay-by-usage link, you should consider defining another domain.

- Whether link is SMTP-only. If a location is connected by SMTP-only links, it must have its own domain. Mail-based replication can occur only between domains; it cannot be used between domain controllers in the same domain.

Retaining Windows NT Domains

Organizations with large Windows NT infrastructures may choose to retain an existing Windows NT domain. Existing Windows NT domains can be upgraded to Windows 2000, sometimes referred to as an *in-place upgrade*. You must weigh the costs of upgrading the Windows NT domain or consolidating the domain against the savings of maintaining and administering fewer domains. It is recommended that you minimize the number of domains by consolidating Windows NT domains before upgrading to Windows 2000.

For information on upgrading existing Windows NT domains to Windows 2000 or consolidating Windows NT domains, see Lesson 1, "Planning a Windows NT 4 Directory Services Migration to Windows 2000 Active Directory," in Chapter 7, "Creating an Active Directory Services Implementation Plan."

Implications of Defining Multiple Domains

Adding a domain increases administrative and hardware costs. When determining whether to define multiple domains, keep the following cost issues in mind:

- Domain administrators. Each time a domain is added, a Domain Admins predefined global group is added as well. More administration is required to monitor the members of this group.

- Security principals. As domains are added, the likelihood that security principals will need to be moved between domains becomes greater. Although moving a security principal between OUs within a domain is a simple operation, moving a security principal between domains is more complex and can negatively affect end users.

- Group policy and access control. Because group policy and access control are applied at the domain level, if your organization uses group policies or delegated administration across the enterprise or many domains, the measures must be applied separately to each domain.

- Domain controller hardware and security facilities. Each Windows 2000 domain requires at least two domain controllers to support fault-tolerance and multimaster requirements. In addition, it is recommended that domain controllers be located in a secure facility with limited access to prevent physical access by intruders.

- Trust links. If a user from one domain must log on in another domain, the domain controller from the second domain must be able to contact the domain controller in the user's original domain. In the event of a link failure, the domain controller may not be able to maintain service. More trust links, which require setup and maintenance, will be necessary to alleviate the problem.

▶   **To define domains**

1. Determine the domains needed by the organization. Domains may need to be defined to meet security requirements, meet administrative requirements, optimize replication traffic, and retain Windows NT domains.

2. Obtain a copy of your design team's network architecture diagram. On the network architecture diagram, use a triangle to indicate domains you're defining.

Design Step Example: Defining Domains

Figure 4.1 shows the network architecture diagram for Pacific Musical Instruments, a manufacturer of traditional instruments of the countries of the Pacific Rim.

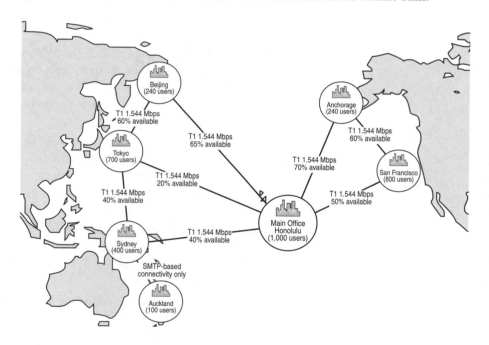

Figure 4.1   Network architecture diagram for Pacific Musical Instruments

Figure 4.2 shows the domains defined for Pacific Musical Instruments. Domains were defined for the following reasons:

- A domain was defined to meet the special password and account lockout settings that Pacific Musical Instruments requires at its Beijing location.

- A domain was defined at the Honolulu headquarters to meet the special legal requirements of Pacific Musical Instruments' personnel files.

- A domain was defined at the Tokyo location because the link to headquarters is only 20% available and could not effectively handle replication traffic.

- A domain was defined at the Sydney location because the link to headquarters is only 40% available and may not be able to effectively handle replication traffic. In addition, Pacific Musical Instruments will be opening up a new manufacturing location in Singapore, which will be linked only to the Sydney location and will likely increase traffic on the Sydney-to-headquarters link.

- A domain was defined at the Auckland location because it can be reached from the Sydney location by SMTP mail only.

- A domain was defined at the San Francisco location because it must be separate from the Honolulu domain and the links to any of the other domain locations were relatively congested and could not effectively handle replication traffic. The Anchorage site will also be served by this domain.

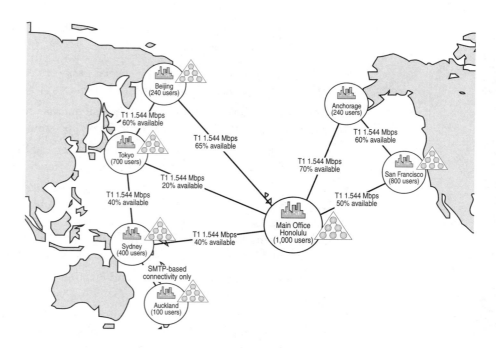

Figure 4.2 Domains defined for Pacific Musical Instruments

Lesson Summary

In this lesson you learned how to define domains for each forest in an organization by assessing an organization's domain needs and determining the number of domains it requires. Two goals should be kept in mind when defining the domains for your organization: to define domains based on the geographical structure of an organization's environment and to minimize the number of domains. It is easier to minimize the number of domains in Windows 2000 because the principles for defining multiple domains in Windows NT no longer apply.

You also learned the reasons for defining multiple domains, which include meeting security requirements, meeting administrative requirements, optimizing replication traffic, and retaining Windows NT domains. The implications of defining multiple domains were discussed, including how adding a domain increases administrative and hardware costs. Finally, you learned to define domains using an organization's network architecture diagram.

Activity 4.1: Defining Domains

In this activity you will read about two organizations that are planning their Active Directory infrastructure. Your task is to analyze each organization's environment to define the domains needed in an Active Directory infrastructure.

Scenario 1: Friendship Vineyards

You are an infrastructure planner on the Active Directory infrastructure design team for Friendship Vineyards, a winery that operates from four locations in South Africa. The business and technical environment analysis documents have already been compiled and copies have been distributed to everyone on the team. You are now in the process of defining the domains for the organization.

Friendship Vineyards is a centralized organization, with IT administration handled from its Cape Town headquarters. Each of the four locations also has a small IT staff to handle basic support tasks. There is one special requirement—that desktops for the distribution personnel at all four locations be restricted to distribution software only. Although Friendship Vineyards is currently running Windows NT 4, its management has decided not to carry the company's current domain structure into the new Windows 2000 environment. A check of the existing DNS namespace reveals that Friendship Vineyards has a Web site, which operates using the DNS name f-100times.com. Your design team has diagrammed the network architecture shown in Figure 4.3.

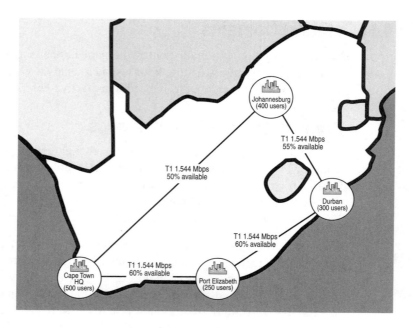

Figure 4.3   Network architecture for Friendship Vineyards

1. On the network architecture diagram, use a triangle to indicate the location of the domain(s) you would define for Friendship Vineyards.

2. Explain your reasoning for defining the domain(s).

Scenario 2: Awesome Computers

You are an infrastructure planner on the Active Directory infrastructure design team for Awesome Computers, a global multibillion-dollar computer manufacturer with more than 65,000 users and computers at more than 30 locations. The company headquarters is located in Atlanta. Six regional offices representing Asia, Africa, Australia, Europe, North America, and South America link to headquarters, and 26 (total) sales offices link to the regional offices. The business and technical environment analysis documents have already been compiled and copies have been distributed to everyone on the team. Your task is to define the domains for the organization.

Each regional office of Awesome Computers runs independently while still a part of the global company. Headquarters oversees each of the regional offices by selecting the administrators and determining the network structure. Each sales office is administered by the regional office to which it connects.

While reading through the business and technical environment analysis documents, you note the following:

- Each of the regional offices requires a separate password and account lockout policy.
- The sales offices in Germany, France, Spain, the Netherlands, Italy, and Switzerland each require localized language settings.
- The Brazilian sales office has a vital accounting database running on Windows NT 4 that must be confined to its own domain. This office also regularly accesses engineering resources at the European location.
- The sales office in Thailand is running several critical Asian distribution applications that will not run under Windows 2000.
- Awesome Computers will soon be acquiring Bits, Bytes & Chips, Inc., a maker of storage media. Bits, Bytes & Chips, Inc., receives 75% of its revenues from sales over the Internet at its Web site, b-100times.com. Awesome Computers will leave the structure of Bits, Bytes & Chips, Inc., undisturbed after the acquisition is complete. However, Bits, Bytes & Chips, Inc., will be part of the same forest as Awesome Computers.
- A check of the existing DNS namespace reveals that Awesome Computers has a Web site, which operates using the DNS name a-100times.com.

Your design team has diagrammed the network architecture shown in Figure 4.4.

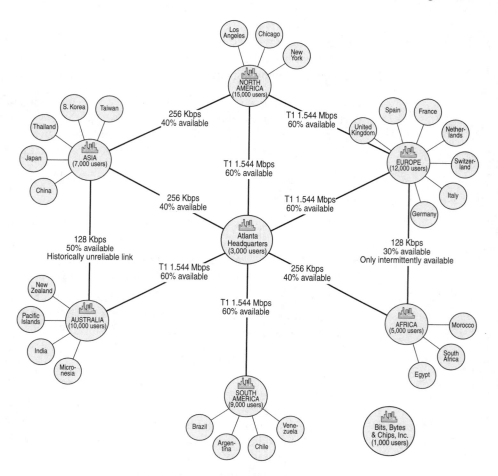

Figure 4.4   Network architecture for Awesome Computers

1. On the network architecture diagram, use a triangle to indicate the location of the domain(s) you would define for Awesome Computers.

2. Explain your reasoning for defining the domain(s).

Lesson 2: Defining a Forest Root Domain

After you define the domains your organization will use for its Active Directory infrastructure, the next step in creating a domain plan is to define a forest root domain. This lesson explains the process of defining a forest root domain, which includes assessing needs and choosing an existing or a dedicated domain for the forest root.

After this lesson, you will be able to

- Identify the factors in an organization's environment that impact the definition of its forest root domain
- Indicate the reasons for using existing or dedicated forest root domains
- Discuss the benefits and implications of using a dedicated forest root domain
- Analyze an organization's environment to define its forest root domain

Estimated lesson time: 10 minutes

Understanding the Forest Root Domain

A *forest root domain* is the first domain you create in an Active Directory forest. For example, in the Active Directory deployment for microsoft.com, the Microsoft domain was created first and is the forest root domain of the hierarchy. The forest root domain must be centrally managed by an IT organization that is responsible for making domain hierarchy, naming, and policy decisions. The Enterprise Admins and Schema Admins predefined universal groups reside only in this domain. Administrators in this domain are those who are key to the network design.

Important After the forest root domain (the first domain in the forest) has been created, you cannot create a new forest root domain, a parent for the existing forest root domain, or rename the forest root domain. For this reason, you should carefully select the forest root domain.

Design Step: Defining a Forest Root Domain

To define a forest root domain, you must complete the following tasks:

1. Assess the domains defined for the organization and its IT management organization.

2. Choose a forest root domain for your organization.

Assessing Forest Root Domain Needs

To define your organization's forest root domain, you must first consult the following documents compiled earlier by your design team:

- Business Structures Worksheet. Assess current administrative structure to locate the IT management organization.

- Network Architecture Worksheet. Assess current network architecture and the domains that have been defined.

- IT Management Organization Worksheet. Assess current IT management organization structure and analyze how the IT management organization handles decisions and changes to determine the location of the forest root.

Note Blank copies of the worksheets are located on the Supplemental Course Materials CD-ROM (\chapt02\worksheets). Completed examples of the worksheets are located in Chapter 2, "Introduction to Designing a Directory Services Infrastructure."

In addition to assessing the information compiled in these documents, it is imperative that you also assess changes currently planned to business structures, network architecture, or the IT management organization to address growth, flexibility, and the ideal design specifications of the organization.

Choosing a Forest Root Domain

When choosing a forest root domain, you will either designate an existing domain as the forest root domain or you can designate an additional, dedicated domain to serve as the forest root domain. The latter method provides certain benefits that may apply to your organization, which are explained later. The forest root domain should be a domain that is centrally managed by an IT department that is capable of making naming and policy decisions.

Reasons for Designating an Existing Domain

Designate an existing domain to serve as the forest root domain when

- Your forest contains only one domain
- Your forest contains multiple domains, and you can select the domain that is the most critical to the operation of your organization from one of them, but you have no desire to
  - Regulate membership in the Enterprise Admins and Schema Admins predefined universal groups in the forest root domain
  - Create a small forest root domain for easier replication
  - Avoid obsolescence of the root domain name

Reasons for Designating a Dedicated Domain

Create a new, dedicated domain to serve as the forest root domain when

- Your forest contains multiple domains, and you *cannot* select the domain that is the most critical to the operation of your organization from one of them. The new domain will be dedicated to the operations associated with enterprise management and should not contain any user or many computer accounts.
- Your forest contains multiple domains, and you *can* select the domain that is the most critical to the operation of your organization from one of them, but you want to
  - Regulate membership in the Enterprise Admins and Schema Admins predefined universal groups in the forest root domain
  - Create a small forest root domain for easier replication
  - Avoid obsolescence of the root domain name

Advantages of Using a Dedicated Domain

Adding a domain to serve as the dedicated domain involves the added costs of an extra domain, as defined in the section "Implications of Defining Multiple Domains" in Lesson 1, "Defining Domains." However, using a dedicated domain can provide your organization with the following advantages:

- Domain administrators in the forest root domain can regulate membership in the Enterprise Admins and Schema Admins predefined universal groups. Using a dedicated root domain, you can restrict the membership of its enterprise-wide administrator groups to only those who need enterprise-wide authority. Those who require administrator capabilities for some of their duties are restricted to regulating membership in administrator groups at the domain level.

- Because a dedicated forest root domain is small, it can be easily replicated across the enterprise to protect the root from catastrophic events. This ability is critical because if all of the domain controllers in the forest root domain are lost in a catastrophic event and none can be restored, the Enterprise Admins and Schema Admins predefined universal groups will also be lost with no way to reinstall the forest root domain.

- Because the only purpose of the forest root domain is to serve as the root, there is little chance of it becoming obsolete. If you designate an existing domain as the forest root domain (based on the fact that it is the most critical domain in the organization), there is always the chance that the organization may change, the domain may no longer be critical, and the domain may become obsolete. Once you've named the root domain you cannot change it without rebuilding the entire Active Directory tree.

▶ **To define a forest root domain**

1. Obtain a copy of your design team's IT Management Organization Worksheet. Analyze the information on the worksheet to determine which domain should be the forest root domain.

2. On the network architecture diagram containing the domains defined for the organization, draw a square around the domain you're defining as the forest root domain.

Design Step Example: Defining a Forest Root Domain

Figure 4.5 shows excerpts from the IT Management Organization Worksheet for Pacific Musical Instruments.

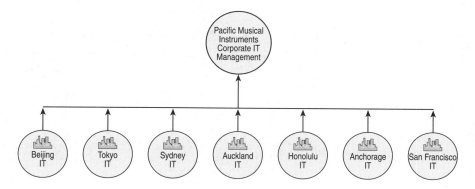

- IT decisions and changes that affect only a regional office are handled by that office's IT department.
- IT decisions that affect the entire organization are handled by the Corporate IT Management department.

Figure 4.5   IT management organization information for Pacific Musical Instruments

Figure 4.2 showed the domains previously defined for Pacific Musical Instruments. Although the Honolulu headquarters domain was considered briefly as the forest root domain, it was not selected because the forest root domain should be a domain that is centrally managed by an IT department that is capable of making naming and policy decisions. At the Honolulu headquarters, two separate departments handle IT management. One department handles IT management for the Honolulu office only, and the other handles IT management for the entire organization. The design team decided to add a dedicated domain as the forest root domain to separate the two IT management departments located in Honolulu and to reap the benefits of using a dedicated forest root domain. Figure 4.6 shows the forest root domain defined for Pacific Musical Instruments.

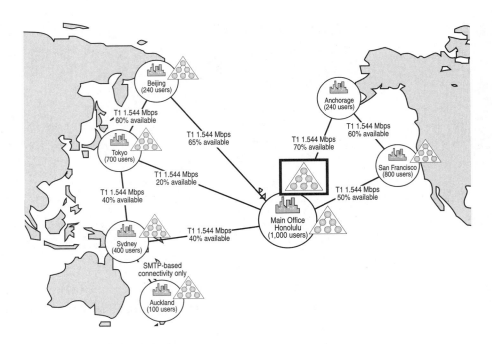

Figure 4.6   Forest root domain defined for Pacific Musical Instruments

Lesson Summary

In this lesson you learned how to define the forest root domain for each forest in an organization by assessing an organization's forest root needs and choosing a forest root domain. When choosing a forest root domain, you will either designate an existing domain as the forest root domain or designate an additional, dedicated domain to serve as the forest root domain. The latter method provides certain benefits that may apply to your organization. The forest root domain should be a domain that is centrally managed by an IT department capable of making naming and policy decisions.

Lesson 3: Defining a Domain Hierarchy

After you define the forest root domain needed for your organization's forests, the next step is to organize the domains in a hierarchy. This lesson explains the process of defining a domain hierarchy, which includes assessing needs, determining the number of domain trees, designating tree root domains, arranging the subdomain hierarchy, and planning cross-link trusts.

After this lesson, you will be able to

- Identify the factors in an organization's environment that impact its domain hierarchy
- Indicate the reasons for using cross-link trusts
- Identify the reason for using multiple trees
- Analyze an organization's environment to define its domain hierarchy

Estimated lesson time: 15 minutes

Understanding Domain Hierarchies

A domain hierarchy is a tree structure of parent and child domains. The way in which domains are arranged in a hierarchy determines the trust relationships between domains. Windows 2000 creates parent-child trusts between parent and child domains in a forest or tree hierarchy. *Parent-child trusts* are implicit, two-way transitive trusts that are created automatically when a domain is added to the hierarchy, as shown in Figure 4.7.

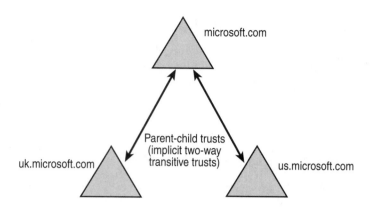

Figure 4.7   Parent-child trusts

The arrangement of domains in a hierarchy does not need to be based on the organization's administrative structure. Domains that function as peers can have parent and child relationships without affecting administrative control. Although administrators in a parent domain can have administrative rights in the child domain, these rights are not automatic and must be explicitly set up. Likewise, group policies set in a parent domain do not automatically propagate to child domains in the forest; they must be explicitly linked. It's important to remember also that the only group that has administrative rights across domains by default is the Enterprise Admins predefined universal group. Rather than arranging domains for administrative capabilities, arrange them in the hierarchy to take advantage of the implicit, two-way transitive trust between parent and child domains, thus optimizing authentication. For example, in Figure 4.7, the uk.microsoft.com and us.microsoft.com domains often require access to resources in the microsoft.com domain. The arrangement shown provides a short, optimal authentication path.

Although the parent-child trusts used in Windows 2000 have reduced administration time compared to the explicit, one-way nontransitive trusts employed by Windows NT, interdomain authentication must follow the established trust path to verify authentication requests. A *trust path* is a series of trust links from one domain to another, established for passing authentication requests. For example, in Figure 4.8, if a user in Domain M requests access to a resource located in Domain P, the domain controller in Domain M must follow the trust path to communicate with the domain controller in Domain P to verify the authentication request.

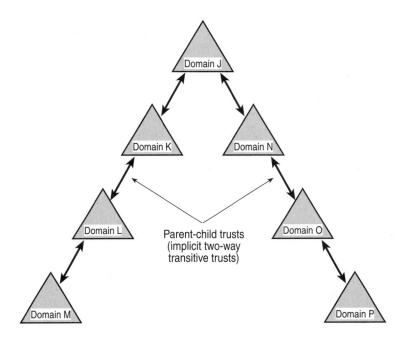

Figure 4.8   Trust paths

The communication process follows these steps:

1. Windows 2000 attempts to locate the resource in Domain M. If the resource is not located, the domain controller in Domain M refers the client to the domain controller in Domain L.

2. Windows 2000 attempts to locate the resource in Domain L. If the resource is not located, the domain controller in Domain L refers the client to the domain controller in Domain K.

3. This process continues up the left side of the hierarchy from Domain K to the top at Domain J and down the right side of the hierarchy until Domain P is reached.

Although this process eventually results in the user being able to access the resource, the process takes time and affects query response performance. In addition, each time clients are referred to another domain controller, the chances of a failure or of encountering a slow link are increased.

Cross-Link Trusts

Windows 2000 provides a means for improving query response performance with cross-link trusts. A *cross-link trust* is a two-way transitive trust that you explicitly create between two Windows 2000 domains that are logically distant from each other in a forest or tree hierarchy in order to optimize the interdomain authentication process. Cross-link trusts are also known as *shortcut trusts*. Cross-link trusts can be created only between Windows 2000 domains in the same forest. Figure 4.9 illustrates a cross-link trust created to shorten the trust path and improve query response performance between Domain M and Domain P described earlier.

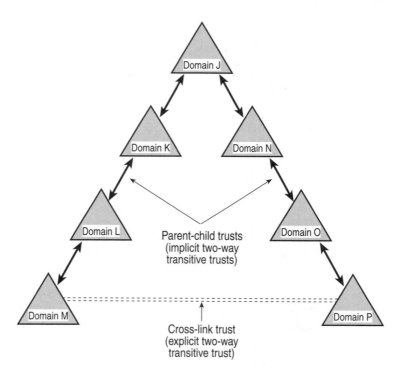

Figure 4.9   Cross-link trust

Because cross-link trusts must be explicitly set up, you must determine whether there is enough authentication traffic between the distant domains to warrant the administrative effort.

Design Step: Defining a Domain Hierarchy

By defining a hierarchy of domains for your organization, you provide a structure for naming domains, which we will explore in Lesson 4, "Naming Domains." To define a domain hierarchy, you must complete the following tasks:

1. Assess the organization's domain hierarchy needs.

2. Determine the domain hierarchy.

Assessing Domain Hierarchy Needs

To define your organization's domain hierarchy, you must first consult the following documents compiled earlier by your design team:

- Information Flow Worksheet. Analyze which domains need access to resources in other domains.

- Network Architecture Worksheet. Assess current network architecture, including the domains defined and the location of the forest root domain.

- DNS Environment Worksheet. Assess current domain structure to determine existing DNS names that may require separate tree structures.

Note Blank copies of the worksheets are located on the Supplemental Course Materials CD-ROM (\chapt02\worksheets). Completed examples of the worksheets are located in Chapter 2, "Introduction to Designing a Directory Services Infrastructure."

In addition to assessing the data compiled in these documents, it is imperative that you also assess changes currently planned to information flow or network architecture to address growth, flexibility, and the ideal design specifications of the organization.

Determining a Domain Hierarchy

To determine a domain hierarchy, you must analyze information about the organization to determine the number of domain trees, designate tree root domains, arrange the subdomain hierarchy, and plan any cross-link trusts.

Determining the Number of Domain Trees

Recall that a *tree* is a grouping or hierarchical arrangement of one or more Windows 2000 domains with contiguous names that you create by adding one or more child domains to an existing parent domain. A forest can have one or more trees. However, one tree per forest is considered ideal because it requires fewer administrative activities. Although the recommended number of trees in a forest is one, you may need to define more than one domain if your organization has more than one DNS name.

Implications of Using Multiple Trees

Using multiple trees increases administrative costs. When determining whether to define multiple trees, keep the following items in mind:

- DNS names. Because each tree requires a separate DNS name, your organization will be responsible for maintaining more DNS names.

- Proxy client exclusion list or proxy autoconfiguration (PAC) file. Because each tree requires a separate DNS name, you must add these names to the list or file.

- Non-Microsoft LDAP clients. These clients may not be able to perform a global catalog search and instead may need to perform an LDAP search of subtree scope that searches each tree separately.

Designating Tree Root Domains

Once you've determined the number of trees in each forest for your organization, you should determine which domain will serve as the tree root domain for each tree. The *tree root domain* is the highest-level domain in the tree, under which its child and grandchild domains are arranged. Typically, the domain you select should be the one that is most critical to the operation of the tree. A tree root domain can also be the forest root domain, as shown in Figure 4.10.

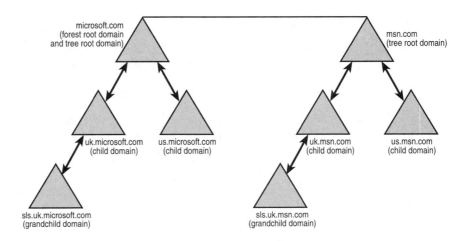

Figure 4.10   Tree and forest root domains

Arranging the Subdomain Hierarchy

After you've determined the number of domain trees and designated the root domain for each tree, the next step in defining a domain hierarchy is to arrange the remaining subdomains in a hierarchy under the root domains. Recall that domains need not be arranged based on administrative structure. You will still be able to represent your administrative structure when you set up OUs and groups, as discussed in Chapter 5, "Creating an Organizational Unit Plan." More importantly, you should arrange domains in a manner that takes advantage of the implicit, two-way transitive trust between parent and child domains. Finally, you should keep your domain tree hierarchy shallow. One level of domains per tree is ideal; for best performance you should restrict the levels to three or four.

Planning Cross-Link Trusts

The final step in defining a domain hierarchy is to determine which domains need to be linked by cross-link trusts. Use the Information Flow Worksheet to determine which domains need access to resources in other domains. If these domains have not already been placed near each other in the hierarchy, you can optimize trust relationships by planning cross-link trusts.

▶ **To define a domain hierarchy**

1. Begin by diagramming the forest root domain at the top of the hierarchy.

2. Determine the number of DNS names to be employed by your organization when Windows 2000 is implemented. Your Active Directory infrastructure will have this number of trees.

3. Diagram the tree root domain for each tree in relation to the existing forest root domain. The tree root domains you select should be the ones that are most critical to the operation of the tree. If there is only one tree, the tree root domain is also the forest root domain.

4. Obtain a copy of your design team's Information Flow Worksheet, which should include a list of the information on the network, such as files, folders, or applications, that is needed by departments but not stored and maintained by that department. Use the information on the worksheet to diagram the remaining subdomains under the forest and tree root domains in a manner that takes advantage of the implicit, two-way transitive trust between parent and child domains.

5. If the domains have not been placed near each other in the hierarchy, designate cross-link trusts on the diagram with a dotted line.

Design Step Example: Defining a Domain Hierarchy

Pacific Musical Instruments currently uses only one registered DNS name, pac-100times.com. The organization does not anticipate needing any other DNS names, so it will have only one tree in its Active Directory infrastructure. Because Pacific Musical Instruments has only one tree, the forest root domain will also serve as the tree root domain.

The finance, human resources, and sales departments at each regional office all require access to resources stored at the Honolulu headquarters. Although each regional office must then go through the root domain to access resources at the Honolulu headquarters, there is no need to use cross-link trusts in this scenario, because the domains are close to each other in the hierarchy. The domain hierarchy diagram for Pacific Musical Instruments is shown in Figure 4.11.

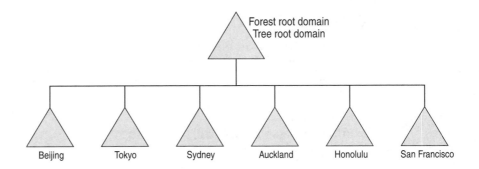

Figure 4.11   Domain hierarchy diagram for Pacific Musical Instruments

Lesson Summary

In this lesson you learned how to define a domain hierarchy for each forest in an organization by assessing needs, determining the number of domain trees, designating tree root domains, arranging the subdomain hierarchy on a diagram, and planning cross-link trusts.

You also learned that the recommended number of trees in a forest is one; however, the number of DNS names employed by your organization determines the number of domain trees needed for the domain hierarchy. The tree root domain is the highest-level domain in the tree, under which its child and grandchild domains are arranged. A tree root domain can also be the forest root domain. After determining the number of trees and the tree root domains, you should arrange the subdomains in a manner that takes advantage of the implicit, two-way transitive trust between parent and child domains. To optimize the inter-domain authentication process, you can explicitly create cross-link trusts, which are two-way transitive trusts between two Windows 2000 domains that are logically distant from each other in a forest or tree hierarchy. A shallow domain tree hierarchy is recommended, with no more than three or four levels of domains.

Lesson 4: Naming Domains

After you define the domain hierarchy for your organization's forests, the next step is to name the domains. This lesson explains how to name domains, which includes assessing domain naming needs and choosing names for each domain in an organization.

After this lesson, you will be able to

- Identify the factors in an organization's environment that impact its domain names
- Recall the guidelines for naming domains
- Analyze an organization's environment to name its domains

Estimated lesson time: 15 minutes

Understanding Domain Names

In Windows 2000 and Active Directory, a *domain name* is a name given to a collection of networked computers that share a common directory. Recall that Active Directory uses the Domain Name System (DNS) as its domain naming and location service, which allows for interoperability with Internet technologies. Therefore, Windows 2000 domain names are also DNS names. When requesting logon to the network, Active Directory clients query their DNS servers to locate domain controllers.

In DNS, names are arranged in a hierarchy and can be partitioned according to the hierarchy. The hierarchy allows parent-child relationships where the name of the child domain is designated by the name of the parent domain preceded by a label. For example, uk.microsoft.com is a child domain of the microsoft.com domain; for the child name the "uk" label is placed before the name of the parent domain, "microsoft.com." Thus, a domain's name identifies its position in the hierarchy.

Design Step: Naming Domains

To name domains, you must complete the following tasks:

1. Assess the organization's domain naming needs.

2. Choose names for each domain in your organization.

Assessing Domain Naming Needs

To define domain names for your organization, you must first consult the following documents compiled earlier by your design team:

- Domain Hierarchy Diagram. Assess the position of domains in the hierarchy to determine the appropriate DNS names.

- DNS Environment Worksheet. Determine existing DNS names.

Note The Domain Hierarchy Diagram is discussed in the previous lesson. A blank copy of the worksheet is located on the Supplemental Course Materials CD-ROM (\chapt02\worksheets). A completed example of the worksheet is located in Chapter 2, "Introduction to Designing a Directory Services Infrastructure."

In addition to assessing the information compiled in these documents, it is imperative that you also assess changes currently planned for domain names and hierarchies to address growth, flexibility, and the ideal design specifications of the organization.

Choosing Domain Names

Because it is nearly impossible to change domain names, the names you select are very important. It's especially critical that you select the correct name for the forest root domain, which you cannot change and which is the basis for its child and grandchild domains. If you adhere to some basic guidelines, you should be able to determine domain names that meet the needs of your organization. The following are guidelines for naming domains:

- Use only the Internet standard characters. Internet standard characters are defined as: A–Z, a–z, 0–9, and the hyphen (-). Although Windows 2000 DNS supports the use of almost any Unicode character in a name, by using only Internet standard characters you ensure that your Active Directory domain names will be compatible with other versions of DNS.

- Differentiate between internal and external namespaces. Because most organizations have an Internet presence, you should use different names for the internal and external root domains to clearly delineate public resources from private resources and prevent unauthorized users from accessing resources on the internal network. For example, a company named Just Togs is represented on the Internet by the DNS name j-100times.com, so the organization should use another DNS name, such as corp.j-100times.com, to represent their Active Directory forest root domain name.

- Base the internal DNS name on the Internet DNS name. If you use an internal DNS name that is related to the Internet DNS name, it will be easier for users to understand the navigational structure. Consider using the Internet DNS name as a suffix for Active Directory domain names. For example, corp.j-100times.com is easily understandable as an extension to j-100times.com.

- Never use the same domain name twice. For example, Just Togs should not use the name j-100times.com for both its Internet and intranet root domains. If a j-100times.com client attempts to connect to either the Internet or the intranet j-100times.com site, the domain that answers first is the one to which the client is connected.

- Use only registered domain names. Register all second-level domain names, whether they are internal or external namespaces, with the InterNIC or other authorized naming authority. For example, Just Togs should register its second-level domain name, j-100times.com. The company does not need to register corp.j-100times.com because it is not a second-level domain name. Internal names that are second-level domain names should be registered to ensure access from outside the corporate firewall. You can find more information about registering domain names at *http://internic.net/*.

Caution Be sure to register and receive verification for domain names *before* creating your Active Directory domain namespace. After you name your forest root domain you cannot change it, and it is difficult to change other domain names.

- Use short, distinct, meaningful names. Use domain names that are easy to use and are representative of your organization's identity.

- Use names that have been reviewed internationally. Review domain names to ensure that they are not derogatory or offensive in another language.

- Use names that will remain static. Use generic names rather than specific ones. For example, Just Togs might use hq.corp.j-100times.com for its Atlanta headquarters domain rather than atlanta.corp.j-100times.com to avoid the need for change if the headquarters is moved.

- Use the International Standards Organization (ISO) standards for names that include countries and U.S. states. The ISO defines two-letter country codes and U.S. state codes, as presented in ISO 3166. You can find more information about ISO 3166 at *http://www.din.de/gremien/nas/nabd/iso3166ma/*.

▶ **To name domains**

1. On the domain hierarchy diagram, assign a DNS name to the forest root domain for each forest in your organization.

2. Assign DNS names to each tree root domain.

3. Assign DNS names to each remaining subdomain. Name each child and grandchild domain according to its position in the hierarchy.

Design Step Example: Naming Domains

Figure 4.11 showed the domain hierarchy diagram for Pacific Musical Instruments. Because the organization already has an Internet presence using the DNS name pac-100times.com, the forest root domain will be named corp.pac-100times.com. Since there is only one tree, the tree root domain is the same as the forest root domain, named corp.pac-100times.com. The child subdomains are named after the regional offices using codes as defined by ISO 3166. The domain hierarchy diagram with domain names is shown in Figure 4.12.

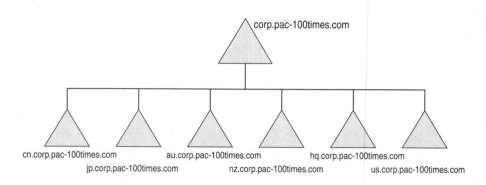

Figure 4.12   Domain hierarchy diagram with domain names for Pacific Musical Instruments

Lesson Summary

In this lesson you learned how to name domains by assessing domain naming needs and choosing names for each domain in an organization. You learned how naming domains is very important because domain names cannot be changed easily and the forest root domain name cannot be changed at all. You also learned some guidelines for naming domains.

Activity 4.2: Defining a Root Domain, Defining a Domain Hierarchy, and Naming Domains

In this activity you will continue creating a domain plan for two organizations that are planning their Active Directory infrastructure. Your task is to analyze each organization's environment to define the root domains, domain hierarchies, and domain names needed for the Active Directory infrastructure.

Scenario 1: Friendship Vineyards

Recall your experience in the previous activity (located after Lesson 1) as an infrastructure planner on the Active Directory infrastructure design team for Friendship Vineyards, a winery that operates from four locations in South Africa. Friendship Vineyards is a centralized organization, with IT administration handled from its Cape Town headquarters. Each of the four locations also has a small IT staff to handle basic support tasks. There is one special requirement—that desktops for the distribution personnel at all four locations be restricted to distribution software only. Although Friendship Vineyards is currently running Windows NT 4, its management has decided not to carry the company's current domain structure into the new Windows 2000 environment. A check of the existing DNS namespace reveals that Friendship Vineyards has a Web site, which operates using the DNS name f-100times.com.

One domain has been defined for the organization. You are now in the process of defining a root domain, defining a domain hierarchy, and naming the domain.

Your design team has defined the domain shown in Figure 4.13.

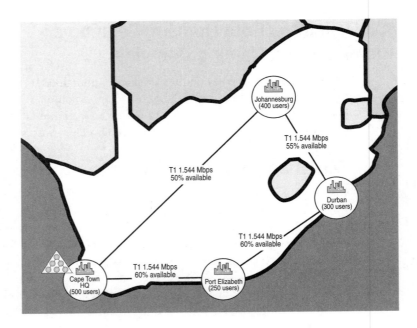

Figure 4.13   Domain defined for Friendship Vineyards

Figure 4.14 shows the excerpts from the IT Management Organization Worksheet for Friendship Vineyards.

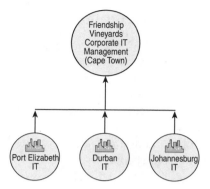

- Basic support tasks for each location are handled by that location's IT department.
- IT decisions that affect the entire organization are handled by the IT Management department at headquarters.

Figure 4.14   IT management organization information for Friendship Vineyards

1. On the network architecture diagram, draw a square around the domain you're defining as the forest root domain. Explain your reasoning for defining the forest root domain.

2. Complete a domain hierarchy diagram for Friendship Vineyards.

3. Name the forest root domain.

Scenario 2: Awesome Computers

Recall your experience in the previous activity (located after Lesson 1) as an infrastructure planner on the Active Directory infrastructure design team for Awesome Computers, a global multibillion-dollar computer manufacturer with more than 65,000 users and computers at more than 30 locations. The company headquarters is located in Atlanta. Six regional offices representing Asia, Africa, Australia, Europe, North America, and South America link to headquarters, and 26 (total) sales offices link to the regional offices. Each regional office of Awesome Computers runs independently while still part of the global company. Headquarters oversees each of the regional offices by selecting the administrators and determining the network structure. Each sales office is administered by the regional office to which it connects.

While reading through the business and technical environment analysis documents, you note the following:

- Each of the regional offices requires a separate password and account lockout policy.

- The human resources, accounting, and distribution departments at each regional office all require access to resources stored at the Atlanta headquarters.

- The sales offices in Germany, France, Spain, the Netherlands, Italy, and Switzerland each require different language settings.

- The Brazilian sales office has a vital accounting database running on Windows NT 4 that must be confined to its own domain. This office also regularly accesses engineering resources at the European location.

- The sales office in Thailand is running several critical Asian distribution applications that will not run under Windows 2000.

- Awesome Computers will soon be acquiring Bits, Bytes & Chips, Inc., a maker of storage media. Bits, Bytes & Chips, Inc., receives 75% of its revenues from sales over the Internet at its Web site, b-100times.com. Awesome Computers will leave the structure of Bits, Bytes & Chips, Inc., undisturbed after the acquisition is complete. However, Bits, Bytes & Chips, Inc., will be part of the same forest as Awesome Computers.

- A check of the existing DNS namespace reveals that Awesome Computers has a Web site, which operates using the DNS name a-100times.com.

Ten domains have been defined for the organization. You are now in the process of defining a root domain, defining a domain hierarchy, and naming the domains.

Your design team has defined the domains shown in Figure 4.15.

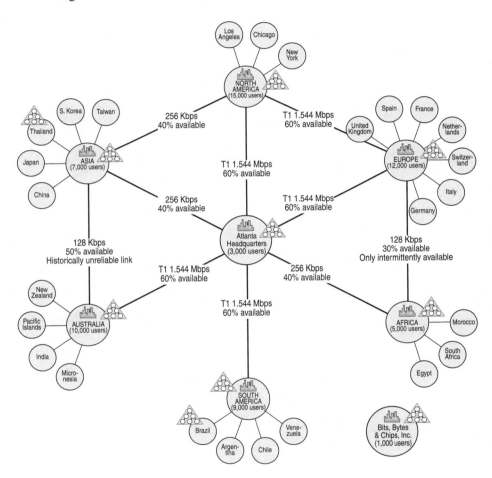

Figure 4.15   Domains defined for Awesome Computers

Figure 4.16 shows the excerpts from the IT Management Organization Worksheet for Awesome Computers.

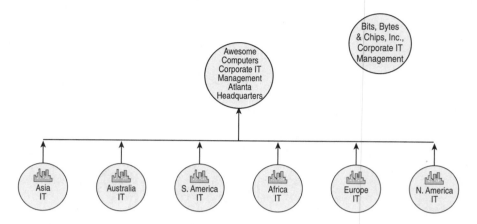

- IT decisions and changes that affect only a regional office are handled by that office's IT department.
- IT decisions that affect only Bits, Bytes & Chips, Inc., are handled by the Bits, Bytes & Chips, Inc., IT department.
- IT decisions that affect the entire organization are handled by the Corporate IT Management department.

Figure 4.16 IT management organization information for Awesome Computers

1. On the network architecture diagram, draw a square around the domain you're defining as the forest root domain. Explain your reasoning for defining the forest root domain.

2. Complete a domain hierarchy diagram for Awesome Computers, including the forest root domain, the tree root domains, and the remaining subdomains. Indicate any cross-link trusts that may be necessary by a dotted line.

3. Name the domains in the domain hierarchy, including the forest root domain, the tree root domains, and the remaining subdomains.

Lesson 5: Planning DNS Server Deployment

After you define the domain hierarchy for your organization's forests and name the domains, the final step in creating a domain plan is to plan DNS server deployment. This lesson explains how to plan DNS server deployment, which includes assessing the organization's current DNS server environment and determining the placement of its DNS servers.

After this lesson, you will be able to

- Identify the factors in an organization's environment that impact its DNS server deployment
- Plan additional zones
- Determine the existing DNS services employed on the DNS servers
- Determine the zone replication method
- Analyze an organization's environment to plan its DNS server deployment

Estimated lesson time: 20 minutes

Understanding DNS Servers

A *DNS server* is a computer that resolves names to IP addresses and IP addresses to names for host devices contained within a portion of the namespace. When a client queries a DNS server for a name or IP address, the server performs one of the following actions: provides the name or IP address, refers the client to another DNS server, or indicates that it cannot fulfill the request. DNS servers are also known as *DNS name servers*.

Note A detailed discussion of DNS is beyond the scope of this course. For a thorough discussion of DNS, refer to the *Microsoft Windows 2000 Server TCP/IP Core Networking Guide* volume of the *Microsoft Windows 2000 Server Resource Kit.*

DNS servers use information stored about zones to handle name resolution. Each DNS server can store information for no zones, one zone, or multiple zones. A *zone* is a contiguous portion of the DNS namespace that is administered separately by a DNS server. The DNS namespace represents the logical structure of your network resources, and DNS zones provide physical storage for these resources. Zones can encompass a single domain or a domain and subdomains. Each zone contains a *zone database file*, a text file containing resource records for the zone. *Resource records* are records that contain information used to process client queries. There are many different types of resource records. When a zone is created, DNS automatically adds two resource records: the Start of Authority (SOA) and the Name Server (NS) records. Table 4.1 describes these resource record types, along with the most frequently used resource records.

Table 4.1   Frequently Used Resource Record Types

Resource record type	Description
Host (A)	Lists the host name to IP address mappings for a forward lookup zone.
Alias (CNAME)	Creates an alias, or alternate name, for the specified host name. You can use a Canonical Name (CNAME) record to use more than one name to point to a single IP address. For example, you can host a File Transfer Protocol (FTP) server, such as ftp.microsoft.com, and a Web server, such as www.microsoft.com, on the same computer.
Host Information (HINFO)	Identifies the CPU and operating system used by the host. Use this record as a low-cost resource-tracking tool.
Mail Exchanger (MX)	Identifies which mail exchanger to contact for a specified domain and in what order to use each mail host.

Resource record type	Description
Name Server (NS)	Lists the name servers that are assigned to a particular domain.
Pointer (PTR)	Points to another part of the domain namespace. For example, in a reverse lookup zone, it lists the IP-address-to-name mapping.
Service (SRV)	Identifies which servers are hosting specific services. For example, if a client needs to find a server to validate logon requests, the client can send a query to the DNS server to obtain a list of domain controllers and their associated IP addresses.
Start of Authority (SOA)	Identifies which name server is the authoritative source of information for data within this domain. The first record in the zone database file must be the SOA record.

Figure 4.17 shows the relationship of DNS servers, domains, zones, zone database files, and resource records.

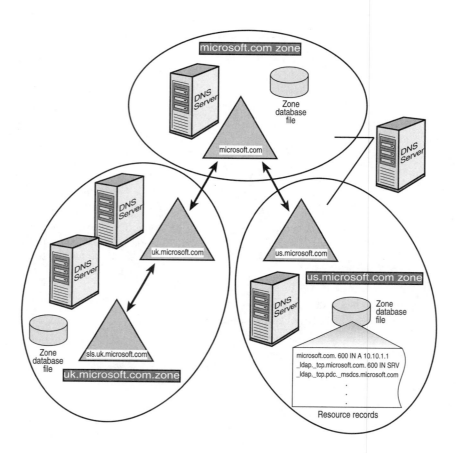

Figure 4.17   Relationship of DNS servers, domains, zones, zone database files, and resource records

Zone Replication

Zone replication is the synchronization of DNS data between DNS servers within a given zone. Replicating zones provides the following benefits:

- Fault tolerance. If a DNS server fails, clients can still direct queries to other DNS servers.
- Query load distribution. Query loads can be balanced among DNS servers.
- WAN traffic reduction. DNS servers can be added in remote locations to eliminate the need for clients to send queries across slow links.

There are two methods for replicating zones: standard zone replication and Active Directory zone replication. The use of Active Directory zone replication is strongly recommended.

Standard Zone Replication

In standard zone replication, primary and secondary zones and primary and secondary DNS servers handle zone replication. A *primary zone* is the master copy of a zone stored in a standard text file on a primary DNS server. A *primary DNS server* is the authoritative server for a primary zone; you must administer and maintain a primary zone on the primary DNS server for the zone. A *secondary zone* is a read-only replica of an existing standard primary zone stored in a standard text file on a secondary DNS server. A *secondary DNS server* is a backup DNS server that receives the zone database files from the primary server in a zone transfer. *Zone transfer* is the process by which DNS servers interact to maintain and synchronize authoritative name data. A zone can have multiple secondary servers, and a secondary server can serve more than one zone. Figure 4.18 shows the use of primary and secondary DNS servers.

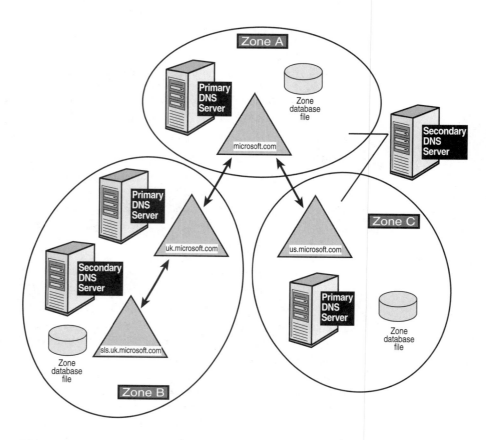

Figure 4.18 Use of primary and secondary DNS servers in zones

There are three types of zone transfers: full zone transfers, incremental zone transfers, and transfers that use the DNS Notify process. In a *full zone transfer (AXFR query)*, the primary DNS server transmits the entire zone database file for the primary zone to the secondary DNS server. In an *incremental zone transfer (IXFR query)*, the servers keep track of and transfer only incremental resource record changes between each version of the zone database file.

Important To perform incremental zone transfer, you must implement a DNS service that supports RFC 1995, which includes Windows 2000 Server. For earlier versions of DNS service, such as those running on Windows NT 4, incremental zone transfer is not supported and only full zone transfers can be used to replicate zones.

Figure 4.19 illustrates the full and incremental zone transfer processes.

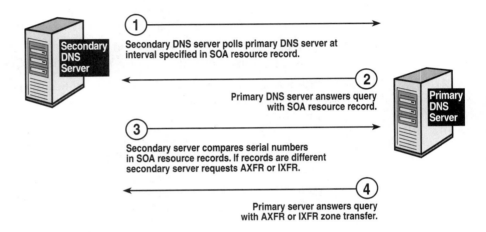

Figure 4.19   Full and incremental zone transfer processes

In the DNS Notify process, the primary server, rather than the secondary server, initiates the zone transfer. The following is a summary of the DNS Notify process:

1. The zone on a primary DNS server is updated, which updates the serial number on the SOA resource record in the primary zone.

2. The primary DNS server sends a notify message to the secondary DNS servers (specified by an administrator) as part of its notify set.

3. When the secondary DNS servers in the notify set receive the notify message, they initiate an AXFR or IXFR zone transfer.

Active Directory Zone Replication

In Active Directory zone replication, Active Directory–integrated zones and domain controllers handle zone replication. Each domain controller functions as a primary DNS server, using Active Directory to store and replicate primary zone files. Active Directory zone replication provides the following advantages over standard zone replication:

- Replication planning is simplified. Because DNS resource records are part of Active Directory and are replicated to each domain controller, it is no longer necessary to maintain zone database files or use zone transfer.

- Replication is multimaster. Updates to zones are allowed at every DNS server/domain controller, rather than just the primary DNS server.

- Efficiency. Because Active Directory zone replication is processed at the property level, it generates less replication traffic than standard zone replication.

- Detailed delegation of administration. Administration for directory-integrated zone data can be delegated for users for each resource record.

Important To replicate zones with Active Directory zone replication, you must implement the Windows 2000 DNS service.

DNS Server Requirements

Existing authoritative DNS servers must meet the following minimum requirements to support Active Directory:

- They must support service (SRV) resource records, as described in RFC 2052.
- They must support dynamic update, as described in RFC 2136.

It is recommended that organizations deploy the Windows 2000 DNS service provided with Windows 2000 Server. Windows 2000 DNS service meets the minimum requirements and provides two additional features:

- Active Directory–integrated zones
- Secure dynamic update

Servers that are not authoritative do not need to meet the DNS server requirements. These servers can usually answer SRV record queries even though they do not support that record type.

Design Step: Planning DNS Server Deployment

To plan DNS server deployment, you must complete the following tasks:

1. Assess the organization's current DNS server environment.
2. Determine the placement of the DNS servers.

Assessing the DNS Server Environment

To plan the DNS server deployment for your organization, you must first consult the following documents compiled earlier by your design team:

- IT Management Organization Worksheet. Assess current IT management organization structure to determine whether it's necessary to delegate management of part of the DNS namespace to another department or location within the organization.

- DNS Environment Worksheet. Assess the organization's current DNS server environment.

Note Blank copies of the worksheets are located on the Supplemental Course Materials CD-ROM (\chapt02\worksheets). Completed examples of the worksheets are located in Chapter 2, "Introduction to Designing a Directory Services Infrastructure."

In addition to assessing the information compiled in these worksheets, it is imperative that you also assess changes currently planned for DNS server environments to address growth, flexibility, and the ideal design specifications of the organization.

Determining Placement of DNS Servers

To determine the placement of your DNS servers, you must plan additional zones, determine the existing DNS services employed on your DNS servers, and determine the zone replication method to use.

Planning Additional Zones

To determine when to divide your DNS namespace into zones, consider if there is a need to

- Delegate management of part of the DNS namespace to another department or location within the organization

- Divide a large zone into smaller zones to distribute traffic loads among multiple servers, improve DNS name resolution performance, or create a more fault-tolerant DNS environment

- Extend the namespace by adding numerous subdomains at once, as in accommodating the opening of a new branch or site

If you can answer "yes" to any of these considerations, you may want to divide your namespace into additional zones.

Determining Existing DNS Services

If your organization is already using a DNS service other than Windows 2000 DNS, you will need to find out whether the service is compatible with Active Directory and how it is currently structured. The following DNS services meet the DNS server requirements to support Active Directory:

- DNS BIND version 8.1.2 or later

- Windows NT 4 DNS

Although these DNS services are compatible with Active Directory, only the Windows 2000 DNS service allows you to use Active Directory–integrated zones, incremental zone transfer, and secure dynamic updates. To take advantage of these features, you can upgrade DNS servers running compatible DNS services to Windows 2000 DNS.

It is important to note that the DNS BIND version 4.*x* does not meet the DNS server requirements to support Active Directory. To implement Windows 2000 in the DNS BIND 4.*x* environment, you will have to upgrade the BIND 4.*x* environment to BIND 8.1.2 or later. From that point you can upgrade your DNS servers to Windows 2000 DNS.

If you cannot upgrade your DNS servers to Windows 2000 DNS, the best solution is to create a delegated subdomain. A *delegated subdomain* is a separate Windows 2000 DNS subdomain set up in the established DNS namespace. The DNS server in the Windows 2000 DNS subdomain is authoritative for that subdomain. You can add child domains to the subdomains as needed.

Determining the Zone Replication Method

Once you've identified the existing DNS service and settled on the DNS service you will use for your Active Directory implementation, you can easily determine the replication method to use. If you are using Windows 2000 DNS service, you can use Active Directory–integrated zone replication. In this case, all of your domain controllers function as primary DNS servers. If you are using DNS BIND version 8.1.2 or later or Windows NT 4 DNS service, you must use standard zone replication. In this case, you must specify primary and secondary DNS servers and zones.

▶   **To plan DNS server deployment**

1. Determine whether your organization needs additional zones.

2. Identify the existing DNS services employed on your DNS servers.

3. Determine whether to use standard or Active Directory–integrated zone replication.

4. If using standard zone replication, specify primary and secondary zones and DNS servers.

Design Step Example: Planning DNS Server Deployment

Pacific Musical Instruments would like to delegate management of part of the us.corp.pac-100times.com domain to the organization's Anchorage location. To do this, the design team plans to split the domain into two zones. Because Pacific Musical Instruments is committed to using Windows 2000 DNS, the company will be able to use Active Directory–integrated zone replication. Because all domain controllers function as primary DNS servers, it is not necessary to define the location of primary and secondary zones and DNS servers. The domain hierarchy diagram showing the planned zones is presented in Figure 4.20.

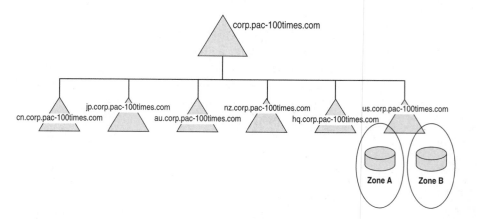

Figure 4.20   Domain hierarchy diagram with planned zones for Pacific Musical Instruments

Lesson Summary

In this lesson you learned how to plan DNS server deployment by assessing the organization's current DNS server environment and determining the placement of its DNS servers. To determine the placement of your DNS servers, you learned how to plan additional zones, determine the existing DNS services employed on the DNS servers, and determine the zone replication method to use.

To plan additional zones, you learned the reasons for dividing your DNS namespace into zones. You also learned that the existing DNS services of DNS BIND version 8.1.2 or later and Windows NT 4 DNS are compatible with Active Directory. Only the Windows 2000 DNS service allows you to use Active Directory–integrated zones, incremental zone transfer, and secure dynamic updates. To take advantage of these features, you can upgrade DNS servers running compatible DNS services to Windows 2000 DNS. You learned that DNS BIND version 4.*x* *does not* meet the DNS server requirements to support Active Directory and that to implement Windows 2000 in the DNS BIND 4.*x* environment, you have to upgrade the BIND 4.*x* environment to BIND 8.1.2 or later. Finally, you learned that if you are using Windows 2000 DNS service, you can use Active Directory–integrated zone replication. If you are using DNS BIND version 8.1.2 or later or Windows NT 4 DNS service, you must use standard zone replication.

Lab 4.1: Creating a Domain Plan

Lab Objectives

After completing this lab, you will be able to

- Define domains
- Define a forest root domain
- Define a domain hierarchy
- Name domains

About This Lab

In this lab, you will analyze portions of the existing environment at a medium-sized company to define domains, define a forest root domain, define a domain hierarchy, name domains, and plan DNS server deployment.

Before You Begin

Before you begin this lab, you must be able to

- Analyze an organization's environment to define its domains
- Analyze an organization's environment to define its forest root domain
- Analyze an organization's environment to define its domain hierarchy
- Analyze an organization's environment to name its domains

Exercise: Creating a Domain Plan

In this exercise, you will analyze the existing environment at a medium-sized company to create a domain plan, which includes a network architecture diagram with the domains and forest root domain indicated and a domain hierarchy diagram with named domains. Review the scenario; then follow the instructions to create the domain plan.

Scenario

Your design team is planning the Active Directory infrastructure for Parnell Aerospace, a developer and manufacturer of commercial and military aircraft. Parnell's headquarters is in Phoenix, Arizona. Last year Parnell Aerospace acquired Lakes & Sons, a developer and manufacturer of small private aircraft. Parnell Aerospace has approximately 63,000 employees worldwide. Six regional offices, in New York, Tokyo, Berlin, London, Paris, and Rio de Janeiro, link to headquarters; each regional office has 5 to 10 sales offices. Lakes & Sons has 5,000 employees in Seattle and 3,000 employees in Minneapolis. Each location has two sales offices.

While reading through the business and technical environment analysis documents, you note the following requirements:

- Because Parnell Aerospace is a defense contractor for the governments of many countries, the company must meet special legal requirements for storing product development files at headquarters.
- The Tokyo location requires special password and account lockout settings.
- German laws require that the Berlin location be administered only by an office in Germany or by company headquarters in Phoenix.
- French law requires that the Paris location have more relaxed Kerberos settings than any of the other locations.
- Lakes & Sons will function independently and have its own Web presence; however, the forest model compiled by the design team requires only one forest.
- At the Phoenix headquarters, two separate departments handle IT management. One department handles IT management for the Phoenix office only, and the other handles IT management for the entire organization.
- At Lakes & Sons, two separate departments handle IT management. One department handles IT management for the Minneapolis office only, and the other group handles IT management for the entire Lakes & Sons organization.

Figure 4.21 shows excerpts from the IT Management Organization Worksheet for Parnell Aerospace.

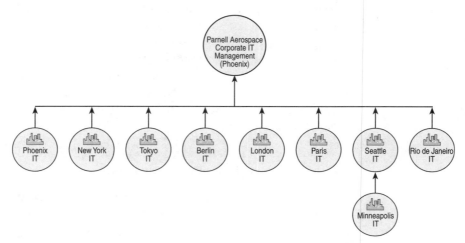

- IT decisions and changes that affect only a regional office are handled by that office's IT department.
- IT decisions that affect the entire organization are handled by the Corporate IT Management department.

Figure 4.21   IT management organization for Parnell Aerospace

- Users at all locations must often access engineering resources at the Phoenix location.

- The Engineering department in Phoenix currently has its own Windows NT 4 domain. They would like to keep their domain, but there are no particular security, administrative, or replication issues that warrant using a separate domain.

- Parnell Aerospace currently has a Web presence and uses the DNS name p-100times.com.

- Lakes & Sons currently has a Web presence and uses the DNS name l-100times.com.

Figure 4.22 shows the network architecture diagram for Parnell Aerospace.

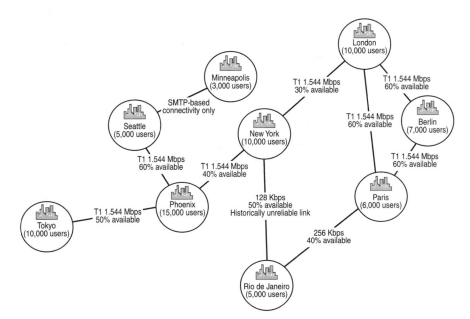

Figure 4.22   Parnell Aerospace network architecture diagram

Exercise Questions

Answer the following questions to create a domain plan.

1. On the network architecture diagram, use a triangle to indicate the location of the domain(s) you would define for Parnell Aerospace. Explain your reasoning for defining the domain(s).

2. On the network architecture diagram, draw a square around the domain you're defining as the forest root domain. Explain your reasoning for defining the forest root domain.

3. Complete a domain hierarchy diagram for Parnell Aerospace. Name the domains in the domain hierarchy.

Review

The following questions are intended to reinforce key information presented in the chapter. If you are unable to answer a question, review the appropriate lesson and then try the question again. Answers to the questions can be found in Appendix A, "Questions and Answers."

1. Your design team is defining domains for an organization. What are the four reasons for defining multiple domains?

2. Your design team is defining the forest root domain for an organization. What are the reasons for designating an existing domain as a forest root domain? What are the reasons for designating a dedicated domain as the forest root domain?

3. Your design team is defining the domain trees for an organization. What is the reason for designating more than one domain tree?

4. Your design team is getting ready to create the w-100times.com forest root domain for Wingtip Toys. What should you do before creating the domain?

5. Your design team is determining the existing DNS service used by an organization. What DNS services meet the DNS server requirements to support Active Directory? What DNS service allows you to use Active Directory–integrated zones?

CHAPTER 5

Creating an Organizational Unit Plan

About This Chapter

After you and your design team finish creating a domain plan, the next stage in designing an Active Directory directory services infrastructure is to create an organizational unit (OU) plan. To create an OU plan, you define an OU structure and then plan user accounts and groups. The end result of an OU plan is a diagram of OU structures for each domain, a list of users in each OU, and a list of groups in each domain. This chapter discusses the process of creating an OU plan.

Real World Read the "Designing in the Real World: Creating an Organization Unit Plan" interview with Xavier Minet, Microsoft Consulting Services, Belgium, for a real-world perspective of creating an organizational unit plan. You can find the interview on the Supplemental Course Materials CD-ROM (\chapt05\OUPlanInterview).

Before You Begin

To complete this chapter, you must have

- Knowledge of Active Directory components and concepts covered in Chapter 1, "Introduction to Active Directory"
- Knowledge of business and technical environment analyses components covered in Chapter 2, "Introduction to Designing a Directory Services Infrastructure"
- Knowledge and skills covered in Chapter 3, "Creating a Forest Plan"
- Knowledge and skills covered in Chapter 4, "Creating a Domain Plan"

Lesson 1: Defining OU Structures

The first step in creating an OU plan is to define OU structures. When you define OU structures, you define the OUs needed for each domain in your organization. This lesson discusses how to define OU structures, which includes defining OU structures to delegate administration, defining OU structures to hide objects, and defining OU structures to administer group policy.

After this lesson, you will be able to

- Identify the three reasons for defining an OU
- Explain the guidelines for defining OU structures
- Identify the factors in an organization's environment that impact its need for OUs
- Identify the tasks in the process of defining OU structures
- Analyze an organization's environment to define its OUs

Estimated lesson time: 30 minutes

Understanding OUs

Recall that an *organizational unit (OU)* is a container used to organize objects within one domain into logical administrative groups. An OU can contain objects such as user accounts, groups, computers, printers, applications, file shares, and other OUs from the same domain. There are three reasons for defining an OU:

- To delegate administration
- To hide objects
- To administer group policy

OUs can be added to other OUs to form a hierarchical structure; this process is known as *nesting* OUs. Each domain defines its own OU structure—the OU structure within a domain is independent of the OU structures of other domains.

Defining OUs to Delegate Administration

The primary reason for defining an OU is to delegate administration. *Delegating administration* is the assignment of IT management responsibility for a portion of the namespace, such as an OU, to an administrator, a user, or a group of administrators or users. In Windows 2000, you can delegate administration for the contents of an OU container (all users, computers, or resource objects in the OU) by granting administrators specific permissions for an OU on the OU's access control list. An *access control list* (ACL) is the mechanism for limiting access to certain items of information or certain controls based on users' identity and their membership in various groups. *Access control entries* (ACEs) in each ACL determine which users or groups can access the OU and what type of access they have.

Because ACEs are inherited by child OUs in an OU hierarchy by default, you can apply permissions to an entire tree of OUs, as shown in Figure 5.1. Inherited ACEs apply only to one domain and do not flow down to child domains. To prevent permissions from being inherited by child objects, you can clear the Allow Inheritable Permissions From Parent To Propagate To This Object check box on the Security tab of the Properties dialog box for the OU.

Permissions flow down to child objects

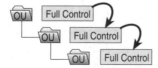

Preventing inheritance stops the flow of permissions

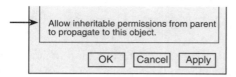

Figure 5.1   Inheriting permissions and blocking inheritance

To delegate administration, you can use the Delegation of Control Wizard or manually modify the access control entries on the Security tab of the Properties dialog box for the OU.

OU Hierarchy Models for Delegation of Administration

Once you determine the OUs needed for your organization, you can add OUs to other OUs to form a hierarchy of administrative control. Hierarchies for delegating administration can reflect various organizational models:

- Location. This structure may be used if administration within a domain is handled by location, as shown in Figure 5.2. The top-level OUs—West, Central, and East—correspond to the regions set up for the microsoft.com organization. The second-level OUs represent the physical locations of the company's eight offices.

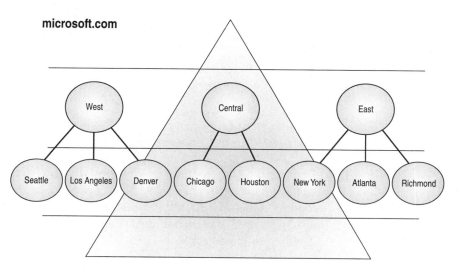

Figure 5.2   An OU structure based on location

- Business function. This structure may be used if administration within a domain is handled by business function, as shown in Figure 5.3. The top-level OUs—Admin, Devel, and Sales—correspond to microsoft.com's business divisions. The second-level OUs represent the functional divisions within the business divisions.

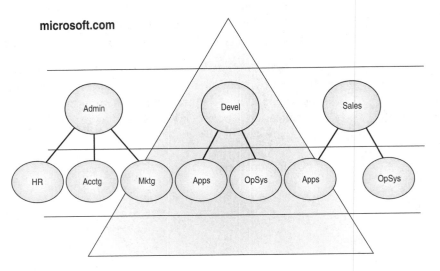

Figure 5.3   An OU structure based on business function

- Object type. This structure may be used if administration within a domain is handled by the types of objects being managed, as shown in Figure 5.4. The top-level OUs—Users, Computers, and Resources—correspond to the types of objects used at microsoft.com. The second-level OUs represent further detailing of the object types.

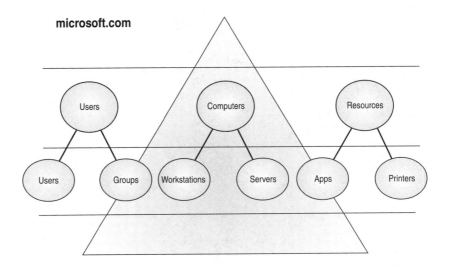

Figure 5.4   An OU structure based on types of objects

- A combination of location, business function, and object type. This structure may be used if administration within a domain is handled by a combination of hierarchy models, as shown in Figure 5.5. The top-level OUs—North America and Europe—correspond to the continents on which microsoft.com has offices. The second-level OUs represent the functional divisions within the company.

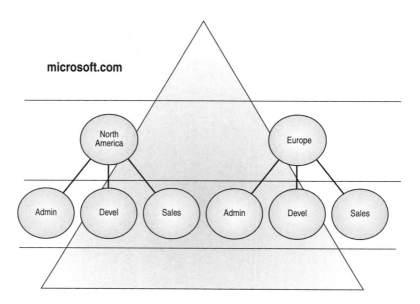

Figure 5.5   An OU structure based on location and business function

Defining OUs to Hide Objects

Your organization may require that certain domain objects be hidden from certain users. Although a user may not have the permission to read an object's attributes, the user can still see that the object exists by viewing the contents of the object's parent container. You can hide objects in a domain by creating an OU for the objects and limiting the set of users who have List Contents permission for that OU.

Defining OUs to Administer Group Policy

Recall that *group policies* are collections of user and computer configuration settings that can be linked to computers, sites, domains, and OUs to specify the behavior of users' desktops. To create a specific desktop configuration for a particular group of users, you create *group policy objects* (GPOs), which are collections of group policy settings. By linking GPOs to OUs, GPOs can be applied to either users or computers in the OU.

How Group Policy Is Processed

Group policy settings are processed in the following order:

1. Local GPO
2. Site GPOs
3. Domain GPOs
4. OU GPOs

GPOs linked to the OU highest in the Active Directory hierarchy are processed first, followed by GPOs linked to its child OU, and so on. Finally, the GPOs linked to the OU that contains the user or computer are processed. At the level of each OU in the Active Directory hierarchy, one, many, or no GPOs can be linked. If several group policies are linked to an OU, they are processed synchronously in an order specified by the administrator.

Figure 5.6 provides an example of how group policy is processed.

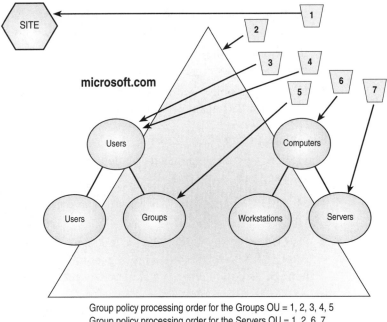

Group policy processing order for the Groups OU = 1, 2, 3, 4, 5
Group policy processing order for the Servers OU = 1, 2, 6, 7

Figure 5.6   Group policy processing

Group Policy Inheritance

In general, group policy is passed down from parent to child containers. Group policy is inherited in the following ways:

- If a policy is configured for a parent OU, and the same policy *is not* already configured for its child OUs, the child OUs, which contain the user and computer objects, inherit the parent's policy setting.

- If a policy is configured for a parent OU, and the same policy *is* configured for a child OU, the child OU's group policy setting overrides the setting inherited from the parent OU.

- Policies are inherited as long as they are compatible. If a policy configured for a parent OU and a policy configured for a child OU are compatible, the child OU inherits the parent's policy, and the child's policy setting is also applied. For example, if the parent OU's policy causes a certain folder to be placed on the desktop and the child OU's policy calls for an additional folder, the users in the child OU see both folders.

- If a policy configured for a parent OU is incompatible with the same policy configured for a child OU, the child OU does not inherit the policy setting from the parent OU. Only the setting configured for the child OU is applied.

- If any of the policy settings of a parent OU are disabled, the child OU inherits them as disabled.

- If any of the policy settings of a parent OU are not configured, the child OU does not inherit them.

Exceptions to Processing Order

The following are exceptions to the default processing order of group policy settings and may affect how GPOs are processed for OUs:

- Member Computer of a Workgroup. These computers process only the local GPO.

- No Override. Any GPO linked to a site, domain, or OU (not the local GPO) can be set to No Override with respect to that site, domain, or OU, so that none of its policy settings can be overwritten. When more than one GPO has been set to No Override, the one highest in the Active Directory hierarchy (or higher in the hierarchy specified by the administrator at each fixed level in Active Directory) takes precedence. No Override is applied to the GPO link.

In Figure 5.7, No Override has been applied to the GPO 4 link to the Users OU. As a result, the policy settings in GPO 4 cannot be overwritten by other GPOs. Processing remains the same.

- Block Policy Inheritance. At any site, domain, or OU, group policy inheritance can be blocked by selecting the Block Policy Inheritance check box on the Group Policy tab of the Properties dialog box for the site, domain, or OU. However, GPO links set to No Override are always applied and cannot be blocked by using Block Policy Inheritance.

  Block Policy Inheritance is applied directly to the site, domain, or OU. It is not applied to GPOs, nor is it applied to GPO links. Thus, Block Policy Inheritance deflects *all* group policy settings that reach the site, domain, or OU from above (by way of linkage to parents in the Active Directory hierarchy) no matter what GPOs those settings originate from.

  In Figure 5.7, Block Policy Inheritance has been applied to the Computers OU. As a result, GPOs 1 and 2, which are applied to the site and the domain, are deflected and do not apply to the Computers OU. Therefore, only GPOs 6 and 7 are processed for the Servers OU.

- Loopback. Loopback is an advanced group policy setting that is useful on computers in certain closely managed environments such as kiosks, laboratories, classrooms, and reception areas. Loopback provides alternatives to the default method of obtaining the ordered list of GPOs whose user configuration settings affect a user.

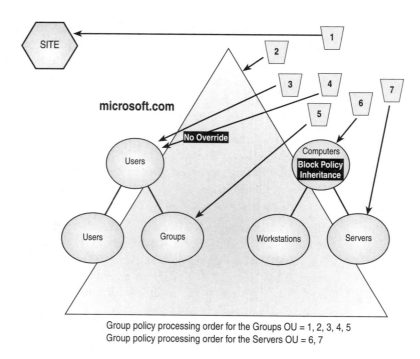

Group policy processing order for the Groups OU = 1, 2, 3, 4, 5
Group policy processing order for the Servers OU = 6, 7

Figure 5.7   Applying No Override and Block Policy Inheritance

Guidelines for Defining OU Structures

Guidelines for defining OU structures include the following:

- Design OUs for simplicity. Previous chapters emphasized the use of minimal numbers of forests and domains in your Active Directory design. However, it is likely that your domains will require a number of OUs to meet administrative requirements. The best practice is to begin with one OU and then add only those OUs that you can justify. You should note the specific reason for creating each OU that you add to your OU plan.

- Assign control to groups rather than users to simplify management tasks. You should also delegate to local groups, rather than global or universal groups. Local groups are ideally suited for resource permissions because, unlike global groups, they can have members from any trusted domain and, unlike universal groups, local group membership is not replicated to the global catalog.

When defining OU structures for your organization, it's also important to keep the following in mind:

- OUs are not security principals. That is, you cannot assign access permissions based on a user's membership in an OU. Access control is the responsibility of global, domain local, or universal groups.
- Users will not use the OU structure for navigation. Although users can see the OU structure of a domain, the most efficient way for users to find resources in Active Directory is to query the global catalog. Therefore, you should define OUs with administration, not users, in mind.

Design Step: Defining OU Structures

To define OU structures, you must complete the following tasks:

1. Define OU structures to delegate administration.
2. Define OU structures to hide objects.
3. Define OU structures to administer group policy.

Important Because there is only one way to delegate administration and there are multiple ways to administer group policy, you must define OU structures to delegate administration first. After an OU structure is defined to handle delegation of administration, you can define additional OUs to hide objects and to administer group policy.

Defining OU Structures to Delegate Administration

To define OU structures to delegate administration, you must complete the following tasks:

1. Assess the organization's IT administration requirements to determine the type of administrative responsibility to delegate.
2. Define OUs to delegate full control.
3. Define OUs to delegate control for object classes.

Assessing IT Administration Requirements

To determine the type of administrative responsibility to delegate, you must first consult the IT Management Organization Worksheet compiled earlier by your design team and analyze how administrative tasks are accomplished. In addition to assessing the information compiled in this worksheet, it is imperative that you assess changes currently planned for IT management to address growth, flexibility, and the ideal design specifications of the organization. You will use these findings to determine the type of administrative responsibility to delegate.

Note A blank copy of the worksheet is located on the Supplemental Course Materials CD-ROM (\chapt02\worksheets). A completed example of the worksheet is located in Chapter 2, "Introduction to Designing a Directory Services Infrastructure."

There are two types of administrative responsibility you can delegate for an OU:

- Full control
- Control for object classes

By default, only domain administrators have full control over all objects in a domain. Domain administrators are responsible for creating the initial OU structure, repairing mistakes, and creating additional domain controllers. It is usually sufficient to allow only domain administrators full control over objects in a domain. However, if there are units in the organization that need to determine their own OU structure and administrative models, you can provide them with this permission by delegating full control.

When determining whether to delegate full control for an OU, you must determine which areas in the organization need to be allowed to change OU properties and to create, delete, or modify any objects in the OU.

If additional OUs are necessary to delegate more restrictive control, you can accomplish this by delegating control of specific object classes for an OU. Although there are many object classes in the schema, you need to consider only the object classes in which administrators will create objects. Such object classes typically include user account objects, computer account objects, group objects, and organizational unit objects. When determining whether to delegate control of object classes, for each object class that your administrators will create in Active Directory you must determine the following:

- Which areas in the organization should be granted full control over objects of this class in the OU

- Which areas in the organization should be allowed to create objects of this class and thus have full control over these objects

- Which areas in the organization should be allowed to modify only specific attributes for or perform specific tasks pertaining to existing objects of this class

Defining OUs to Delegate Full Control or Control of Object Classes

After you determine the type of administrative responsibility to delegate, you can create OUs to delegate full control or control of object classes.

▶ **To define OUs to delegate full control or control of object classes**

1. Diagram the desired OU.

2. Diagram a security group and list administrators who require full control or control of a specific object class in the group.

3. If the OU is allowed to set its own membership, place the administrator group inside the OU. If the OU is not allowed to set its own membership, place the administrator group outside the OU.

Defining OU Structures to Hide Objects

To define OU structures to hide objects, you must complete the following tasks:

1. Assess the organization's IT administration requirements to determine the need to hide objects from users.

2. Define OUs to hide objects.

Assessing the Need to Hide Objects

To define OU structures to hide objects, you must first consult the Technical Standards Worksheet compiled earlier by your design team to determine the objects that must be hidden from users and the users from which the objects must be hidden. In addition to assessing the information in this worksheet, it is imperative that you assess changes currently planned for IT management to address growth, flexibility, and the ideal design specifications of the organization. You will use these findings to determine whether to define OUs to hide objects.

Note A blank copy of the worksheet is located on the Supplemental Course Materials CD-ROM (\chapt02\worksheets). A completed example of the worksheet is located in Chapter 2, "Introduction to Designing a Directory Services Infrastructure."

When determining whether to define OUs to hide objects, you must assess the following:

- Which objects need to be hidden
- Which groups need to access the OU where the hidden objects reside to perform specific administrative tasks
- Which groups need read access to the OU where the hidden objects reside
- Which groups need full control of the OU where the hidden objects reside

Defining OUs to Hide Objects

After you determine whether it's necessary to define OUs to hide objects, you can define the necessary OUs.

▶ **To define an OU to hide objects**

1. Diagram the OU in which you will place the objects to be hidden.
2. List the groups that you want to have full control of the OU.
3. List the groups that you want to have generic read access to the OU and its contents.
4. List any groups that you want to have specific permissions, such as creating a specific object class, for the OU.
5. Specify the objects that you want to hide in the OU.

Defining OU Structures to Administer Group Policy

To define OU structures to administer group policy, you must complete the following tasks:

1. Assess the organization's group policy requirements and the existing OU structure you created to delegate administration to determine which group policies require the creation of additional OUs for administration.

2. Define OU structures to administer group policy.

Assessing the Need to Define OU Structures to Administer Group Policy

To define OU structures to administer group policy, you must first consult the Technical Standards Worksheet compiled earlier by your design team and the existing OU structure you created to delegate administration and hide objects to determine which group policies require the creation of additional OUs for administration. In addition to assessing the information in this worksheet, it is imperative that you assess changes currently planned for IT management to address growth, flexibility, and the ideal design specifications of the organization. You will use these findings to determine whether to define additional OUs to administer group policy.

Note A blank copy of the worksheet is located on the Supplemental Course Materials CD-ROM (\chapt02\worksheets). A completed example of the worksheet is located in Chapter 2, "Introduction to Designing a Directory Services Infrastructure."

When determining whether to define OUs to administer group policy, you must determine the following:

- What group policy settings are necessary for the domain

- To which users or computers do the group policy settings apply

- Which of the group policy settings *are not* handled by GPOs linked to the site, domain, or existing OUs created to delegate administration or hide objects

Defining OUs to Administer Group Policy

After you determine whether to create OUs to administer group policy, you can define the necessary OUs.

▶ **To define OUs to administer group policy**

1. Diagram the OU that will administer the desired group policy settings.

2. List the users or computers to which the group policy setting(s) for the OU apply.

3. Diagram a security group and place administrators who require control of the OU in the group.

4. Diagram the GPO and indicate its group policy settings.

5. Indicate the groups that have administrative control for the GPO.

6. Indicate any processing exceptions (such as No Override or Block Policy Inheritance) for the GPO.

7. Link the GPO to the OU.

Design Step Examples: Defining OU Structures

The following scenarios are examples of defining OU structures to delegate administration, defining OU structures to hide objects, and defining OU structures to administer group policy.

Defining OU Structures to Delegate Administration

Figure 5.8 shows an example of defining an OU structure to delegate full administrative control of the OU. The Silk unit of Miller Textiles was a recent acquisition, with locations in Tokyo and Osaka. The Silk unit is maintaining its own IT Management department. Therefore, Silk has become its own OU in the asia.m-100times.com root domain. The Silk Admins group is allowed to set its own membership and is set inside the Silk OU. The Tokyo Admins and Osaka Admins groups are not allowed to set their own memberships and are set in the Silk OU, outside of their respective OUs.

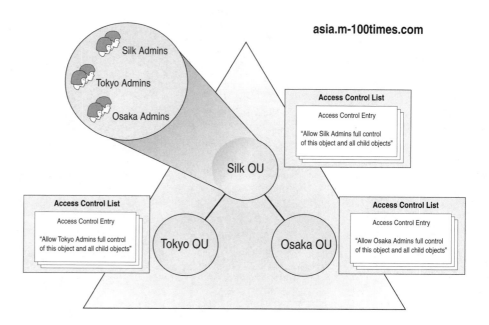

Figure 5.8   Defining OUs to delegate full administrative control

Figure 5.9 shows an example of defining an OU structure to delegate control of object classes. The Tokyo location for the Silk unit of Miller Textiles currently contains two Windows NT 4 resource domains, Natural and Synthetic. When the organization migrates to Windows 2000, the resource domains will be consolidated and replaced by OUs. The Natural and Synthetic administrators currently use their domains to share files controlled by group membership and to reset passwords for team members. Groups were created to administer group objects and user objects and then granted the appropriate level of control for the Natural and Synthetic OUs.

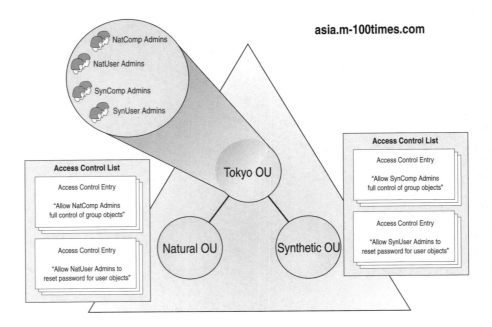

Figure 5.9   Defining OUs to delegate control of object classes

Defining OU Structures to Hide Objects

Figure 5.10 shows an example of defining an OU to hide objects. The
na.m-100times.com domain has locations in San Francisco, Kansas City,
and Raleigh. The OUs in the top half of the diagram were already defined
to delegate administration. Because Miller Textiles requires administrative
accounts in each location to be hidden from users, it was necessary to create
three new OUs to hide the accounts.

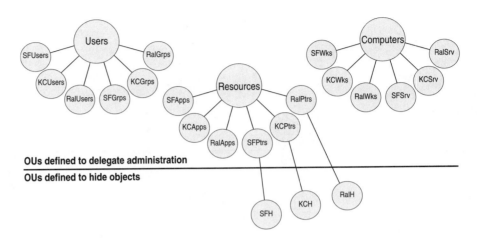

na.m-100times.com

OUs defined to delegate administration

OUs defined to hide objects

Figure 5.10   Defining OUs to hide objects

Defining OU Structures to Administer Group Policy

Figure 5.11 shows an example of defining OUs to administer group policy. The na.m-100times.com domain has locations in San Francisco, Kansas City, and Raleigh. The OUs in the top half of the diagram were already created to delegate administration. Because Miller Textiles requires one group policy to provide folder redirection for users in the Managers group and another group policy to publish software on management workstations, six new OUs were necessary to administer the group policies. Group Policy 1 redirects the My Documents folder for the Managers group only. Group Policy 2 publishes software for installation on managers' workstations only.

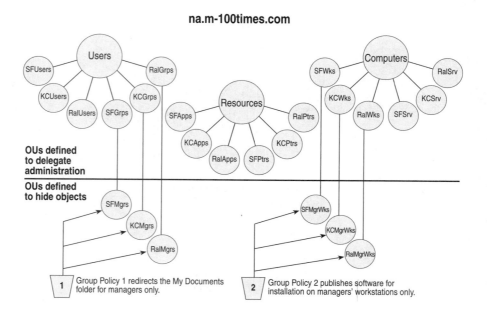

Figure 5.11   Defining OUs to administer group policy

Lesson Summary

In this lesson you learned that defining OU structures is a three-step process: (1) define OU structures to delegate administration, (2) define OU structures to hide objects, and (3) define OU structures to administer group policy. Because there is only one way to delegate administration and there are multiple ways to administer group policy, you must define the OU structures to delegate administration first. After an OU structure is defined to handle delegation of administration, you can define additional OUs to hide objects and to administer group policy.

You learned how OU structures to delegate administration can be arranged in a hierarchy to reflect various organizational models: location, business function, object type, or a combination of any of the models. You also learned how you can hide objects in a domain by defining an OU for the objects and limiting the set of users who have List Contents permission for that OU. Finally, you learned how you can link GPOs to OUs to apply group policy settings to either users or computers in the OU.

Activity 5.1: Defining OU Structures

In this activity you will read about an organization that is planning its Active Directory infrastructure. Your task is to analyze the organization's environment to define the OU structures needed in an Active Directory infrastructure. You will define the OU structures by creating a diagram.

Scenario: Arbor Shoes

You are an infrastructure planner on the Active Directory infrastructure design team for Arbor Shoes, a distributor of upscale non-leather shoes operating from three locations in San Francisco, Houston, and Boston. The business and technical environment analysis documents, the forest plan, and the domain plan have already been compiled, and copies have been distributed to everyone on the team. You are now in the process of defining the OU structures for the organization.

Arbor Shoes is a centralized organization, with major IT administration issues handled from its headquarters in Boston. Each of the three locations also has a small autonomous IT staff to handle support tasks. Your design team has created the domain hierarchy diagram shown in Figure 5.12.

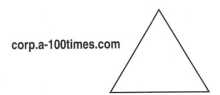

corp.a-100times.com

Figure 5.12   Domain hierarchy diagram for Arbor Shoes

While reading through the business and technical environment analysis documents, you note the following:

- One administrative group at each location handles the administration of users.

- A second administrative group at each location handles the administration of computers.

- A third administrative group at each location handles the administration of resources.

- Arbor Shoes requires a specific logon and logoff script for all users at each location, except for users in the Finance department. The Finance department at each location requires a separate logon script but no logoff script.

1. Diagram the OU structures needed to delegate administration for the corp.a-100times.com domain. Explain your reasoning for defining each OU.

2. Diagram the OU structures needed to hide objects. Explain your reasoning for defining each OU.

3. Diagram the OU structures needed to administer group policy. Explain your reasoning for defining each OU.

Lesson 2: Planning User Accounts and Groups

After you define OU structures, the next step in creating an OU plan is to plan user accounts and groups. When you plan user accounts and groups, you define the user accounts and groups needed for each domain in your organization. This lesson discusses how to plan user accounts and groups, which includes naming and placing user accounts and naming and defining groups.

After this lesson, you will be able to

- Identify the factors in an organization's environment that impact its naming conventions
- Analyze an organization's environment to establish naming conventions for users and groups
- Identify factors in an organization's environment that impact the placement of user accounts
- Analyze an organization's environment to place user accounts
- Identify factors in an organization's environment that impact its need for groups
- Analyze an organization's environment to define groups

Estimated lesson time: 25 minutes

Understanding Users and Groups

Before launching into a discussion of users and groups, it's important to understand the difference between OUs and groups. In the previous lesson, you learned that OUs contain objects such as user accounts, groups, computers, printers, applications, file shares, and other OUs from the same domain. OUs are defined mainly to delegate the administration of their contents. Groups also contain objects such as user accounts, contacts, computers, and other groups. However, groups are defined mainly to assign permissions to users or to restrict user access to various objects in the domain. Planning user accounts and groups is the second part of creating an organizational unit plan.

User Accounts

A domain *user account* provides a user with the ability to log onto the domain to gain access to network resources. Each person who regularly uses the network should have a unique user account.

You create a domain user account in a container or in an OU on a domain controller. The domain controller replicates the new user account information to all domain controllers in the domain. After Windows 2000 replicates the new user account information, all of the domain controllers in the domain tree can authenticate the user during the logon process. During the logon process, each user provides his or her user name and password. By using this information, Windows 2000 authenticates the users and then builds an access token that contains information about the user and security settings. The access token identifies the user to computers running Windows 2000 and pre–Windows 2000 computers on which the user tries to gain access to resources. Windows 2000 provides the access token for the duration of the logon session.

Groups

A *group* is a collection of user accounts. Groups simplify administration by allowing you to assign permissions to a group of users rather than having to assign permissions to each individual user account. *Permissions* control what users can do with a resource, such as a folder, file, or printer. When you assign permissions, you give users the capability to gain access to a resource and define the type of access that they have. For example, if several users need to read the same file, you would add their user accounts to a group. Then, you would give the group permission to read the file.

In addition to user accounts, you can add other groups, contacts, and computers to groups. You add groups to other groups to create a consolidated group and reduce the number of times that you need to assign permissions. However, you should use caution to add only those groups that are absolutely necessary. You add computers to groups to simplify the process of giving a user logged on to one computer access to a resource on another computer.

Group Types

You can create groups for security-related purposes, such as assigning permissions, or for nonsecurity purposes, such as sending e-mail messages. To facilitate this, Windows 2000 includes two group types: *security* and *distribution*. The group type determines how you use the group. Both types of groups are stored in the database component of Active Directory, which allows you to use them anywhere in your network.

Windows 2000 uses only security groups, which you use to assign permissions to gain access to resources. Programs that are designed to search Active Directory can also use security groups for nonsecurity-related purposes, such as retrieving user information for use in a Web application. A security group also has all the capabilities of a distribution group. Because Windows 2000 uses only security groups, this lesson focuses on security groups.

Group Scopes

When you create a group you must select a group type and a group scope. *Group scopes* allow you to use groups in different ways to assign permissions. The scope of a group determines where in the network you are able to use the group to assign permissions to the group. The three group scopes are global, domain local, and universal.

Global security groups are most often used to organize users who share similar network access requirements. A global group has the following characteristics:

- Limited membership. You can add members only from the domain in which you create the global group.

- Access to resources in any domain. You can use a global group to assign permissions to gain access to resources that are located in any domain in the domain tree or forest.

Domain local security groups are most often used to assign permissions to resources. A domain local group has the following characteristics:

- Open membership. You can add members from any domain.

- Access to resources in one domain. You can use a domain local group to assign permissions to gain access only to resources located in the same domain where you create the domain local group.

Universal security groups are most often used to assign permissions to related resources in multiple domains. A universal security group has the following characteristics:

- Open membership. You can add members from any domain.

- Access to resources in any domain. You can use a universal group to assign permissions to gain access to resources that are located in any domain.

- Available only in native mode. Universal security groups are not available in mixed mode.

Group Nesting

Adding groups to other groups, or *nesting,* creates a consolidated group and can reduce network traffic between domains and simplify administration in a domain tree. For example, you could create separate regional manager groups for the managers in each region. Then, you could add all of the regional manager groups to a worldwide managers group. When all managers need access to resources, you assign permissions only to the worldwide managers group.

Guidelines for group nesting include the following:

- Minimize levels of nesting. Tracking permissions and troubleshooting becomes more complex with multiple levels of nesting. One level of nesting is the most effective to use.

- Document group membership to keep track of permissions assignments. Providing documentation of group membership can eliminate the redundant assignment of user accounts to groups and reduce the likelihood of accidental group assignments.

To efficiently use nesting it is important to understand the membership rules of groups.

Rules for Group Membership

The group scope determines the membership of a group. Membership rules determine the members that a group can contain. Table 5.1 describes group membership rules, including what each group scope can contain in native and mixed mode.

Table 5.1   Group Scope Membership Rules

Group scope	In native mode, group can contain	In mixed mode, group can contain
Global	User accounts and global groups from the same domain	Users from the same domain
Domain local	User accounts, universal groups, and global groups from any domain; domain local groups from the same domain	User accounts and global groups from any domain
Universal	User accounts, other universal groups, and global groups from any domain	Not applicable; universal groups cannot be created in mixed mode

Design Step: Planning User Accounts and Groups

Planning user accounts and groups is a two-step process:

1. Name and place user accounts.

2. Name and define groups.

Naming and Placing User Accounts

To name and place user accounts, you must complete the following tasks:

1. Assess the organization's existing user account naming conventions and OU structure to determine current user account naming requirements and the OU structure.

2. Determine the user account naming convention.

3. Place user accounts in the appropriate OUs.

Assessing User Account Naming Conventions and the OU Structure

To determine current user account naming conventions, you must first consult the Technical Standards Worksheet compiled earlier by your design team to find out the current user account naming requirements. In addition to assessing the information in this worksheet, it is imperative that you assess changes in user account names currently planned to address growth, flexibility, and the ideal design specifications of the organization.

Note A blank copy of the worksheet is located on the Supplemental Course Materials CD-ROM (\chapt02\worksheets). A completed example of the worksheet is located in Chapter 2, "Introduction to Designing a Directory Services Infrastructure."

To place user accounts in the appropriate OUs, use the OU structure diagram to determine

- The user accounts administered by each administrative group
- The user accounts affected by each GPO

Determining User Account Naming Conventions

By establishing a naming convention for user accounts, you can standardize how users are identified in the domain. A consistent naming convention will help you and your users remember user logon names and locate them in lists. Table 5.2 summarizes some points you might want to consider in determining a user account naming convention for your organization.

Table 5.2 User Account Naming Convention Considerations

Consideration	Explanation
Domain user accounts	The user's logon name (distinguished name) must be unique to the directory. The user's full name (relative distinguished name, also referred to as display name or account name) must be unique within the OU where you create the domain user account.
20 characters maximum	User logon names can contain up to 20 uppercase or lowercase characters. Although the field accepts more than 20 characters, Windows 2000 recognizes only the first 20.
Invalid characters	The following characters are invalid: " / \ [ ] : ;	= , + * ? < >

Consideration	Explanation
User logon names are not case sensitive	You can use a combination of special and alphanumeric characters to help uniquely identify user accounts. User logon names are not case sensitive, but Windows 2000 preserves the case.
Accommodate duplicate employee names	If two users were named John Doe, you could use the first name and the last initial and then add letters from the last name to differentiate the duplicate names. In this example, one user account logon name could be Johnd and the other Johndo. Another possibility would be to number each user logon name—for example, Johnd1 and Johnd2.
Identify the type of employee	In some organizations, it is useful to identify temporary employees by their user account. To identify temporary employees, you can use a T and a hyphen in front of the user's logon name—for example, T-Johnd. Alternatively, use parentheses in the name—for example, John Doe (Temp).
E-mail compatibility	Some e-mail systems may not accept characters, such as spaces and parentheses—"()".

Placing User Accounts in the Appropriate OUs

After you determine the user account naming convention, you can place user accounts in the appropriate OUs. To determine the OU for a user account, you must identify the administrative groups that administer the account and any GPOs that must apply to the account. The OU for the user account is the OU that is administered by the administrative group and the GPO.

▶ **To name and place user accounts**

1. Select a naming scheme that ensures that unique user account names are generated for all users in the forest.
2. Ensure that all administrators adhere to the naming scheme.
3. List the administrative groups that must administer the account.
4. List the GPOs that must apply to the account.
5. Place the account in the OU administered by the designated administrative group and the designated GPO. List the accounts contained in each OU.

Naming and Defining Groups

To name and define groups, you must complete the following tasks:

1. Assess the organization's existing group naming conventions and OU structure to determine group naming requirements and the definition of appropriate groups.
2. Determine the group naming convention.
3. Define the appropriate global and domain local groups.
4. Define the appropriate universal groups.

Assessing Group Naming Conventions and the OU Structure

To determine group naming requirements, you must first consult the Technical Standards Worksheet compiled earlier by your design team to find out the current group naming requirements. In addition to assessing the information in this worksheet, it is imperative that you assess changes to group names currently planned to address growth, flexibility, and the ideal design specifications of the organization.

Note A blank copy of the worksheet is located on the Supplemental Course Materials CD-ROM (\chapt02\worksheets). A completed example of the worksheet is located in Chapter 2, "Introduction to Designing a Directory Services Infrastructure."

Use the list of accounts contained in each OU to define the appropriate global, domain local, and universal groups.

Determining the Group Naming Convention

By establishing a naming convention for groups, you can standardize how groups are identified in the domain. A consistent naming convention will help you and your users remember group names and locate them in lists. Table 5.3 summarizes some points you might want to consider in determining a group naming convention for your organization.

Table 5.3   Group Naming Convention Considerations

Consideration	Explanation
Groups	The group name must be unique to the directory.
64 characters maximum	Group names can contain up to 64 uppercase or lowercase characters.
Invalid characters	The following characters are invalid: " / \ [ ] : ;	= , + * ? < >
Group names are not case sensitive	You can use a combination of special and alphanumeric characters to help uniquely identify groups. Group names are not case sensitive, but Windows 2000 preserves the case.

Defining the Appropriate Global and Domain Local Groups

Depending on the administration required for the group, you can define global and domain local groups in either domains or organizational units. The group scope determines the domain from which members can be added and the domain in which the rights and permissions assigned to the group are valid.

To define appropriate global and domain local groups:

- Identify users with common job responsibilities and add the user accounts to a global group. For example, in a finance department, user accounts for all accountants are added to a global group called Finance.

- Identify the resources to be shared, such as files or printers, and add the resources to a domain local group for that resource. For example, color printers in a company are added to a domain local group called Color Printers.

- Identify all global groups that share the same access needs for resources and make them members of the appropriate domain local group. For example, add the global groups Finance, Sales, and Management to the domain local group Color Printers.

- Assign the required permissions for the resource to the domain local group. For example, assign the necessary permissions to use color printers to the Color Printers group. Users in the Finance, Sales, and Management global groups receive the required permissions because their global group is a member of the domain local group Color Printers.

This strategy gives you the most flexibility for growth and reduces permissions assignments. Although there are other methods for defining groups, these methods have the following limitations:

- Placing user accounts in domain local groups and assigning permissions to the domain local groups does not allow you to assign permissions for resources outside of the domain, reducing the flexibility when your network grows.

- Placing user accounts in global groups and assigning permissions to the global groups can complicate administration if you are using multiple domains. If global groups from multiple domains require the same permissions, you have to assign permissions for each global group.

Defining the Appropriate Universal Groups

Use universal groups to grant or deny access to resources that are located in more than one domain. Because universal groups and their members are listed in the global catalog, when membership of any universal group changes, the changes must be replicated to every global catalog in the forest. This action can cause excessive network traffic. Therefore, you should define universal groups with caution.

Follow these guidelines to ensure minimal impact on replication traffic:

- Add global groups, not users, to universal groups. The global groups are the members of the universal group. Keep the number of group members in universal groups as low as possible and minimize the number of individual users.

- Change the membership of universal groups as infrequently as possible. By requiring all members of universal groups to be global groups and making individual membership changes in the global groups, the membership changes you make to the global groups will not affect the universal groups or replication traffic.

▶ **To name and define groups**

1. Select a naming scheme that ensures that unique group names are generated for all groups in the forest.

2. Ensure that all administrators adhere to the naming scheme.

3. List the user accounts that must be added to a global group.

4. List the resources that must be added to a domain local group.

5. List all global groups that share the same access needs for resources and note the domain local group to which they must be added.

6. List the global groups that must be added to a universal group or groups.

Design Process Examples: Planning User Accounts and Groups

The following scenarios are examples of naming and placing user accounts and naming and defining groups.

Naming and Placing User Accounts

Consolidated Messenger, a worldwide fictitious delivery service, has 21 new users that need accounts at their location in Dallas. Consolidated Messenger has selected a user account naming scheme that ensures that unique user account names are generated for all users in the forest. Three years ago, the company instituted a naming scheme that creates the account name by taking the user's first initial followed by the first six letters of his or her last name. In case of the same last name, the first two letters of the first name will be used. For temporary employees, "T-" will precede the user account name. Consolidated Messenger will continue to use the naming scheme. All administrators have been trained and recognize the importance of adhering to the naming scheme. All administrators are aware of the procedures to follow in the event of exceptions to the naming scheme.

Table 5.4 provides fictitious names and hiring information for the new employees. The table also lists the administrative groups that must administer each account and the GPOs that apply to some of the accounts.

Table 5.4   New Hire List

User name	User logon name	Title	Department	Status	Administrative group	GPOs
Alboucq, Steve	t-salbouc	Representative	Delivery	Temp	DelAdmin	1
Egert, Amy	aegert	Manager	Human Resources	Perm	AdAdmin	
Guo, Bei-Jing	bguo	Developer	IT	Perm	ITAdmin	
Hjellen, Robin	rhjelle	Representative	Dispatch	Perm	DspAdmin	
Koduri, Sunil	skoduri	Representative	Delivery	Perm	DelAdmin	
Lyon, Robert	rlyon	Representative	Human Resources	Perm	HRAdmin	
Lysaker, Jenny	jlysake	Representative	Delivery	Perm	DelAdmin	
Miksovsky, Jan	t-jmiksov	Representative	Delivery	Temp	DelAdmin	1
Ota, Lani	lota	Representative	Dispatch	Perm	DspAdmin	
Ramirez, Francisco	t-framire	Representative	Delivery	Temp	DelAdmin	1
Richardson, Miles	mrichar	System Administrator	IT	Perm	DomainAdmins	
Samarawickrama, Prasanna	psamara	Representative	Delivery	Perm	Perm	
Smith, James	t-jasmith	Representative	Delivery	Temp	DelAdmin	1
Smith, Jeff	jesmith	Representative	Delivery	Perm	DelAdmin	
Smith, Jeff	jsmith	Representative	Payroll	Perm	FinAdmin	4
Spencer, Phil	pspence	Representative	Delivery	Perm	DelAdmin	
Steiner, Alan	asteine	Manager	Dispatch	Perm	DspAdmin	
Thomas, Stephen	t-sthomas	Representative	Delivery	Temp	DelAdmin	1
Van Dam, Tanya	tvandam	Representative	Delivery	Perm	DelAdmin	
Wood, John	jwood	Representative	Dispatch	Perm	DspAdmin	
Yim, Kevin	kyim	Manager	Delivery	Perm	OpsAdmin	

Figure 5.13 shows the OU structure diagram for the corp.dallas.c-100times.com domain.

corp.dallas.c-100times.com

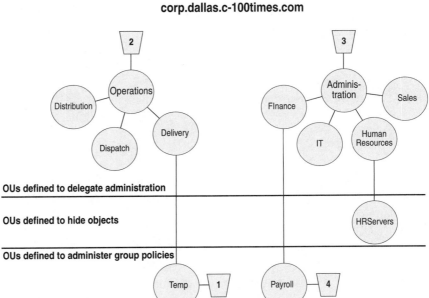

Figure 5.13   OU structure diagram for corp.dallas.c-100times.com domain

Table 5.5 is a list of administrative groups that can administer users in each OU.

Table 5.5   Administrative Groups in Consolidated Messenger OUs

OU	Administrative groups
Operations	SysAdmin
	OpsAdmin
Distribution	SysAdmin
	OpsAdmin
	DstAdmin

continued

OU	Administrative groups
Dispatch	SysAdmin
	OpsAdmin
	DspAdmin
Delivery	SysAdmin
	OpsAdmin
	DelAdmin
Administration	SysAdmin
	AdAdmin
Finance	SysAdmin
	AdAdmin
	FinAdmin
Payroll	SysAdmin
	AdAdmin
	FinAdmin
IT	SysAdmin
	AdAdmin
	ITAdmin
Human Resources	SysAdmin
	AdAdmin
	HRAdmin
Sales	SysAdmin
	AdAdmin
	SlsAdmin
Temp	SysAdmin
	TmpAdmin

Table 5.6 shows the new user accounts placed in the OU administered by the designated administrative group and the designated GPO.

Table 5.6   New User Accounts Placed in OUs

OU	New user accounts
Operations	mrichar (or Administration OU)
Dispatch	rhjelle, lota, asteine, jwood
Delivery	skoduri, jlysake, psamara, jesmith, pspence, tvandam, kyim
Temp	t-salbouc, t-jmiksov, t-framire, t-jasmith, t-sthomas
Administration	mrichar (or Operations OU)
Payroll	jsmith
IT	bguo
Human Resources	aegert, rlyon

Naming and Defining Groups

Consolidated Messenger has selected a group naming scheme that ensures that unique group names are generated for all groups in the forest. Three years ago, the company instituted a naming scheme for administrative groups that uses a two- or three-letter abbreviation for the group followed by "Admin." User group names consist of one word that describes the group. Consolidated Messenger will continue to use the naming scheme. All administrators have been trained and recognize the importance of adhering to the naming scheme. All administrators are aware of the procedures to follow in the event of exceptions to the naming scheme.

Table 5.7 provides the job function and number of employees in each job function in Consolidated Messenger's Operations division.

Table 5.7   Consolidated Messenger Operations Division Employee Information

Job function	Number of employees
Distribution Tracker	50
Distribution Handler	100
Domestic Dispatcher	50
International Dispatcher	25
Delivery Representative	200
Manager	10

Table 5.8 lists the information access requirements for various employee functions.

Table 5.8   Employee Access Requirements

Employee	Need access to
Domestic Dispatchers, International Dispatchers, Managers	Customer database, full access
Delivery Representatives	Customer database, read-only access
All employees	Company policies, read-only access
Distribution Trackers, Managers	Tracking database, full access
Distribution Handlers	Tracking database, read-only access
All employees	Company announcements through e-mail
All employees, except Delivery Representatives	Shared installation of Microsoft Office applications
Managers, Managers from other domains	Delivery time reports

To meet the needs listed in the table, Consolidated Messenger has planned the groups listed in Table 5.9.

Table 5.9   Consolidated Messenger Groups

Group name	Type and scope	Members
Trackers	Security, global	All Distribution Trackers
Handlers	Security, global	All Distribution Handlers
DomDispatchers	Security, global	All Domestic Dispatchers
IntDispatchers	Security, global	All International Dispatchers
DeliveryReps	Security, global	All Delivery Representatives
Managers	Security, global	All Managers
AllEmployees	Security, global	All employees
CustDatabase	Security, domain local	Domestic Dispatchers, International Dispatchers, Managers
CustDatabase2	Security, domain local	Delivery Representatives
CompanyPol	Security, domain local	All employees
TrackDatabase	Security, domain local	Distribution Trackers, Managers
TrackDatabase2	Security, domain local	Distribution Handlers
MSOffice	Security, domain local	Distribution Trackers, Distribution Handlers, Domestic Dispatchers, International Dispatchers, Managers
DeliveryTimeReports	Security, domain local	Managers
E-mail	Distribution, domain local	All employees

The Consolidated Messenger network does not require universal groups because the information provided indicates that no groups need access to resources in multiple domains and also need to have members from multiple domains.

Lesson Summary

To begin this lesson, you were reminded that the purpose of defining OUs is to delegate administration, while the purpose of groups is to provide users with access to resources. In this lesson you learned how planning user accounts and groups is a two step-process: (1) naming and placing user accounts and (2) naming and defining groups. You learned how naming conventions help you and your users remember user logon names and locate them in lists. To place user accounts in the appropriate OUs, you must use the OU structure diagram to determine the user accounts administered by each administrative group and the user accounts affected by each GPO. You also learned how a consistent group naming convention will help you and your users remember group names and locate them in lists. To define the appropriate global, domain local, and universal groups, you identify the users to be assigned to various global groups, the resources to be assigned to various domain local groups, and the resources that are located in more than one domain to be assigned to universal groups.

Activity 5.2: Planning User Accounts

In this activity you will read about an organization that is planning its Active Directory infrastructure. Your task is to analyze the organization's environment to plan the user accounts needed in an Active Directory infrastructure.

Scenario: Dearing School of Fine Art

You are an infrastructure planner on the Active Directory infrastructure design team for the Dearing School of Fine Art (DSFA), an art school located in Washington, D.C. The business and technical environment analysis documents, the forest plan, the domain plan, and the OU structure diagram have already been compiled and copies have been distributed to everyone on the team. You are now in the process of planning the naming and placing of user accounts for new students in the fiber arts department.

While looking over the Technical Standards Worksheet, you find that DSFA has selected a user account naming scheme that ensures that unique user account names are generated for all users in the forest. This naming scheme uses the first eight letters of a user's first and last names. In case of the same first and last names, the user's middle initial is used. For part-time students, "PT-" will precede the user account name.

Table 5.10 provides fictitious names and enrollment information for the new students. The table also lists the administrative groups that must administer each account.

Table 5.10   New Student List

Student name	Department	Status	Administrative group
Akhtar, Sarah	Fiber Arts	Part Time	PTFiberAdmin
Barnhill, Josh	Painting	Full Time	FTPaintAdmin
Berry, Jo	Fiber Arts	Full Time	FTFiberAdmin
Dunn, Matthew	Drawing	Full Time	CompArtAdmin
Dunn, Micheal	Drawing	Part Time	PTDrawAdmin
Hart, Sherri	Painting	Full Time	FTPaintAdmin

continued

Student Name	Department	Status	Administrative group
Jacobson, Lisa	Drawing	Full Time	CompArtAdmin
Khanna, Karan	Painting	Full Time	FTPaintAdmin
Phua, Meng	Fiber Arts	Full Time	FTFiberAdmin
Schäfer, Christina	Painting	Part Time	PTPaintAdmin
Tobey, Chris	Drawing	Full Time	FTDrawAdmin
Wolfe-Hellene, Marta	Fiber Arts	Part Time	PTFiberAdmin
Young, Rob	Drawing	Full Time	FTDrawAdmin

Your design team has created the OU structure diagram shown in Figure 5.14.

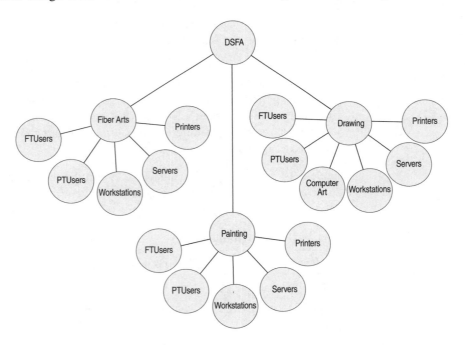

Figure 5.14   OU structure diagram for the Dearing School of Fine Art

Table 5.11 is a list of administrative groups that can administer users in each OU.

Table 5.11 Administrative Groups in DSFA OUs

OU	Administrative groups
FTUsers (Fiber Arts)	SysAdmin
	FiberAdmin
	FTFiberAdmin
PTUsers (Fiber Arts)	SysAdmin
	FiberAdmin
	PTFiberAdmin
FTUsers (Painting)	SysAdmin
	PaintAdmin
	FTPaintAdmin
PTUsers (Painting)	SysAdmin
	PaintAdmin
	PTPaintAdmin
FTUsers (Drawing)	SysAdmin
	DrawAdmin
	FTDrawAdmin
PTUsers (Drawing)	SysAdmin
	DrawAdmin
	PTDrawAdmin
Computer Art	SysAdmin
	DrawAdmin
	CompArtAdmin

In the table below, place the new student accounts, by account name, in the appropriate OU.

OU	New student accounts
FTUsers (Fiber Arts)	_____
PTUsers (Fiber Arts)	_____
FTUsers (Painting)	_____
PTUsers (Painting)	_____
FTUsers (Drawing)	_____
PTUsers (Drawing)	_____
Computer Art	_____

Activity 5.3: Planning Groups

In this activity you will read about an organization that is planning its Active Directory infrastructure. Your task is to analyze the organization's environment to plan the groups needed in an Active Directory infrastructure.

Scenario: The Ski Haus

You are an infrastructure planner on the Active Directory infrastructure design team for The Ski Haus, an international retailer of ski apparel. The Ski Haus uses two domains, one for resources at their Denver, Colorado, location and another for resources at their Geneva, Switzerland, location.

The Product Design department at each location maintains a separate database of ski hat designs. Product Design users at each location must have full control of the ski hat design database in their own domain. Product Design users at both locations must have read permissions on both ski hat design databases. Product Design users at both locations must have change permissions on the ski sweater design database in the Geneva location.

1. Explain how your design team will use security groups to allow the Product Design users in each domain full control of the ski hat design databases in their domains.

2. Explain how your design team will use security groups to allow the Product Design users in each domain read permission to the Denver and Geneva ski hat design databases.

3. Explain how your design team will use security groups to allow all Product Design users in both domains change permission to the ski sweater design database in Geneva.

Lab 5.1: Defining an OU Structure and Security Groups

Lab Objectives

After completing this lab, you will be able to

- Define an OU structure
- Define security groups

About This Lab

In this lab, you will analyze portions of the existing environment at a medium-sized company to define an OU structure and security groups.

Before You Begin

Before you begin this lab, you must be able to

- Analyze an organization's environment to define its OUs
- Analyze an organization's environment to place user accounts
- Analyze an organization's environment to define groups

Exercise 5.1: Defining an OU Structure

In this exercise, you will analyze the existing environment at a medium-sized company to define an OU structure and security groups. Review the scenario; then follow the instructions to define the OU structure and security groups.

Scenario

Your design team is planning the Active Directory infrastructure for Uncle Bob's Root Beer, a worldwide producer of a root beer soft drink. Uncle Bob's has four regional offices in Melbourne, Chicago, Berlin, and New Delhi. There are 107 bottling plants worldwide. The corporate headquarters is located in Melbourne. Each regional office has a human resources, finance, sales, production, and distribution department. In addition, Melbourne also has a new products department. Uncle Bob's infrastructure plan uses one domain.

While reading through the business and technical environment analysis documents, you note the following:

- The IT management organization in each regional office administers user accounts and user desktop configurations, manages servers, and enforces network security.

- At the corporate headquarters, some administrators have administrative authority over the entire network in order to complete performance and security audits.

- In order to keep new products secure in the competitive soft drink industry, the New Products department has its own IT management organization that administers user accounts, manages users, and enforces network security.

- Though the IT management organization in each regional office administers user accounts for the Production department, each Production department administers access to its servers.

- All users in the company use the same e-mail and word processing applications.

- The Distribution department at each regional office uses its own proprietary distribution tracking software.

- The company requires that all human resources (HR) servers be hidden from non-HR personnel.

- Each regional office staffs a help desk whose users are permitted to reset passwords.

Exercise Questions

Based on your notes, follow the instructions below to define an OU structure.

1. Create an OU structure diagram for Uncle Bob's Root Beer that supports the needs indicated in the scenario.

2. Complete the table below to document each OU in your design, the reason for creating it, and the users and computers that it contains.

OU created	Reason created	Users and computers contained in the OU

Exercise 5.2: Defining Groups

In this exercise, you will design security groups to provide users with access to network resources.

Scenario

Your design team is planning the security groups needed in connection with the Production department at the Chicago regional office of Uncle Bob's Root Beer. Recall that the Production department has its own IT management organization to manage resources, including servers. Users from all departments and locations of the company must be able to access information on the servers in the Chicago Production department. The table below identifies the resources managed by the Production department, the users that require access to the resources, and the level of access they require.

Resource	Users requiring access	Access level
Formulas	Chicago Production Server Administrators	Full control
Formulas	Chicago Production Managers	Change
Formulas	Chicago Production Specialists	Read
Formulas	All Production Managers company-wide	Read
Production Logs	Chicago Production Server Administrators	Full control
Production Logs	Chicago Production Managers	Change
Production Logs	Chicago Production Specialists	Read
Production Logs	Chicago Distribution Managers	Read
Production Logs	All Production Managers company-wide	Read
Bottling Logs	Chicago Production Server Administrators	Full control
Bottling Logs	Chicago Production Managers	Change
Bottling Logs	Chicago Production Specialists	Read
Bottling Logs	Chicago Distribution Managers	Read
Bottling Logs	All Production Managers company-wide	Read
Customer Service Logs	Chicago Production Server Administrators	Full control
Customer Service Logs	Chicago Production Managers	Change
Customer Service Logs	Chicago Production Specialists	Read

continued

Resource	Users requiring access	Access level
Customer Service Logs	Chicago Distribution Managers	Read
Customer Service Logs	All Production Managers company-wide	Read
Customer Service Logs	All Distribution Managers company-wide	Read

Exercise Questions

Complete the table below to document your security group design. Include the name of each security group, the group scope, and the members of the group. Also note whether the members are individuals or list group names if the members are groups.

Group	Scope	Members
_____	_____	_____
_____	_____	_____
_____	_____	_____
_____	_____	_____
_____	_____	_____
_____	_____	_____
_____	_____	_____
_____	_____	_____
_____	_____	_____
_____	_____	_____
_____	_____	_____
_____	_____	_____
_____	_____	_____
_____	_____	_____
_____	_____	_____
_____	_____	_____
_____	_____	_____

Review

The following questions are intended to reinforce key information presented in the chapter. If you are unable to answer a question, review the appropriate lesson and then try the question again. Answers to the questions can be found in Appendix A, "Questions and Answers."

1. Your design team is getting ready to define OU structures for your organization's Active Directory infrastructure design. What are the three reasons for defining an OU? What is the primary reason?

2. Your design team has defined an OU to delegate control of user objects. You have diagrammed the desired OU, diagrammed a security group, and listed the administrators who require control of the user object class in the group. You want to allow the OU to set its own membership. Where should the administrator group be placed?

3. Your design team has defined a forest, domains, and OUs. Where should user accounts be placed?

4. Your design team is assigning users to groups. Which group scope is most often used to assign permissions to resources?

5. Your organization is running Windows 2000 in native mode. The design team is adding users to groups. Why shouldn't the team add individual users to universal groups?

C H A P T E R   6

Creating a Site Topology Plan

About This Chapter

After you and your design team finish creating the OU Plan, the next stage in designing an Active Directory directory services infrastructure is to create a site topology plan. An Active Directory site topology is a logical representation of an organization's physical network. Creating a site topology plan includes defining sites, placing domain controllers, defining a replication strategy, and placing global catalog servers and operations masters within a forest. This chapter shows you how to create a site topology plan.

Before You Begin

To complete this chapter, you must have

- Knowledge of Active Directory components and concepts covered in Chapter 1, "Introduction to Active Directory"
- Knowledge of business and technical environment analyses components covered in Chapter 2, "Introduction to Designing a Directory Services Infrastructure"
- Knowledge and skills covered in Chapter 3, "Creating a Forest Plan"
- Knowledge and skills covered in Chapter 4, "Creating a Domain Plan"
- Knowledge and skills covered in Chapter 5, "Creating an Organizational Unit Plan"

Lesson 1: Defining Sites

The first step in creating a site topology plan is to define sites. To define sites, you must assess the organization's need for sites and then determine the sites for each forest in the organization. This lesson discusses how to define sites.

After this lesson, you will be able to

- Explain the purpose of sites
- Identify the factors in an organization's environment that impact its need for sites
- Analyze an organization's environment to define its sites

Estimated lesson time: 15 minutes

Understanding Sites

Recall that a *site* is a set of Internet Protocol (IP) subnets connected by a highly reliable and fast link (usually a LAN). Typically, networks with a bandwidth of at least 512 kilobits per second (Kbps) are considered fast networks. An average available bandwidth of 128 Kbps and higher is sufficient for designating a site. *Average available bandwidth* is the amount of bandwidth that is actually available for use during peak traffic after normal network traffic is handled.

In Active Directory, site structure mirrors the location of user communities. Site structure concerns the physical environment and is maintained separately from the logical environment, the domain structure. Because sites are independent of the domain structure, a single domain can include a single site or multiple sites, and a single site can include multiple domains, as shown in Figure 6.1.

The main purpose of a site is to physically group computers to optimize network traffic. Sites act to confine authentication and replication traffic to only the devices within a site. Because network traffic is prevented from unnecessarily crossing slow WAN links, traffic is limited. Sites have two main roles:

- To determine the nearest domain controller during workstation logon
- To optimize the replication of data between sites

Because site names are used in the records registered in DNS by the domain locator, they must be valid DNS names. Recall that valid DNS names consist of the standard characters A–Z, a–z, 0–9, and hyphen (-).

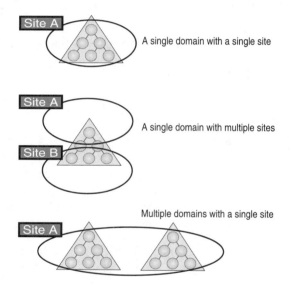

A single domain with a single site

A single domain with multiple sites

Multiple domains with a single site

Figure 6.1   The relationship of site and domain structures

Design Step: Defining Sites

To define sites, you must complete the following tasks:

1. Assess the organization's need for sites.
2. Determine the sites for the organization.

Assessing the Need for Sites

To define sites, you must first consult the Network Architecture Worksheet compiled earlier by your design team. Use the Network Architecture Worksheet to determine

- The locations in which the organization has offices
- The speed of the LANs in each location and the percentage of average available bandwidth on each link during normal business hours
- The TCP/IP subnets in each location

Note A blank copy of the worksheet is located on the Supplemental Course Materials CD-ROM (\chapt02\worksheets). A completed example of the worksheet is located in Chapter 2, "Introduction to Designing a Directory Services Infrastructure."

In addition to assessing the information in this worksheet, it is imperative that you assess any changes to the network architecture currently planned to address growth, flexibility, and the ideal design specifications of the organization.

Defining Sites for the Organization

Define a site for

- Each LAN or set of LANs that are connected by a high-speed backbone
- Each location that does not have direct connectivity to the rest of the network and is only reachable using SMTP mail

If an entire network consists of fast, reliable links, the network can be considered a single site. Similarly, if bandwidth between networks is plentiful and it is acceptable for a client on one network to communicate with a server on another network, the networks may together be considered a single site.

Subnets that are not defined in the directory are not considered part of a site. The subnets may be undefined because they have not yet been added to the network. Any clients on undefined subnets must then communicate randomly with all domain controllers in a domain, which may result in authentication delays.

To eliminate these delays, you can associate the clients with a site by creating default subnets and then associating the subnets with a site. The default subnets are shown in Table 6.1.

Table 6.1   Default Subnets

Subnet ID	Mask	Description
128.0.0.0	192.0.0.0	Captures all clients on Class B networks that are not yet defined in the directory.
192.0.0.0	224.0.0.0	Captures all clients on Class C networks that are not yet defined in the directory.

No default subnet is provided for clients on Class A networks that are not yet defined in the directory.

▶ **To define sites**

1. Determine the site(s) needed to encompass each
   - LAN or set of LANs that are connected by a high-speed backbone
   - Location that does not have direct connectivity to the rest of the network and is only reachable using SMTP mail
2. Create a site diagram:
   - Use an oval to represent each site.
   - Name each site using a valid DNS name.
   - List the set of IP subnets that constitute each site.

Design Step Example: Defining Sites

Figure 6.2 shows the network architecture diagram for Margo Tea Company, a producer of herbal teas with seven locations. The company headquarters is located in Cincinnati, with regional offices in Pittsburgh and Louisville. The Toledo, Lexington, and Charleston locations are sales offices, and the company's distribution center is located in Columbus. The company operates within a single domain. Each location has a high-speed backbone that connects a set of 10–100 Kbps LANs.

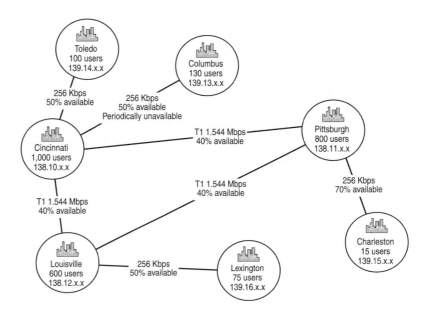

Figure 6.2   Network architecture diagram for Margo Tea Company

Figure 6.3 shows the site diagram for Margo Tea Company. A site was defined for each location because each location has a high-speed backbone that connects a set of 10–100 Kbps LANs.

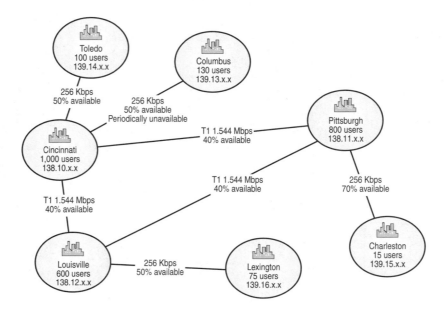

Figure 6.3   Site diagram for Margo Tea Company

Lesson Summary

In this lesson you learned how to define sites for an organization by assessing an organization's site needs and determining the location of its sites. You also learned the guidelines for defining a site: define a site for each LAN or set of LANs that are connected by a high-speed backbone and define a site for each location that does not have direct connectivity to the rest of the network and is reachable only by SMTP mail. Finally, you learned to create a site diagram that includes the name of each site and a listing of the set of IP subnets that constitute each site.

Lesson 2: Placing Domain Controllers in Sites

The second step in creating a site topology plan is to place domain controllers in sites. To place domain controllers, you must assess the organization's need for domain controllers and then determine the location of domain controllers for the organization. This lesson discusses how to place domain controllers in sites.

After this lesson, you will be able to

- Identify the factors in an organization's environment that impact its need for domain controllers
- Analyze an organization's environment to place domain controllers in sites

Estimated lesson time: 30 minutes

Understanding Domain Controller Placement

Recall that a *domain controller* is a computer running Windows 2000 Server that authenticates user logons and maintains the security policy and the master database for a domain. Because the availability of Active Directory depends on the availability of domain controllers, a domain controller must always be available so that the users can be authenticated. The need to have an available domain controller determines the sites in which domain controllers are placed. By placing domain controllers in sites to provide fault tolerance, you can ensure the availability of required functions.

When you install the first domain in a forest, a default site object named Default-First-Site-Name is created in the Sites container. The first domain controller is automatically installed into this site. You can change the name of the first site object. When you add subsequent domain controllers, the Active Directory Installation Wizard determines the site into which they are installed. The wizard checks existing sites for the subnet of the domain controller you are installing. If the subnet is found in an existing site, the domain controller is installed in that site. If the subnet is not found in an existing site, the wizard installs the new domain controller in the site of the first domain controller. If you need to create a new site for the new domain controller, you can create the site after Active Directory is installed and then move the domain controller from the site of the first domain controller to the new site.

Naming Domain Controllers and Computers

By default, a Windows 2000 domain controller and/or computer that is added to a domain will assign itself a fully qualified DNS name that consists of the computer's host name followed by the DNS name of the domain the computer has joined. For example, in Figure 6.4, the domain controllers DC01 and DC02 are located in the domain uk.microsoft.com, and the domain controller DC01 is located in the domain us.microsoft.com, so the fully qualified DNS names for the domain controllers become DC01.uk.microsoft.com, DC02.uk.microsoft.com, and DC01.us.microsoft.com.

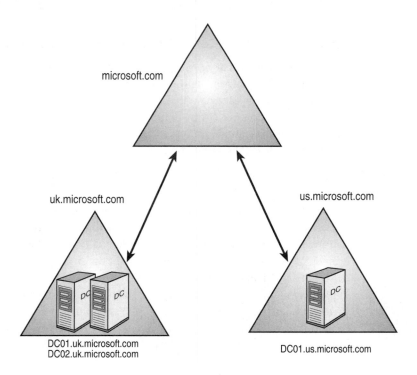

Figure 6.4   Domain controller naming

Design Step: Placing Domain Controllers

To place domain controllers, you must complete the following tasks:

1. Assess the organization's need for domain controllers.
2. Determine the location of domain controllers for the organization.

Assessing the Need for Domain Controllers

To place domain controllers, you must first consult the

- Site diagram compiled earlier by your design team to view the sites defined for your network and determine the possible locations for domain controllers
- Network Architecture Worksheet, including defined domains, compiled earlier by your design team to find out location of domains for the organization

Note A blank copy of the worksheet is located on the Supplemental Course Materials CD-ROM (\chapt02\worksheets). A completed example of the worksheet is located in Chapter 2, "Introduction to Designing a Directory Services Infrastructure."

In addition to assessing the information in these documents, it is imperative that you assess any changes that may be planned for the sites or domains to address growth, flexibility, and the ideal design specifications of the organization.

Determining the Location of Domain Controllers

For optimum network response time and application availability, place at least

- One domain controller in each site

  A domain controller in each site provides users with a local computer that can service query requests for their domain over LAN connections.
- Two domain controllers in each domain

  By placing at least two domain controllers in each domain, you provide redundancy and reduce the load on the existing domain controller in a domain. Recall that a domain controller can service only one domain.

Note When a single site includes multiple domains, you cannot place a domain controller in the site and expect it to service more than one domain.

The following are reasons for placing additional domain controllers in a site:

- There are a large number of users in the site, and the link to the site is slow or near capacity.

  If a site has slow logon times and slow authentication when attempting to access user resources, capacity may be insufficient. By monitoring domain controller usage you can determine whether there is enough processing power and bandwidth to service requests. If performance is lagging, you should consider adding another domain controller to the site.

- The link to the site is historically unreliable or only intermittently available.

  If a single domain controller in a site fails, clients can connect to other domain controllers in other sites in the domain by crossing site links. However, if site links are unreliable, users on that site will not be able to log on to their computers. In this case, you should consider adding another domain controller to the site.

In some situations, it may *not* be efficient to place a domain controller in a site. These situations include

- Sites with small numbers of users

  For sites with a small number of users, using available bandwidth to log on and query the directory may be more economical than adding a domain controller.

- Small sites that have client computers but no servers

  For sites with no servers, a domain controller is not necessary. Users will still be able to log on using cached credentials if the site link fails. Because there are no server-based resources at the site, there is no need for further authentication.

Using Active Directory Sizer

To determine the number of domain controllers you need, you may want to use Active Directory Sizer, a tool for estimating the hardware required for deploying Active Directory based on your organization's profile, domain information, and site topology. We will experiment with Active Directory Sizer in Lesson 4, "Placing Global Catalog Servers and Operations Masters." For more information on Active Directory Sizer, visit *http://www.microsoft.com/windows2000/library/ resources/reskit/tools/new/adsizer-o.asp*.

▶ **To place domain controllers**

1. On the site diagram, place a domain controller in each site except for sites with small numbers of users or no servers. Use a rectangle containing the domain controller's host name to represent the domain controller.

2. Determine whether you need to place additional domain controllers in any of the sites and indicate them on the site diagram in the same manner.

3. Ensure that there are at least two domain controllers in each domain by placing any additional domain controllers needed in the appropriate site.

Design Step Example: Placing Domain Controllers

Review Figure 6.3, which shows the site diagram for Margo Tea Company. Recall from Lesson 1 that Margo Tea Company requires only one domain. Figure 6.5 shows the location of domain controllers for Margo Tea Company. The reasons for locating domain controllers in this manner are

- One domain controller is placed in each site except the Charleston sales office to meet minimum requirements.

- A second domain controller is placed in each of the Cincinnati, Louisville, and Pittsburgh regional offices to handle the relatively large number of users in each of these sites.

- A second domain controller is placed in the Columbus distribution center because it has a periodically unavailable link to the Cincinnati headquarters location.

- A domain controller is not placed in the Charleston location because of the relatively small number of users in this location and because the link is operating well below capacity.

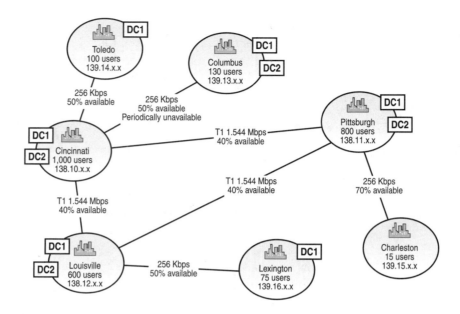

Figure 6.5   Domain controller locations for Margo Tea Company

Lesson Summary

In this lesson you learned how to place domain controllers for an organization by assessing an organization's need for domain controllers and determining where domain controllers should be placed. You learned that for optimum network response time and application availability, you should place at least one domain controller in each site and two domain controllers in each domain. You also learned when to consider placing additional domain controllers in a site, such as when there are a large number of users in the site and the link to the site is slow or near capacity, or when the link to the site is historically unreliable or only intermittently available. Finally, you learned to indicate the placement of domain controllers on the site diagram.

Activity 6.1: Defining Sites and Placing Domain Controllers in Sites

In this activity you will read about an organization that is planning its Active Directory infrastructure. Your task is to analyze the organization's environment to define the sites and domain controllers needed in an Active Directory infrastructure. You will define sites and place domain controllers by creating a site diagram and indicating the location of all domain controllers.

Scenario: Ramona Publishing

You are an infrastructure planner on the Active Directory infrastructure design team for Ramona Publishing, a publisher of Spanish language books with seven locations in Miami, Mexico City, Buenos Aires, Los Angeles, New York, San Juan, and Madrid. The business and technical environment analysis documents, the forest plan, the domain plan, and the OU plan have already been compiled, and copies have been distributed to everyone on the team. You are now in the process of defining sites and placing domain controllers for the organization.

Your design team has created the network architecture diagram for Ramona Publishing, shown in Figure 6.6. Domain locations have also been included on the diagram. Each location has a high-speed backbone that connects a set of 10–100 Kbps LANs.

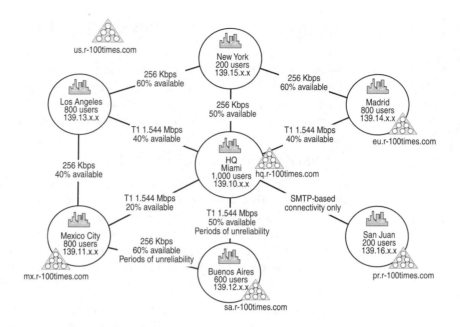

Figure 6.6 Network architecture diagram for Ramona Publishing

1. Diagram the sites needed for Ramona Publishing. Explain your reasoning for defining each site.

2. Place the domain controllers needed for Ramona Publishing. Explain your reasoning for placing each domain controller.

Lesson 3: Defining a Replication Strategy

The third step in creating a site topology plan is to define a replication strategy. To define a replication strategy, you must assess the physical connectivity of the organization's network, plan a site link configuration for each network connection, plan whether to disable site link transitivity (if necessary), and plan preferred bridgehead servers (if necessary). This lesson discusses how to define a replication strategy.

After this lesson, you will be able to

- Explain how information is replicated within sites and between sites
- Explain the purpose of site links, site link bridges, and bridgehead servers
- Explain site link transitivity
- Identify the factors in an organization's environment that impact its replication strategy
- Analyze an organization's environment to define its replication strategy

Estimated lesson time: 40 minutes

Understanding Replication

Replication is the process of copying data from a data store or file system to multiple computers to synchronize the data. In Windows 2000, each domain controller maintains a replica of all Active Directory objects contained in the domain to which it belongs. Replication ensures that changes made to a replica on one domain controller are synchronized to replicas on all other domain controllers within the domain. If domains are linked in a forest, some of the data is synchronized to replicas on other domain controllers in other domains.

Replication Triggers

The following actions trigger replication between domain controllers:

- Creating an object
- Modifying an object
- Moving an object
- Deleting an object

Information Replicated

Three types of objects are stored in Active Directory. Each type of object is stored in a tree, called a naming context (NC). The three naming contexts are

- Schema NC. Contains objects that can be created in the directory and the attributes those objects can have. Objects in the schema NC must be replicated to all domain controllers in all domains in the forest.
- Configuration NC. Contains objects that represent the logical structure of the deployment, including the domain structure and replication topology. Objects in the configuration NC must be replicated to all domain controllers in all domains in the forest.
- Domain NC. Contains all of the objects in a domain. Objects in the domain NC can be replicated only to domain controllers within the domain. For the purpose of finding information throughout the domain tree or forest, selected attributes for all objects in all domains are stored in the global catalog.

How Information Is Replicated

Recall that Active Directory replicates information in two ways: *intrasite* (within a site) and *intersite* (between sites). Table 6.2 compares the intrasite and intersite replication.

Table 6.2   Intrasite and Intersite Replication Comparison

	Intrasite replication	Intersite replication
Compression	To save CPU time, replication data is not compressed.	To save WAN bandwidth, replication data greater than 50 KB is compressed.
Replication model	To reduce replication latency, replication partners notify each other when changes need to be replicated and then push the information for processing.	To save WAN bandwidth, replication partners do not notify each other when changes need to be replicated.
Replication frequency	Replication partners poll each other periodically.	Replication partners poll each other at specified intervals, only during scheduled periods. If updates are necessary, operations are scheduled to pull the information for processing.
Transport protocols	Remote procedure call (RPC)	IP or SMTP

For intrasite replication, the Windows 2000 Knowledge Consistency Checker (KCC) on each domain controller helps to automatically generate and optimize a replication topology among domain controllers in the same domain. To accomplish this, the KCC automatically creates connection objects between domain controllers. A *connection object* is an Active Directory object that represents a communication channel used to replicate information from one domain controller to another. Under normal conditions, Active Directory automatically creates and deletes connection objects. However, you can manually create connection objects to force replication if you are certain the connection is required and you want the connection to persist until you manually remove it.

For intersite replication to occur, you must customize how Active Directory replicates information by setting up site links. *Site links* are logical, transitive connections between two or more sites that mirror the network links and allow replication to occur. Once you have created site links, the KCC will then automatically generate the replication topology by creating the appropriate connection objects. It's important to note the difference between site links and connection objects. Site links are used by the KCC to determine replication paths between two sites and *must* be created manually. Connection objects actually connect domain controllers and are created by the KCC, though you can also manually create them if necessary.

Configuring Site Links

To ensure efficient replication and fault tolerance, you must configure the following information for site links:

- Intersite transport. The method of transport used for replication, either
  - Directory Service Remote Procedure Call (DS-RPC), designated in Windows 2000 as IP,

    or

  - Inter-Site Messaging–Simple Mail Transport Protocol (ISM-SMTP), designated in Windows 2000 as SMTP

- Site link cost. A value assigned to the site link that indicates the cost of the connection in relation to the speed of the link. Higher costs are used for slow links, and lower costs are used for fast links.

- Replication frequency. A value assigned to the site link that indicates the number of minutes Active Directory should wait before using a connection to check for replication updates.

- Replication availability. A schedule assigned to the site link that indicates when the link is available for replication.

Site Link Transitivity

By default, all site links are transitive, which simply means that if sites A and B are linked and sites B and C are linked, then site A and site C are transitively linked. Site link transitivity is enabled or disabled by selecting the Bridge All Site Links check box in the Properties dialog box for either the IP or the SMTP intersite transport. By default, site link transitivity is enabled for each transport.

If you disable site link transitivity for a transport, all site links for that transport are affected and none of them are transitive. You must manually create site link bridges to provide transitive replication. The following are some reasons why you may want to disable site link transitivity:

- To have total control over replication traffic patterns
- To avoid a particular replication path, such as a path that involves a firewall
- If your IP network is not fully routed

Caution Carefully consider the needs of your organization before disabling site link transitivity.

Site Link Bridges

A *site link bridge* connects two or more site links in a transport where transitivity has been disabled in order to create a transitive and logical link between two sites that do not have an explicit site link. For example, in Figure 6.7, site link Ber-Lu connects the Bern and Lucerne sites. Site link Lu-Zur connects the Lucerne and Zurich sites. Site link bridge Ber-Lu-Zur connects site links Ber-Lu and Lu-Zur.

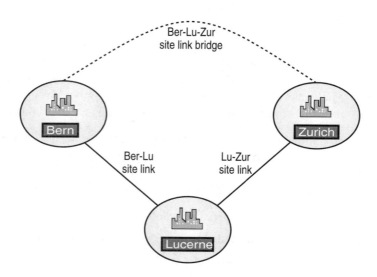

Figure 6.7   A site link bridge

Because site links are transitive by default, it is seldom necessary to create site link bridges. In other words, if site link transitivity is enabled, then manually creating a site link bridge will be redundant and will have no effect. However, if site link transitivity is disabled, you will need to manually create a site link bridge if a transitive link is required to handle your organization's replication strategy.

Bridgehead Servers

After you have configured site links, the KCC will then automatically designate a domain controller in each site, for each intersite transport, as the bridgehead server. A *bridgehead server* is a single domain controller in a site, the contact point, used for replication between sites. The KCC automatically creates connection objects between bridgehead servers. When a bridgehead server receives replication updates from another site, it replicates the data to the other domain controllers within its site.

A bridgehead server is designated automatically by the KCC. You can also specify a preferred bridgehead server if you have a computer with appropriate bandwidth to transmit and receive information. If you specify a preferred bridgehead server rather than use the one designated by the KCC, you can select the optimum conditions for the connection between sites. To designate a preferred bridgehead server, select the desired intersite transport or transports on the Server tab in the Properties dialog box for the domain controller you want to make a bridgehead server. You can specify multiple preferred bridgehead servers, but only one will be active at any time in a single site.

Caution By specifying preferred bridgehead servers, you limit the ability of the KCC to provide failover should the bridgehead servers you designated as preferred go offline. If an active preferred bridgehead server fails, Active Directory will select another preferred bridgehead server from the set you designated. If no other preferred bridgehead servers are specified or no other preferred bridgehead servers are available, replication will not occur to that site.

How Intersite Replication Works

The following steps, illustrated in Figure 6.8, show how intersite replication works:

1. At the interval determined by the selected replication frequency, the bridgehead server in the Zurich site polls the bridgehead server in the Lucerne site for any updated data.

2. If the bridgehead server in the Lucerne site finds that it has updated Active Directory data, it compresses the data (if larger than 50 KB) and sends it to the bridgehead server in the Zurich site.

3. When the bridgehead server in the Zurich site has received all of the data, it then replicates the data to the other domain controllers in the site, without compressing the information.

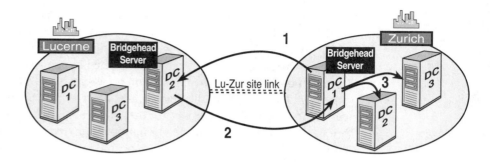

Figure 6.8   The intersite replication process

Note that polling and pull replication, rather than notification and push replication, are used between bridgehead servers during intersite replication. Pull replication is the most efficient for intersite replication because the destination domain controller knows which replication data to request. In contrast, notification and push replication are more efficient for intrasite replication, when domain controllers are well connected and not restrained by site link schedules.

Design Step: Defining a Replication Strategy

An organization's replication strategy determines when and how information is replicated. To define a replication strategy, you must complete the following tasks:

1. Assess the physical connectivity of the organization's network.
2. Plan a site link configuration for each network connection.
3. Plan site link transitivity disabling (optional).
4. Plan preferred bridgehead servers (optional).

Assessing Physical Connectivity

To define a replication strategy, you must first consult the site diagram containing domain controller locations that your design team compiled earlier to view the network links, sites, and domain controllers defined for your network and determine what site links are needed. You should also consider whether there is any need to disable site link transitivity and to create site link bridges. Then consider whether specifying preferred bridgehead servers is required. In addition to assessing these needs, it is imperative that you assess any changes that may be planned for the sites or domain controller locations to address growth, flexibility, and the ideal design specifications of the organization.

Planning a Site Link Configuration

For each site link, you will need to specify the following information: site link name, method of replication transport, site link cost, replication frequency, and replication availability.

For the site link name, you should set up a site link naming convention. This naming convention should easily convey the sites connected by the link. For example, if your sites are named Chicago and Redmond, you might name the site link Chi-Red or Red-Chi.

To select the method of replication transport for a site link, either Directory Service Remote Procedure Call (DS-RPC, designated in Windows 2000 as IP) or Simple Mail Transport Protocol (designated in Windows 2000 as SMTP), you'll need to know how the sites are connected. A site link that uses IP replication transport is designed for faster connections and uses remote procedure calls (RPCs) for direct synchronous replication using TCP/IP. A site link that uses SMTP replication transport is designed for slower and less reliable connections and uses e-mail messages to handle replication updates. Because SMTP replication transport is asynchronous, sending and receiving updates automatically according to the e-mail system, it ignores replication schedules.

Important If you choose to use SMTP transport, you must complete the process of installing and configuring a certificate authority. You must have an Enterprise certificate authority (CA) available and SMTP must be installed on all domain controllers that will use the site link. The CA signs SMTP messages that are exchanged between domain controllers, ensuring the authenticity of directory updates.

The site link cost can be a number between 1 and 32,767. The default cost is 100. Lower values indicate better connectivity and higher usage priority. The values you assign for the site link cost depend on the intersite link speeds and the replication transports used in your organization. For example, if you have three different types of connections (T1, 256 Kbps, and 64 Kbps), you will need three site link cost values. In addition, if you use both replication transports with each type of connection, you will need six site link cost values. The values you assign should reflect the relative bandwidth of the connections. For example, you may want to use 1–25 for fast, low-cost links; 26–50 for medium-cost links; and 51 and higher for high-cost links. Because Active Directory always chooses the connection on a per-cost basis, the cheapest connection will be used if it is available. You can assign identical costs to site links; the KCC treats these sites equally.

To set the replication frequency, indicate the number of minutes the replication partners on the site link should wait during scheduled periods before polling each other for changes.

To set the replication availability, you must consider when you want to allow replication along the site links. Consider allowing low-cost links to be available for longer periods of time, while allowing high-cost links to be available only at very specific times. For replication to occur across all links, you must schedule a common time period for the links to be available.

Planning Site Link Transitivity Disabling (optional)

By default, site link transitivity in Windows 2000 is enabled. You should disable site link transitivity only if it is absolutely necessary to have total control over replication traffic patterns. Disabling site link transitivity often creates work for the administrator and may cause replication between sites to fail. If you disable site link transitivity, you must create site link bridges between site links if you want to make them transitive.

Planning Preferred Bridgehead Servers (optional)

By specifying a preferred bridgehead server rather than using the one designated by the KCC, you can select the optimum conditions for the connection between sites.

▶ **To define a replication strategy**

1. Identify sites connected with very fast (2Mbps or higher), low-cost connections.

2. Identify sites connected with medium-speed, medium-cost connections.

3. Identify sites connected with low-speed, unreliable, or high-cost connections.

4. Designate each connection as a site link on the site diagram by placing the name of the site link on the connection between two sites.

5. Create a site link table that includes the site link name, method of replication transport, site link cost, replication frequency, and replication availability for each site link.

6. (optional) On the site link table, list the transport(s) for which you need to disable site link transitivity.

7. (optional) For each transport listed, create a site link bridge table that indicates the name of each site link bridge required and the name of the site links contained in the site link bridge.

8. (optional) On the site link table, create a preferred bridgehead server table that lists the names of the domain controllers that you want to make preferred bridgehead servers for each site.

Design Step Example: Defining a Replication Strategy

Review Figure 6.5, which shows the site diagram, including domain controllers, for Margo Tea Company. Figure 6.9 shows a site diagram with site links added for Margo Tea Company. Site link names are indicated by the first three letters of each connected site name.

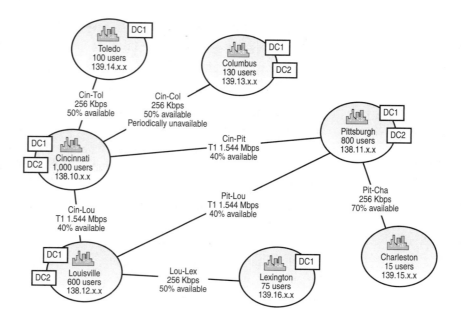

Figure 6.9   Site links for Margo Tea Company

Table 6.3 shows the site link configurations planned for Margo Tea Company.

Table 6.3   Site Link Configurations for Margo Tea Company

Site link	Transport	Cost	Frequency	Availability
Cin-Pit	IP	25	15 min	always
Pit-Lou	IP	25	15 min	always
Cin-Lou	IP	25	15 min	always
Pit-Cha	IP	50	1 hr	2300 to 0500 daily
Cin-Tol	IP	50	1 hr	2300 to 0500 daily
Cin-Col	IP	50	15 min	always
Lou-Lex	IP	50	1 hr	2300 to 0500 daily

Margo Tea Company has no plans to disable site link transitivity. The company has also decided to let the KCC select the bridgehead servers and has not designated any preferred bridgehead servers.

Lesson Summary

In this lesson you learned how to define a replication strategy by assessing the physical connectivity of the organization's network, planning a site link configuration for each network connection, planning site link transitivity disabling (which is optional), and planning preferred bridgehead servers (which is also optional). You learned how to plan a site link configuration by selecting the site link name, method of replication transport, site link cost, replication frequency, and replication availability. You learned that site link transitivity in Windows 2000 is enabled by default and that you should disable site link transitivity only if it is absolutely necessary to have total control over replication traffic patterns. If you disable site link transitivity, you must create site link bridges between site links you want to make transitive. You also learned that a bridgehead server is designated automatically by the KCC and that you can specify a preferred bridgehead server if you have a computer with enough bandwidth to transmit and receive information. If you specify a preferred bridgehead server rather than use the one designated by the KCC, you can select the optimum conditions for the connection between sites. Finally, you learned to indicate your replication strategy by placing site links on the site diagram and by creating a site link table, site link bridge table (optional), and a preferred bridgehead server table (optional).

Lesson 4: Placing Global Catalog Servers and Operations Masters

The final step in creating a site topology plan is to place global catalog servers and operations masters. To place global catalog servers and operations masters, you must assess the organization's need for global catalog servers and operations masters and then determine their location. This lesson discusses how to place global catalog servers and operations masters.

After this lesson, you will be able to

- Identify the factors in an organization's environment that impact its need for global catalog servers
- Identify the factors in an organization's environment that impact its need for operations masters
- Analyze an organization's environment to place global catalog servers in sites
- Analyze an organization's environment to assign operations master roles
- Use Active Directory Sizer to determine the number and placement of domain controllers and global catalog servers

Estimated lesson time: 30 minutes

Understanding Global Catalog Servers

Recall that a *global catalog server* is a Windows 2000 domain controller that holds a copy of the global catalog for the forest. A global catalog server must be available when a user logs on to a Windows 2000 native-mode domain or logs on with a user principal name because in native mode a domain controller must send a query to a global catalog server to determine the user's membership in universal groups. Because universal groups can be used to deny access to resources, knowledge of universal group membership is necessary in order to enforce access control. Consequently, if a global catalog server is not available during user logon, the domain controller refuses the logon request. Therefore, it is imperative that you plan the location of global catalog servers carefully.

By default, the initial domain controller in a forest is designated as a global catalog server. However, you can configure any domain controller or designate additional domain controllers to serve this function.

Understanding Operations Masters

Operations master roles are special roles assigned to one or more domain controllers in an Active Directory domain to allow the domain controllers to perform single-master replication for specific operations. Active Directory supports multimaster replication of the database between all domain controllers in the domain. However, some changes are impractical to perform in multimaster fashion, so one or more domain controllers can be assigned to perform single-master operations (operations that are not permitted to occur at different places in a network at the same time).

In any Active Directory forest, five operations master roles must be assigned to one or more domain controllers. Some roles must appear in every forest. Other roles must appear in every domain in the forest. You can change the assignment of operations master roles after Setup, but in most cases this will not be necessary. You must be aware of operations master roles assigned to a domain controller if problems develop on a domain controller or if you plan to take it out of service.

Forest-Wide Operations Master Roles

Every Active Directory forest must have the following roles:

- Schema master

  The schema master domain controller controls all updates and modifications to the schema. To update the schema of a forest, you must have access to the schema master. At any time, there can be only one schema master in the entire forest.

- Domain naming master

  The domain controller holding the domain naming master role controls the addition or removal of domains in the forest. At any time, there can be only one domain naming master in the entire forest.

Domain-Wide Operations Master Roles

Every domain in the forest must have the following roles:

- Relative ID master

  The relative ID master allocates sequences of relative IDs to each of the various domain controllers in its domain. Whenever a domain controller creates a user, group, or computer object, it assigns the object a unique security ID. The security ID consists of a domain security ID (that is the same for all security IDs created in the domain) and a relative ID that is unique for each security ID created in the domain. At any time, only one domain controller can act as the relative ID master in each domain in the forest.

- Primary domain controller (PDC) emulator

  If the domain contains computers operating without Windows 2000 client software or if it contains Windows NT backup domain controllers (BDCs), the PDC emulator acts as a Windows NT primary domain controller. It processes password changes from clients and replicates updates to the BDCs. In a Windows 2000 domain operating in native mode, the PDC emulator receives preferential replication of password changes performed by other domain controllers in the domain. If a password was recently changed, that change takes time to replicate to every domain controller in the domain. If a logon authentication fails at another domain controller due to a bad password, that domain controller will forward the authentication request to the PDC emulator before rejecting the logon attempt. At any time, only one domain controller can act as the PDC emulator in each domain in the forest.

- Infrastructure master

  The infrastructure master is responsible for updating the security identifiers and distinguished names in cross-domain object references whenever the name of an object is renamed or changed. At any time, only one domain controller can act as the infrastructure master in each domain.

Figure 6.10 shows how the operations master roles are distributed throughout a forest by default. Domain A was the first domain created in the forest (the forest root domain). It holds both of the forest-wide operations master roles. The first domain controller in each of the other domains is assigned the three domain-specific roles.

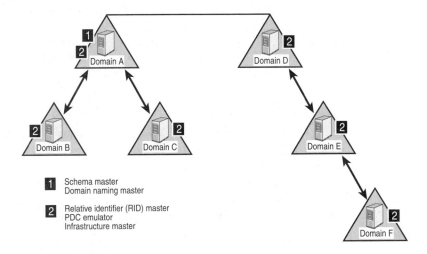

Figure 6.10 Operations master role default distribution in a forest

Design Step: Placing Global Catalog Servers and Operations Masters

To place domain global catalog servers and operations masters, you must complete the following tasks:

1. Locate domain controllers.

2. Determine the location of global catalog servers for the organization.

3. Determine the location of operations masters for the organization.

Locating Domain Controllers

To place global catalog servers and operations masters, you must first consult the site diagram containing domain controller locations and site links that was compiled earlier by your design team to view the network links, sites, domain controllers, and site links defined for your network. From this diagram, you can determine which domain controllers to designate as global catalog servers and operations masters. In addition to locating domain controllers, it is imperative that you assess any changes that may be planned for the sites or domain controller locations to address growth, flexibility, and the ideal design specifications of the organization.

Determining the Location of Global Catalog Servers

For optimum network response time and application availability, designate at least one domain controller in each site as the global catalog server. A global catalog server in each site provides users with a local computer that can service query requests for their domain over LAN connections. When considering which domain controllers to designate as global catalog servers, base your decision on the ability of your network structure to handle replication and query traffic.

To determine whether to designate additional domain controllers in a site as global catalog servers, the rules for designating additional domain controllers in a site apply. However, you must balance the need for additional global catalog servers with the increased replication traffic that these servers will generate.

If your organization uses Microsoft Exchange 2000, you should try to place a global catalog server in each site that contains an Exchange server. This is because Exchange 2000 uses Active Directory as its directory service, and all mailbox names are resolved by queries through Active Directory to the global catalog server. In a large Exchange environment, a global catalog server may need to handle a large number of queries, so placing a global catalog server in each site that contains an Exchange server can ensure that all queries are handled promptly.

Using Active Directory Sizer

To determine the number of global catalog servers you need, you may want to use Active Directory Sizer, a tool for estimating the hardware required for deploying Active Directory based on your organization's profile, domain information, and site topology. For more information on Active Directory Sizer, visit *http:// www.microsoft.com/windows2000/library/resources/reskit/tools/new/adsizer-o.asp*.

▶ **To place global catalog servers**

1. On the site diagram, designate a domain controller in each site as the global catalog server. Use a circle containing "GC" to represent the global catalog server.

2. Determine whether you need to designate additional domain controllers as global catalog servers and indicate them on the site diagram.

Determining the Location of Operations Masters

In a small Active Directory forest with only one domain and one domain controller, that domain controller is assigned all the operations master roles. When you create the first domain in a new forest, all of the operations master roles are automatically assigned to the first domain controller in that domain. When you create a new child domain or the root domain of a new domain tree in an existing forest, the first domain controller in the new domain is automatically assigned the relative identifier master, PDC emulator master, and infrastructure master roles. Because there can be only one schema master and one domain naming master in the forest, these roles remain in the first domain created in the forest.

The default operations master locations work well for a forest deployed on a few domain controllers in a single site. In a forest with more domain controllers, or in a forest that spans multiple sites, you may want to transfer the default operations master role assignments to other domain controllers in the domain or forest.

Planning the Operations Master Role Assignments by Domain

Follow these guidelines when assigning operations master roles for a domain:

- If a domain has only one domain controller, that domain controller must hold all of the domain roles.

- If a domain has more than one domain controller,

  - Choose two, well-connected domain controllers that are direct replication partners. Make one of the domain controllers the operations master domain controller. Make the other the *standby* operations master domain controller. The standby operations master domain controller is used in case of failure of the operations master domain controller.

- In domains that are not large, assign both the relative identifier master and PDC emulator roles to the operations master domain controller. In very large domains, you can reduce the peak load on the PDC emulator by placing the relative identifier master and the PDC emulator roles on separate domain controllers, both of which are direct replication partners of the standby operations master domain controller. However, to avoid the administrative tasks associated with separating the roles, it's best to keep them together unless the load on the operations master domain controller justifies separating the roles.

- The infrastructure master role should not be assigned to the domain controller that is hosting the global catalog. However, you should assign the infrastructure master role to any domain controller that is well connected to a global catalog (from any domain) in the same site. If the operations master domain controller meets these requirements, use it unless the load justifies the extra management burden of separating the roles. If the infrastructure master and global catalog are on the same domain controller, the infrastructure master will not function. The infrastructure master will never find data that is out of date, and so will never replicate any changes to the other domain controllers in the domain. If all of the domain controllers in a domain are also hosting the global catalog, all of the domain controllers will have the current data and it does not matter which domain controller holds the infrastructure master role.

Planning the Operations Master Roles for the Forest

Once you have planned all of the domain roles for each domain, consider the forest roles. The schema master and the domain naming master roles should always be assigned to a domain controller designated as the global catalog server. This ensures that when the domain naming master creates an object representing a new domain, no other object has the same name. The load of these operations master roles is very light, so, to simplify management, place these roles on the operations master domain controller of one of the domains in the forest.

Planning for Growth

Normally, as your forest grows, you will not need to change the locations of the various operations master roles. But when you are planning to decommission a domain controller, change the global catalog status of a domain controller, or reduce the connectivity of parts of your network, you may need to revise the operations master role assignments.

▶ **To place operations masters**

1. On the site diagram, designate the appropriate domain controller(s) with the relative identifier master, PDC emulator master, and infrastructure master roles. Use a diamond shape containing "RID," "PDC," and "IM" to represent each role.

2. On the site diagram, indicate the domain controller designated as the global catalog server with the schema master and domain naming master roles. Use a diamond shape containing "SM" and "DN" to represent each role.

Note After you've added the global catalog servers and operations masters to your site diagram that already contains sites, domain controllers, and site links, you have a complete site topology diagram.

Design Step Example: Placing Global Catalog Servers and Operations Masters

Review Figure 6.9, which shows the site diagram for Margo Tea Company. Figure 6.11 shows the location of global catalog servers and operations masters for Margo Tea Company. The reasons for locating global catalog servers in this manner are

- One global catalog server is placed in each site except the Charleston sales office to meet minimum requirements. In addition, there are Microsoft Exchange 2000 servers in the Cincinnati, Pittsburgh, and Louisville sites, so by placing a global catalog server in each of these sites, query traffic can be handled promptly.

- A global catalog server is not placed in the Charleston location because of the relatively small number of users in this location and because the link is operating well below capacity.
- Because locating additional global catalog servers in each site will increase replication traffic, no additional global catalog servers are placed.

The reasons for locating operations masters in this manner are

- Because the domain has more than one domain controller, DC1 in the Cincinnati site was chosen as the operations master domain controller. The standby operations master controller is DC2 in the Cincinnati site.
- Because the domain is not very large, both the relative identifier master and PDC emulator roles were assigned to the operations master domain controller.
- Because the infrastructure master role should not be assigned to the domain controller that is hosting the global catalog, it was assigned to DC2.
- Because the schema master and the domain naming master roles should always be assigned to a domain controller designated as the global catalog server, and because their load is very light, the forest-wide roles were assigned to DC1.

More Info For further information on designing an Active Directory infrastructure design, view the online seminar "Designing the Active Directory Structure," located on the Supplemental Course Materials CD-ROM (\chapt06\OnlineSeminars\Designing). Click the Portal_ActiveDirectoryStructure file to begin the seminar.

You can also view the online seminar "Comparative Active Directory Designs," located on the Supplemental Course Materials CD-ROM (\chapt06\OnlineSeminars\Comparative). Click the Portal_ActiveDirectoryDesigns file to begin the seminar.

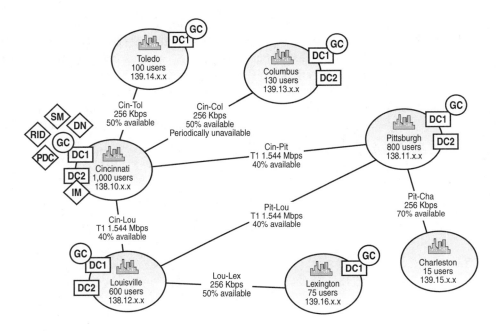

Figure 6.11   Global catalog server and operations masters locations for Margo Tea
Company

Lesson Summary

In this lesson you learned how to place global catalog servers and operations
masters for an organization by assessing an organization's need for global
catalog servers and operations masters. You learned that for optimum network
response time and application availability, you should designate at least one
domain controller in each site as the global catalog server. You also learned
that you must balance the need for additional global catalog servers with the
increased replication traffic that the additional servers will generate. You learned

some guidelines for assigning domain-wide operations master roles, which include not assigning the infrastructure master role to the domain controller that is hosting the global catalog. You learned some guidelines for assigning forest-wide operations master roles, which include always assigning the schema master and the domain naming master roles to the domain controller designated as the global catalog server. Finally, you learned to indicate the placement of global catalog servers and operations masters on the site diagram to create a completed site topology diagram.

Activity 6.2: Using Active Directory Sizer

In this activity you will use Active Directory Sizer to determine the number and location of domain controllers and global catalog servers for an organization that is planning its Active Directory infrastructure. To complete this activity, you will need to download and install Active Directory Sizer from *http:// www.microsoft.com/windows2000/library/resources/reskit/tools/new/adsizer-o.asp*.

Scenario: Margo Tea Company

Throughout this chapter we have used the scenario for Margo Tea Company as an example for defining sites, placing domain controllers, defining a replication strategy, and placing global catalog servers and operations masters within a forest. We performed these tasks manually to create a site topology plan. When you're creating a site topology plan, it's also a good idea to use the Active Directory Sizer tool to consider a more conservative estimation of the hardware required for deploying Active Directory. Active Directory Sizer uses data you input to estimate the

- Number of domain controllers per domain per site
- Number of global catalog servers per domain per site
- Number of CPUs per machine and type of CPU
- Number of disks needed for Active Directory data storage
- Amount of memory required
- Network bandwidth utilization
- Domain database size
- Global catalog database size
- Intersite replication bandwidth required

The procedures below walk you through the use of Active Directory Sizer to determine the number and placement of domain controllers and global catalog servers for Margo Tea Company.

▶ **To determine the number of domain controllers and global catalog servers**

1. Click Start, point to Programs, point to Active Directory Sizer, then click Active Directory Sizer.

2. Click File, then select New.

3. In the Active Directory Sizer Wizard, enter **Margo Tea Co.** as the name for the domain, then click Next.

4. On the User Accounts screen, enter **2720** for the total number of users and **80%** for the percentage of users active during peak hours. Use **25** for additional attributes. Click Next.

5. On the second User Accounts screen, use **7** for the average number of groups a user will belong to. Enter **45** days for password expiration frequency. For the average logon rate per second during peak hours, type **100** for interactive, **10** for batch, and **10** for network, then click Next.

6. On the Computers And Other Objects screen, enter **2720** for the number of Windows 2000 computers, **270** for the number of other computers, and **300** for the number of other objects to be published in Active Directory, then click Next.

7. On the second Computers And Other Objects screen, use the defaults for desired average CPU utilization and preferred CPU type. Click Next.

8. On the Administration screen, use **Weekly** as the time interval. For the average number of objects, type **55** for objects you plan to add, **25** for objects you plan to delete, and **500** for objects you plan to modify, and then click Next.

9. On the Exchange 2000 screen, select **Yes** to plan to use Microsoft Exchange 2000. Then use **25** for the average number of messages sent per day and the default for the average number of recipients for each message. Click Next.

10. On the Services Using Active Directory screen, select **Yes** to indicate that you plan to use Active Directory enabled DNS, **270** for the number of dial-in connections, and the defaults for Dynamic Host Configuration Protocol (DHCP) lease and NoRefreshInterval. Click Next.

11. On the second Services Using Active Directory screen, leave each of the estimates boxes blank (default). To actually complete this section, you must consult the documentation for Active Directory–enabled applications you want represented in the Sizer's estimates. Click Next.

12. On the Conclusion screen, click Finish.

The number of domain controllers and global catalog servers needed for this domain are displayed in the right pane.

Note In Active Directory Sizer, bridgehead servers are also domain controllers and global catalog servers.

Use the Active Directory Sizer tool with caution. Because Active Directory Sizer indicates only the number of domain controllers needed to satisfy logon, authentication, and replication requirements of the organization, it does not reflect the best practice of placing redundant domain controllers in each site.

▶ **To determine the location of domain controllers and global catalog servers and to plan sites**

1. Right-click Site Configuration in the left pane, and then click Add Site.

2. In the New Site dialog box, in the Site Name box, type **Cincinnati**, and then click Apply. Do the same for the **Toledo**, **Columbus**, **Pittsburgh**, **Charleston**, and **Louisville** sites. Then in the Site Name box, type **Lexington** and click OK.

3. Right-click Default-First Site in the left pane, and then click Distribute Users.

4. In the Distribute Users dialog box, click Default-First Site in the Source Site window, and then type **1000** in the Users To Move box. Click **Cincinnati** in the Destination Site window, and then click Apply.

5. Repeat the previous step for each of the remaining sites as indicated in the following table:

Users to move	Destination site
100	Toledo
130	Columbus
800	Pittsburgh
15	Charleston
600	Louisville
75	Lexington

6. Click OK.

The new server distributions for each site are located in the right pane.

Lab 6.1: Creating a Site Topology Plan

Lab Objectives

After completing this lab, you will be able to create a site topology plan.

About This Lab

In this lab, you will analyze portions of the existing environment at a medium-sized company to create a site topology plan.

Before You Begin

Before you begin this lab, you must be able to

- Analyze an organization's environment to define its sites

- Analyze an organization's environment to place domain controllers in sites

- Analyze an organization's environment to define its replication strategy

- Analyze an organization's environment to place global catalog servers in sites

- Analyze an organization's environment to assign operations master roles

Exercise: Creating a Site Topology Plan

In this exercise, you will analyze the existing environment at a medium-sized company to manually create a site topology plan. Review the scenario; then follow the instructions to create a site topology plan.

Scenario

Your design team is planning the Active Directory infrastructure for Fabrikam, Inc., a Japanese retailer of silk fabrics. Fabrikam, Inc., has three regional offices, located in Osaka, Tokyo, and Nagoya. The Nagoya location also serves as the company headquarters. There are 150 retail stores across Japan aligned under each regional office. There are five distribution centers, located in Sapporo, Kawasaki, Yokohama, Kyoto, and Fukuoka.

Your design team has created a network architecture diagram for Fabrikam, Inc., shown in Figure 6.12. Domain locations have also been included on the diagram. Each location has a high-speed backbone that connects a set of 10–100 Kbps LANs.

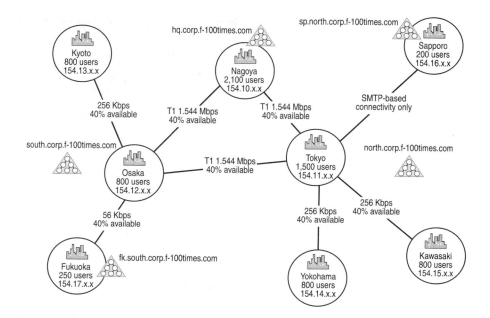

Figure 6.12   Network architecture diagram for Fabrikam, Inc.

Exercise Questions

Follow the instructions below to create a site topology plan.

1. Begin your site topology diagram by indicating the sites needed for Fabrikam, Inc. Explain your reasoning for defining each site.

2. Indicate the domain controllers needed for Fabrikam, Inc., on your site topology diagram. Explain your reasoning for placing each domain controller as you did.

3. Indicate the site links needed for Fabrikam, Inc., on your site topology diagram. Name each site link by using the first two letters of each connected site name. Indicate the site link configurations for each site link in the table below.

Site link	Transport	Cost	Frequency	Availability
_____	_____	____	_____	_____
_____	_____	____	_____	_____
_____	_____	____	_____	_____
_____	_____	____	_____	_____
_____	_____	____	_____	_____
_____	_____	____	_____	_____
_____	_____	____	_____	_____
_____	_____	____	_____	_____

4. Indicate the location of global catalog servers and operations masters for Fabrikam, Inc., on your site topology diagram. Explain your reasoning for placing each global catalog server and operations master.

Review

The following questions are intended to reinforce key information presented in the chapter. If you are unable to answer a question, review the appropriate lesson and then try the question again. Answers to the questions can be found in Appendix A, "Questions and Answers."

1. You are defining sites for an organization that has three sets of LANs, each connected by a T1 line. How many sites should you define?

2. You have placed the minimum number of domain controllers into sites for your organization. What are the reasons for placing additional domain controllers into sites?

3. You are configuring site links and you want to set up a site link table for your site topology plan. What configuration information should you include in the table?

4. Describe how Active Directory data is replicated between bridgehead servers during intersite replication. Then describe how Active Directory is replicated from the bridgehead server to other domain controllers within a site.

5. You are assigning the infrastructure master role to a domain controller that has been designated as the global catalog server. Explain why you should do this only under certain conditions and explain those conditions.

C H A P T E R 7

Creating an Active Directory Implementation Plan

About This Chapter

After you and your design team finish creating a site topology plan, the Active Directory directory services infrastructure design is complete and you are ready to begin thinking about implementing Active Directory. However, before you implement Active Directory, you must create an implementation plan that considers the issues involved in moving from your organization's current directory service to Active Directory. If your organization is running Microsoft Windows NT as its primary network operating system and using Windows NT directory services, you must gather information about the current setup and plan how you will make the transition to Windows 2000 Active Directory. If your organization is running another directory service, you must also gather information about the current setup and plan your transition to Windows 2000 Active Directory. This chapter explores directory service migration and synchronization issues that make up your Active Directory implementation plan.

Before You Begin

To complete this chapter, you must have

- Knowledge of Active Directory components and concepts covered in Chapter 1, "Introduction to Active Directory"

- Knowledge of business and technical environment analyses components covered in Chapter 2, "Introduction to Designing a Directory Services Infrastructure"

- Knowledge and skills covered in Chapter 3, "Creating a Forest Plan"

- Knowledge and skills covered in Chapter 4, "Creating a Domain Plan"

- Knowledge and skills covered in Chapter 5, "Creating an Organizational Unit Plan"

- Knowledge and skills covered in Chapter 6, "Creating a Site Topology Plan"

Lesson 1: Planning a Migration from Windows NT 4 Directory Services to Windows 2000 Active Directory

To implement Windows 2000 Active Directory in an organization running Microsoft Windows NT as its primary network operating system and using Windows NT directory services, you must plan how you will make the transition. To plan a Windows NT 4 directory services migration to Windows 2000 Active Directory, you must assess the organization's goals for migration, determine the migration method(s), and plan the migration steps. This lesson discusses how to a plan a migration from Windows NT 4 directory services to Windows 2000 Active Directory.

After this lesson, you will be able to

- Identify the factors in an organization's environment that determine its migration strategy

- Indicate the reasons for using the domain upgrade method

- Indicate the reasons for using the domain restructure method

- Explain the steps involved in planning a domain upgrade

- Explain the steps involved in planning a domain restructure

- Explain the steps involved in planning the consolidation of resource domains into organizational units (OUs)

- Analyze an organization's Windows NT 4 directory services environment to plan its migration to Windows 2000 Active Directory

Estimated lesson time: 30 minutes

Understanding Migration

Migration is the process of making existing applications and data work on a different computer or operating system. To migrate to Active Directory directory services, you must migrate a Windows NT Server 3.51 or 4 deployment to Windows 2000 Server. You cannot migrate a pre–Windows NT Server 3.51 deployment or Windows NT Server 4 Enterprise Edition to Windows 2000 Server, and you can migrate Windows NT Server 4 Enterprise Edition only to Windows 2000 Advanced Server. Table 7.1 shows the supported migration paths to Windows 2000 Server.

Table 7.1   Supported Migration Paths to Windows 2000 Server

Server role in Windows NT Server 3.51 or 4	Server role in Windows 2000 Server
Primary domain controller (PDC)	Domain controller
Backup domain controller (BDC)	Domain controller or member server
Member server	Member server
Standalone server	Member server or standalone server

Migration Methods

There are two methods for migrating to Windows 2000 Server:

- Domain upgrade
- Domain restructure

Domain Upgrade

A *domain upgrade* is the process of installing an existing Windows NT domain structure and its users and groups intact into the Windows 2000 DNS–based domain hierarchy, as shown in Figure 7.1. This method also retains most Windows NT system settings, preferences, and program installations. A domain upgrade is the easiest way to migrate to Windows 2000 Server and may also be referred to as an "in-place upgrade" or simply an "upgrade."

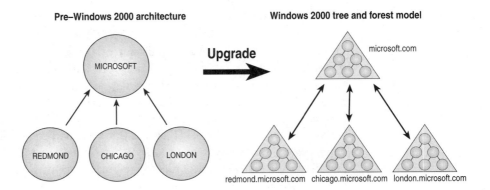

Figure 7.1   Domain upgrade

Although a domain upgrade can upgrade the PDC and BDCs in a Windows NT domain from Windows NT Server to Windows 2000 Server, all servers in a Windows NT domain need not be upgraded to take advantage of Windows 2000 features. Your organization can operate in mixed mode to handle the interoperability of Windows 2000 domain controllers and Windows NT BDCs.

When you use the domain upgrade method to migrate an existing Windows NT deployment, the following are preserved:

- Groups, user accounts, and passwords
- Access to Windows NT domains using existing Windows NT trust relationships
- Access to Windows NT servers, Windows 95, and Windows 98 clients

An upgrade is accomplished in two steps. First, the Windows NT PDC and BDCs are upgraded to Windows 2000 Server. Second, the Active Directory Installation Wizard is used to promote the Windows 2000 servers to Active Directory domain controllers, either as forest root domains, tree root domains, or child domains in a tree. Because member servers are not domain controllers, it is not necessary to install Active Directory on these servers; they need only be upgraded to Windows 2000 Server.

Domain Restructure

A *domain restructure* is a redesign of the Windows NT domain structure, which often results in fewer, consolidated domains, as shown in Figure 7.2. This method of migration allows organizations to redesign the structure to take full advantage of Windows 2000 features. A domain restructure migrates the existing Windows NT environment into a "pristine" Windows 2000 forest using a nondestructive copy. A *pristine forest* is an ideal Windows 2000 forest that is isolated from the Windows NT production environment and that operates in native mode. Domain accounts exist in both Windows NT and Windows 2000, and the Windows NT environment is retained until it is ready to be decommissioned. This method requires more administrative overhead, resources, and time. A domain restructure may also be referred to as a "domain consolidation" or simply a "restructure."

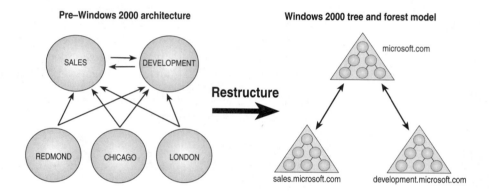

Figure 7.2   Domain restructure

Windows 2000 provides the following functionality to allow domain restructuring:

- The ability to move security principals from one domain to another

  Because users retain their SIDhistory when moved between domains, they are able to maintain the same access to resources they had before the move. SIDhistory is an attribute of Active Directory security principals that is used to store the former security IDs (SIDs) of moved objects, such as users and groups.

- The ability to move domain controllers from one domain to another

  Windows 2000 domain controllers can be moved between domains while retaining their settings, applications, and services and without having to completely reinstall the operating system.

A domain restructure is accomplished in several steps:

1. A pristine forest is created.
2. Trust relationships are established between the target Windows 2000 domain and the existing Windows NT resource domains to maintain access to resources in the resource domains during restructuring.
3. Windows NT global and shared local groups are cloned into the pristine forest.
4. User accounts are cloned into the pristine forest.
5. Computer accounts are moved to the pristine forest.
6. After testing and modification, the Windows NT domain is eventually retired.

The upgrade and restructure migration methods can be used separately or combined depending upon the needs of the organization. An organization may find it necessary to upgrade first and then restructure while another organization may recognize a need to restructure from the start. The upgrade strategy depends largely upon the current Windows NT domain model used by the organization.

Migrating Resource Domains

As discussed in Chapter 4, in Windows NT, domains are the smallest units of administrative delegation and additional domains are sometimes created for the purpose of containing the resources over which administrators have control. As discussed in Chapter 5, in Windows 2000, OUs allow you to partition domains to delegate administration, eliminating the need to define domains just for delegation. You can delegate administration for the contents of an OU container (all users, computers, or resource objects in the OU) by granting administrators specific permissions for an OU. By consolidating resource domains into OUs during Windows NT migration to Windows 2000, an organization can take full advantage of the OU feature. You can consolidate resource domains into OUs after a domain upgrade or a domain restructure.

Migration and the Production Environment

Because migration involves the transitioning of domains, groups, and users from Windows NT to the Windows 2000 environment, it's possible that an organization's everyday computing environment, called the *production environment*, may be affected by the migrations performed using the upgrade method. Possible effects include slowed response times and other interruptions in service. The IT management organization must determine what disruptions to the production environment, if any, are tolerable during the migration process and then take steps to minimize problems. You can take the following steps to minimize problems during an upgrade:

- Run tests of the planned upgrade in a test environment and monitor the test results.
- Perform upgrades during non-peak hours.
- Upgrade small domains first, monitor the effects of the upgrade, and adjust processes when upgrading larger domains.

Despite taking steps to minimize problems, the production environment may still be affected by the upgrade process. The safest way to migrate to Windows 2000 is to use the restructure method and create a parallel, pristine Windows 2000 forest that can be tested before it is actually implemented. Because the restructure method requires a great deal of hardware, testing, and administrative time, the IT management organization must weigh the costs of planning the restructure against the inconveniences to the production environment caused by the migration.

Migration and Windows 2000 Domain Modes

When you migrate a domain controller to Windows 2000 Server, the domain controller is set to run in mixed mode. Mixed mode allows the domain controller to interact with any domain controllers in the domain that are running previous versions of Windows NT. You can allow a domain to run in mixed mode indefinitely, or you can set the mode to native mode.

When all the domain controllers in the domain run Windows 2000 Server, and you do not plan to add any more pre–Windows 2000 domain controllers to the domain, you can switch the domain from mixed mode to native mode.

During the conversion from mixed mode to native mode,

- Support for pre–Windows 2000 replication ceases. Because pre–Windows 2000 replication is gone, you can no longer have any domain controllers in your domain that are not running Windows 2000 Server.

- You can no longer add pre–Windows 2000 domain controllers to the domain.

- The server that served as the primary domain controller during migration is no longer the domain master; all domain controllers act as peers.

Note The change from mixed mode to native mode is one-way only; you cannot change from native mode to mixed mode.

Although all the domain controllers in the domain must be migrated to Windows 2000 Server in order to make the switch to native mode, it is not necessary to upgrade all or any of the member servers to make the switch. As long as all domain controllers have been migrated, you can switch to native mode and still have Windows NT, Windows 95, or Windows 98 computers participating in the domain.

Active Directory Migration Tool

The Active Directory Migration Tool (ADMT) is provided to migrate existing Windows NT 4 and earlier domains into Windows 2000. It can also be used to consolidate multiple Windows 2000 domains (within the same forest or within different forests) into a single domain. ADMT allows you to test the migration settings and analyze the migration impact before and after the migration process.

To assist you in the migration process, ADMT employs the following wizards:

- User Migration, to identify and migrate user accounts and migrate roaming profiles
- Group Migration, to identify and migrate global and shared local groups
- Computer Migration, to identify and migrate workstations and member servers
- Security Translation, to migrate local profiles and update service account user rights
- Reporting, to generate migration reports
- Service Account Migration, to migrate service accounts and identify service accounts not running under local system authority
- Exchange Directory Migration, to update Exchange after migrating users
- Undo, to undo the last migration operation
- Retry Tasks, to retry a task involving a migration agent
- Trust Migration, to establish trusts between domains
- Group Mapping And Merging, to map a group in the source domain to a different group in the target domain

ADMT is used with the restructure method of migration. To use ADMT, you first design and build a pristine Windows 2000 forest separate from your existing domain structure. Then you use ADMT to migrate user accounts, groups, and computer accounts, in stages, from your production environment to the new Windows 2000 forest. Eventually, you will decommission the old domain structure. ADMT is not used with the upgrade method of migration because this method requires no restructuring of the domain architecture. However, after upgrading your Windows NT domains you may need to restructure. If so, you can create a new Windows 2000 forest and use ADMT to migrate the upgraded domains into the new forest.

How ADMT Works

When migrating objects from computers in a source domain to a target domain, ADMT installs services, called agents, on the source computers. These agents are dispatched from the computer on which ADMT is running and are installed on other computers using the security credentials of the user account used to run ADMT. Once installed, the agents run as a service using the local system security credentials. There is no need to load software on the source computers prior to the migration.

You can download ADMT from the Microsoft Web site. For more information about ADMT, visit *http://www.microsoft.com/windows2000/library/planning/activedirectory/admt.asp*.

Note A discussion of the actual process of migrating to Active Directory is beyond the scope of this training kit. This lesson covers the tasks necessary to plan a migration from Windows NT 4 directory services to Active Directory. For more information, refer to *the Microsoft Windows 2000 Server Deployment Planning Guide* volume of the *Microsoft Windows 2000 Server Resource Kit*.

More Info For further information on migrating from Windows NT 4 to Windows 2000, view the online seminar "How to Migrate Your Windows NT 4.0 Directory Services to Windows 2000 Active Directory," located on the Supplemental Course Materials CD-ROM (\chapt07\Migration). Click the Portal_Migration file to begin the seminar. You can also read the white paper "Planning Migration from Windows NT to Windows 2000," on the Supplemental Course Materials CD-ROM (\chapt07\PlanningDomainMigration).

Design Step: Planning a Windows NT 4 Directory Services Migration to Windows 2000 Active Directory

To plan a Windows NT 4 directory services migration to Windows 2000 Active Directory, you must complete the following tasks:

1. Assess the organization's goals for migration.
2. Determine the migration method(s).
3. Plan the migration steps.
4. Plan the consolidation of resource domains into OUs, if applicable.

Assessing Migration Goals

To assess the organization's migration goals, you must first consult the following documents compiled earlier by your design team:

- Windows NT Domain Architecture Worksheet. Examine the existing Windows NT domains and trust relationships and determine those that should be included in the Active Directory forest. Examine the existing Windows NT domain controllers and determine the number and location of domain controllers to be upgraded.

- DNS Environment Worksheet. Examine the existing DNS namespace and determine whether or how it should be included in Active Directory.

Note Blank copies of the worksheets are located on the Supplemental Course Materials CD-ROM (\chapt02\worksheets). Completed examples of the worksheets are located in Chapter 2, "Introduction to Designing a Directory Services Infrastructure." The Forest Model is discussed in Chapter 3, "Creating a Forest Plan."

In addition to assessing the information in these worksheets, it is imperative that you assess any changes to the domain architecture currently planned to address growth, flexibility, and the ideal design specifications of the organization.

Determining the Migration Method

By asking yourself a few simple questions, you can determine whether to migrate to Windows 2000 by using the domain upgrade method, the domain restructure method, or the domain upgrade followed by the domain restructure method.

- Use the domain upgrade method when both of the following are true:
    - The current Windows NT domain structure functions well.
    - The current production environment can withstand possible negative effects as a result of the migration process.

- Use the domain restructure method when one of the following is true:
    - The current Windows NT domain structure does not function well and will not function well even with a few simple modifications.
    - The current production environment cannot withstand any negative effects as a result of the migration process.

- Use the domain upgrade method followed by the domain restructure method when both of the following are true:
    - The current Windows NT domain structure would function well with a few simple modifications.
    - The current production environment can withstand possible negative effects as a result of the migration process.

Planning the Migration

Depending upon the method(s) selected for the migration, you must plan one or more of the following:

- The domain upgrade
- The domain restructure
- The consolidation of resource domains into OUs

Planning a Domain Upgrade

Important Before planning a domain upgrade, you must first complete the design of your Active Directory infrastructure, which includes a forest plan, domain plan, OU plan, and site topology plan as described in Chapters 3 through 6.

To plan a domain upgrade, you will need to determine a recovery plan, the order for upgrading domains, a strategy for upgrading domain controllers, and when to switch to native mode.

Determining a Recovery Plan A recovery plan helps you prevent accidental data loss during the upgrade process. A recovery plan should include the following steps:

1. Ensure each Windows NT domain has at least one BDC. If the PDC upgrade fails, the BDC can be promoted and continue to function, preventing the domain from becoming orphaned. Maintaining one BDC also ensures the ability to roll back to Windows NT domains after upgrading.

2. Back up network services. If services such as file and print services, DHCP, or WINS are running on the PDC or BDCs, back them up and test the backup.

3. Create a spare BDC. By creating a spare BDC, synchronizing it with the PDC, and taking it offline during the PDC upgrade, you can create an image of the Windows NT domain information as it is before the PDC upgrade.

4. Synchronize all BDCs with the PDC. Force all BDCs, including the spare BDC, to synchronize with the PDC. Check to be sure all BDCs have the current domain information and that information is being replicated.

5. Take the spare BDC offline and place it in a secure area. This action provides safe storage of the Windows NT domain information image.

6. Perform a complete backup. Backup domain-based information immediately before the PDC is upgraded.

Determining the Order for Upgrading Domains You should upgrade domains in the following order:

1. Forest root domain. If a Windows NT domain is to become the forest root, it should be upgraded first.

   Note The forest root domain does not have to be an upgraded Windows NT domain. The Windows NT domains you upgrade can join an existing Windows 2000 forest root domain.

2. Small account domains. By upgrading small account domains early, you allow users to take advantage of Windows 2000 features as soon as possible while limiting the number of users initially impacted by the upgrade. After the first small account domain is upgraded, you can determine the impact of the upgrade on users, learn from it, and adjust the process to streamline the upgrade of the remaining domains.

3. Larger account domains and remaining account domains. By upgrading the larger account domains after the small account domains, you allow users to take advantage of Windows 2000 features as soon as possible while incorporating the experience of upgrading the smaller domains first.

   Note If you plan to upgrade resource domains, follow Steps 4 and 5. However, if you plan to consolidate resource domains into OUs, refer to the section entitled "Planning the Consolidation of Resource Domains into OUs," later in this lesson, for further information.

4. Resource domains that require the Windows 2000 platform or features. By upgrading the resource domains that require the Windows 2000 platform or features early, you can take advantage of new applications such as Microsoft IntelliMirror or Remote OS Installation as soon as possible.

5. Remaining resource domains. If you plan to consolidate resource domains, upgrade those you've identified as target domains early. You must have a target domain in order to consolidate domains. Then upgrade the remaining resource domains that will be consolidated into the target domains.

Note It is not necessary to upgrade *all* account domains before upgrading resource domains.

Determining a Strategy for Upgrading Domain Controllers   You should upgrade domain controllers in the following order:

1. The PDC in the first domain to be upgraded.

2. The BDCs in the first domain to be upgraded, except for the spare one you set aside.

3. The PDC in the second domain to be upgraded.

4. The BDCs in the second domain to be upgraded, except for the spare one you set aside.

5. Continue upgrading the PDC followed by the BDCs for each remaining domain to be upgraded, in order.

Determining When to Switch to Native Mode   Although you can allow a domain to run in mixed mode indefinitely, it's best to plan the switch to native mode as soon as possible in order to take advantage of all Windows 2000 features. However, once you switch a domain to native mode, you cannot switch it back to mixed mode or to a Windows NT domain. Therefore, you must carefully consider the advantages of operating in native mode and the reasons why you may want to consider operating in mixed mode.

The advantages of operating in native mode are

- Universal groups and domain local groups are available; also group nesting is permitted.

- Active Directory multimaster replication is enabled between all domain controllers, rather than just the domain controller assigned the PDC emulator role.

The main reasons for remaining in mixed mode are

- To maintain a BDC in the domain. Some applications, such as those that must avoid pass-through authentication, may operate only on a Windows NT BDC. For the application to run, the BDC cannot be upgraded and demoted to a member server and can operate only in Windows 2000 mixed mode.

- The inability to provide physical security for BDCs. Because of the multi-master directory update capability in Windows 2000, domain controllers require a secured physical environment. Because of the single master directory update capability in Windows NT, BDCs require a less secure physical environment. If the BDC cannot be secured, it should not be upgraded and the domain should continue to operate in mixed mode.

- To allow rollback to Windows NT domains. In some organizations, it may be necessary to roll back to Windows NT for technical, administrative, or political reasons. Maintaining at least one BDC in the domain and running in mixed mode allows the domain to roll back to Windows NT.

► **To plan a domain upgrade**

1. List the steps in your recovery plan.

2. List the domains to be upgraded, in order.

3. List the strategy for upgrading domain controllers in each domain.

4. Indicate when you plan to switch to native mode.

Planning a Domain Restructure

To plan a domain restructure, you will need to establish a restructure timeframe, design a pristine forest, identify the trust relationships for resource domains, and map the groups and users to be migrated.

Note Because a domain restructure migrates the existing Windows NT environment into a pristine Windows 2000 forest using a nondestructive copy, domain accounts exist in both Windows NT and Windows 2000 and the Windows NT environment is retained until it is ready to be decommissioned. Therefore, fallback is possible at any time and a separate recovery plan is not needed.

Establishing a Restructure Timeline   Depending on the needs of the organization, you can plan a domain restructure in three different timeframes:

- Following a domain upgrade. In situations where the current Windows NT domain structure would function well with a few simple modifications, plan a domain restructure after a domain upgrade. The domain upgrade handles the least complex parts of the migration, such as upgrading domains in which the trust structure remains unchanged and in which there are no administrative issues. The domain restructure handles more detailed aspects of migration, such as restructuring the domains to reduce complexity or bringing the resource domains into the forest in a secure manner. The most likely time for a domain restructure is after a domain upgrade.

- In place of a domain upgrade. In situations where the current Windows NT domain structure does not function well and will not function well even with a few simple modifications or when the current production environment cannot withstand any negative effects as a result of the migration process, plan a domain restructure in place of a domain upgrade. A restructure occurring in this timeframe requires the design of a pristine forest followed by the slow migration of users, groups, and resources into the forest to allow the organization to continue normal operations. When the migrations are completed successfully, the restructured environment becomes the production environment.

- Post migration. In situations where the current Windows 2000 domain structure becomes unsuitable, such as after organizational changes or acquisitions, a domain restructure may be required. These situations may occur months or years after the initial migration from Windows NT and may require the transitioning of domains or the complete design of a pristine forest.

Designing a Pristine Forest   To design a pristine forest you must follow the steps for designing an Active Directory infrastructure, which includes creating a forest plan, domain plan, OU plan, and site topology plan as described in Chapters 3 through 6. After the pristine forest is actually created, switch the domains to native mode.

Identifying the Trust Relationships for Resource Domains   To ensure that users can continue to access resources in resource domains during the domain restructure process, you must identify the explicit one-way nontransitive trust relationships that are necessary between Windows NT resource domains and the Windows 2000 domain to which you are transitioning users. These trusts are also necessary to allow administration of the Windows NT source domain from the Windows 2000 domain.

Mapping the Groups and Users to be Migrated   To ensure that users can log on to the Windows 2000 domain and access resources in the Windows NT resource domain, you must identify the Windows NT global and domain local groups to be moved into the pristine forest and the location to which they will be moved. Because a global group can contain members only from its own domain, when a user is moved from the Windows NT domain to the Windows 2000 domain, the global groups of which the user is a member are also moved. Similarly, when a global group is moved from the Windows NT domain to the Windows 2000 domain, the members of the global group are also moved.

▶ **To plan a domain restructure**

1. Indicate when the restructure should take place.

2. Create an Active Directory infrastructure plan for the pristine forest.

3. On the Windows NT Architecture Worksheet, indicate the trust relationships that must be set up in order for users to continue to access resource domains during the migration process.

4. List the present location of Windows NT users and groups and their location in the pristine forest.

Planning the Consolidation of Resource Domains into OUs

To plan the consolidation of resource domains into OUs, you will need to map the resources to be migrated and identify the trust relationships needed for domains outside the target forest.

To ensure that users can access the appropriate resources, you must identify the Windows NT resources to be consolidated and the OU to which they will be consolidated. If there are Windows NT or Windows 2000 domains outside the target OU's forest and the users in these domains require access to the resources you are consolidating into the target OU, you must establish the appropriate explicit one-way nontransitive trust relationships with those domains.

▶   **To plan the consolidation of resource domains into OUs**

1. List the present location of resources in Windows NT and the OUs to which the resources will be consolidated.

2. Indicate the trust relationships that must be set up in order for users outside of the forest to access resources when they are consolidated in the target OU.

Design Step Example: Planning a Windows NT 4 Directory Services Migration to Windows 2000 Active Directory

You may recall that Windows NT domains can be grouped into one of four domain models based on administrative needs:

- Single domain model
- Single master domain model
- Multimaster domain model
- Multiple trust domain model

Each domain model requires a different strategy when migrating to Windows 2000.

Migration Strategies for the Single Domain Model

In the single domain model, all servers, users, and other resources are contained in the domain. The single Windows NT domain is migrated using the upgrade method, and the Windows NT domain simply becomes the forest root domain in the new Windows 2000 tree, as shown in Figure 7.3.

Single Windows NT domain model   Single Windows 2000 domain

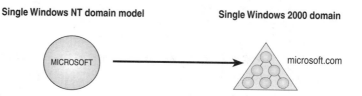

Figure 7.3   Migrating a Windows NT single domain model

Migration Plan

Because this migration strategy uses the domain upgrade method, the migration plan includes

- A recovery plan
- A strategy for updating domain controllers
- A plan to switch to native mode

Because there is only one domain to be upgraded, there is no need for a list of domains to be upgraded.

Migration Strategies for the Single Master Domain Model

The single master domain model places all user accounts and groups into one master domain, called the *account domain*, for centralized administration. All printers and servers are grouped into other domains, called *resource domains*. Users with access rights in the account domain (the trusted domain) can access resources in the resource domain (the trusting domain) through one-way non-transitive trusts.

If the domains in the single master domain model are migrated using the upgrade method, the master account domain becomes the forest root domain in the new Windows 2000 tree. At this point, the forest root domain is running Windows 2000 in mixed mode and the resource domains are still running Windows NT, as shown in Figure 7.4. Functionality, performance, and security continue as normal in the following manner:

- The one-way nontransitive trust relationships between the master domain and the resource domains remain valid.

- Clients in the network continue to authenticate to the master domain using the Windows NT Net Logon service.

- Single master replication occurs between the new domain controller and the Windows NT 4 BDCs in the forest root domain.

- The new domain controller appears as a Windows NT 4 PDC to each pre–Windows 2000 client.

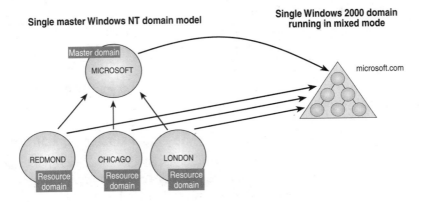

Figure 7.4   Partial migration of a Windows NT single master domain model

To complete the migration to Windows 2000, each of the resource domains can be migrated using the upgrade method to become the child domains of the forest root domain, as shown in Figure 7.5. The resource domains should then be consolidated into OUs, which can be used to organize users and resources within the domains.

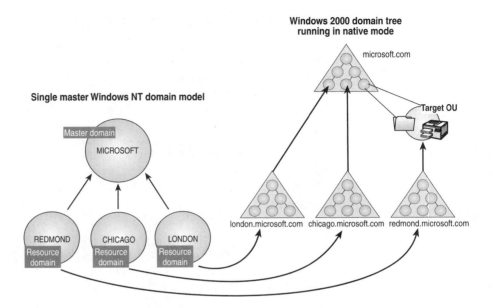

Figure 7.5   Complete migration of a Windows NT single master domain model

Migration Plan

Because this migration strategy uses the domain upgrade method followed by a consolidation of resource domains into OUs, the migration plan includes

- A recovery plan
- A list of domains to be upgraded
- A strategy for upgrading domain controllers in each domain
- A list of the present locations of Windows NT resources and the OUs to which the resources will be consolidated
- An indication of the trust relationships that must be set up in order for users outside of the forest to access resources when the resources are consolidated in the target OU
- A plan to switch to native mode

Multimaster Domain Model Migration Strategy

The multimaster domain model is similar to the single master model, except it groups all user accounts and groups into more than one master account domain for decentralized administration. Printers and servers are grouped into resource domains. Like the single master domain model, users with access rights in the account domains can access resources in the resource domains through one-way nontransitive trusts.

If the domains in the multimaster domain model are migrated using the upgrade method, any one of the master account domains or a new, dedicated domain must become the forest root domain. Then the remaining account domains become the child domains of the forest root domain, and the resource domains become the child domains of the account domains. The resource domains should then be consolidated into OUs to organize users and resources within the domains. Figure 7.6 shows a new dedicated domain as the forest root domain, the placement of the account domains (sales.microsoft.com and development.microsoft.com), and the placement of the resource domains (london.microsoft.com, chicago.microsoft.com, and redmond.microsoft.com).

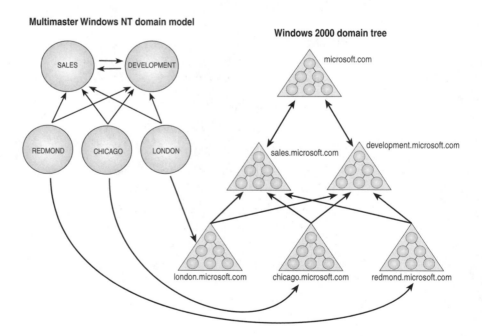

Figure 7.6   Migrating a Windows NT multimaster domain model

Migration Plan

Because this migration strategy uses the domain upgrade method followed by a consolidation of resource domains into OUs, the migration plan is similar to the one used for the single master domain model.

Multiple Trust Domain Model Migration Strategy

The multiple trust domain model is a web of independently managed trust relationships set up to accommodate decentralized administration and is extremely difficult to manage. If the multiple trust domain model is migrated using the upgrade method, one of the existing domains or a new, dedicated domain must become the forest root domain. The remaining domains become the child domains of the forest root domain. Domains should then be consolidated into OUs to organize users and resources within the domains. Figure 7.7 shows one of the domains selected to be the forest root domain and the placement of the remaining domains.

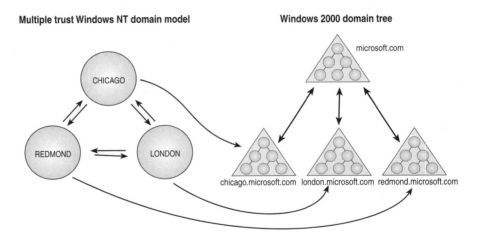

Figure 7.7   Migrating a Windows NT multiple trust domain model

Migration Plan

Because this migration strategy uses the domain upgrade method followed by a consolidation of resource domains into OUs, the migration plan is similar to the one used for the single master domain model.

Lesson Summary

In this lesson you learned how to plan a Windows NT 4 directory services migration to Windows 2000 Active Directory by assessing the organization's goals for migration, determining the migration method(s), and planning the migration steps. You learned how to determine the migration method(s) by analyzing how the current Windows NT domain structure functions and determining whether the current production environment can withstand possible negative effects as a result of the migration process. You learned that to plan a domain upgrade, you will need to determine a recovery plan, the order for upgrading domains, a strategy for upgrading domain controllers, and when to switch to native mode. To plan a domain restructure, you will need to establish a restructure timeframe, design a pristine forest, identify the trust relationships for resource domains, and map the groups and users to be migrated. Finally, you learned that to plan the consolidation of resource domains into OUs, you will need to map the resources to be migrated and identify the trust relationships needed for domains outside the target forest.

Lesson 2: Planning Directory Service Synchronization with Active Directory

To implement Windows 2000 Active Directory in an organization running another directory service, you must plan your transition. Active Directory is designed to extend Windows 2000 interoperability and allows you to synchronize directory information with other directory services. Active Directory is able to synchronize with Microsoft Exchange Server 5.5 directory service, Novell NetWare Bindery or Novell Directory Services (NDS), and other LDAP-compliant directory services. This lesson discusses how to plan the synchronization of your existing directory service with Windows 2000 Active Directory.

After this lesson, you will be able to

- Identify the tools needed to synchronize Exchange Server 5.5 directory service with Active Directory

- Identify the tools needed to synchronize Novell NetWare Bindery or NDS with Active Directory

- Identify the tools needed to synchronize other LDAP-compliant directory services with Active Directory

- Explain how to plan the synchronization of Exchange Server 5.5 directory service with Active Directory

- Explain how to plan the synchronization of Novell NetWare Bindery or NDS with Active Directory

Estimated lesson time: 30 minutes

Understanding Directory Service Synchronization

Recall that a directory service is a network service that identifies resources on a network and makes them accessible to users and applications. There are many types of directory services. Some, such as Active Directory, are designed for network computing, whereas others are designed to handle particular applications, such as e-mail. Because Active Directory is designed to extend Windows 2000 interoperability, it has the ability to synchronize directory information with other directory services. *Directory synchronization* is the sharing of data between two directory services so that changes made to objects in one directory are propagated automatically to the other directory. When data is synchronized between directory services, system administration is more efficient because there is no longer a need to manage multiple directories.

Note A discussion of the actual process setting up synchronization with Active Directory is beyond the scope of this training kit. This lesson covers the tasks necessary to plan Active Directory synchronization with Exchange Server 5.5, Novell Directory Services (NDS), and NetWare 3.*x* Binderies. Refer to the *Microsoft Windows 2000 Server Deployment Planning Guide* volume of the *Microsoft Windows 2000 Server Resource Kit* for more information.

Active Directory is currently able to synchronize with the directory services used by the following:

- Microsoft Exchange Server 5.5
- Novell NetWare Bindery or NDS
- Other LDAP-compliant directory services

Note For Exchange 2000 Server, the successor to Exchange Server 5.5, the Exchange Server directory service is seamlessly integrated with Active Directory and no synchronization is necessary.

Synchronizing with Microsoft Exchange Server 5.5

When an Exchange Server 5.5 directory is synchronized with Active Directory, both directories are maintained in their own information stores. Information is replicated between the directory services in a manner similar to that of Windows 2000 replication. By synchronizing the Microsoft Exchange Server 5.5 directory with Windows 2000 Server Active Directory, you can use Exchange Server to initially populate a new Active Directory with user attributes and objects. In addition, because Exchange Server supports third-party e-mail directory services, you can copy third-party directory user attributes and objects into Exchange Server and then synchronize the third-party data into Active Directory.

Note To synchronize data between Active Directory and Exchange Server 5.5, Exchange Server 5.5 Service Pack 1 or later must be installed.

To set up synchronization between Active Directory and Exchange Server 5.5, you must install the Active Directory Connector (ADC). The installation files for ADC are located on the Windows 2000 Server CD in the Valueadd\Msft\Mgmt\ADC folder. After installation, you can use the Active Directory Connector Management tool to set up *connection agreements*, which define how synchronization will occur. For each connection agreement, you can specify

- The direction of replication: two-way, from Exchange to Windows, or from Windows to Exchange
- The method of authentication used for the replication
- The replication schedule
- The objects to be replicated
- How the replication of deleted objects is handled

You can also set up a *primary connection agreement*, which allows you to create new objects in the destination directory in addition to replicating information about existing objects. It is recommended that you set up only one primary connection agreement per Exchange Server and Active Directory synchronization to ensure that duplicate objects are not created in the destination directory.

Synchronizing with Novell NetWare Bindery or NDS

Some organizations that use Novell NetWare will find it convenient and cost effective to introduce Active Directory while continuing to use their existing Novell directory. As with Exchange Server, when you synchronize a Novell NetWare Bindery or NDS directory with Active Directory, you maintain both directories in their own information stores rather than replace one directory with the other. Information is replicated between the directory services in a manner similar to that of Windows 2000 replication.

To enable users of Novell directory services to implement synchronization, Microsoft developed Microsoft Directory Synchronization Services (MSDSS), which is included with Services for NetWare version 5 (SFNW5). MSDSS is managed by using a Microsoft Management Console (MMC) snap-in, and supports Active Directory synchronization with the following Novell directory services:

- NDS for Novell NetWare 4, 4.1, 4.11, 4.2, 5, 5 with NDS 8, and 5.1
- Bindery for Novell NetWare 3.1, 3.11, 3.12, and 3.2, as well as NetWare 4.*x* configured in bindery emulation mode.

Using MSDSS, you can choose one-way or two-way synchronization when you initially set up a synchronization session for a pair of containers. One-way synchronization is available for either Bindery or NDS and lets you manage objects in both directories from Active Directory. Two-way synchronization is available for NDS only and lets you manage shared data, such as user account information, from either directory.

For both Bindery and NDS, MSDSS synchronization maps Novell user, group, and distribution list objects to Active Directory user, group, and distribution list objects. For NDS only, MSDSS maps Novell OUs and organizations to Active Directory OUs. Also for NDS only, MSDSS synchronization provides optional custom object mapping that lets you map objects in dissimilar directory structures to each other.

A Word About Migrating Novell Bindery or NDS Directories to Windows 2000 Active Directory

Rather than synchronize with Active Directory, some organizations may want to migrate their Novell Bindery or NDS directory to Active Directory. MSDSS migration and the Microsoft File Migration Utility (also included with SFNW5), enable you to migrate your Novell Bindery or NDS directory to Active Directory and your file system to the Windows 2000 NTFS version 5 file system (NTFS5). The File Migration Utility supports migration for the following Novell directory services:

- NDS for Novell NetWare 4.2, 5, and 5.1
- Bindery for Novell NetWare 3.12

Using MSDSS migration, you can choose whether to migrate NDS or Bindery objects and files to Active Directory immediately or to implement a phased migration. In an immediate migration, you perform a quick, secure, one-time migration of NDS or Bindery objects and files to Active Directory. In a phased migration, (often employed by organizations with complex directory scenarios) you set up and maintain synchronization for a period of weeks or months, keeping both directories available for the migration of users, computers, services, and applications in planned stages. By moving from a Novell-based directory to Active Directory over a period of time, you minimize the disruption of users.

MSDSS migration enables you to automatically migrate Bindery or NDS directory objects that store the largest amount of information and the most important information, such as user accounts, groups, and distribution lists (for both Bindery and NDS), and (for NDS only) OUs and organizations. All other object classes, such as machine accounts, printer objects, application objects, and object security permissions must be migrated manually.

By using the File Migration Utility in conjunction with MSDSS, you can migrate all or part of your NetWare folders and files to one or more Windows 2000–based file servers. The NetWare structure, the existing rights, and the existing permissions are maintained in the Windows 2000 file system, NTFS version 5 (NTFS5).

More Info Read the white papers "MSDSS Deployment: Understanding Synchronization and Migration" and "MSDSS Deployment: Implementing Synchronization and Migration," for a discussion of how MSDSS enables interoperability between Active Directory and the Novell NetWare operating system's Novell Directory Service (NDS) and NetWare 3.x Binderies. You can find the white papers on the Supplemental Course Materials CD-ROM (\chapt07\MSDSSund and \chapt07\MSDSSimp).

Synchronizing with Other LDAP-Compliant Directory Services

Some organizations have sophisticated directory management needs, including the need to synchronize more than two directory services, the need for business rule-based processing, or the need to join namespaces to manage objects and attributes across multiple isolated data stores. For these organizations, Microsoft

Metadirectory Services (MMS) is available through a service engagement with trained providers.

MMS allows the integration of identity and directory from multiple repositories with Active Directory. This allows organizations to manage diverse information and reduces the cost of directory management. MMS allows the integration of information from platforms such as Microsoft Windows 2000, Microsoft Active Directory, Microsoft Windows NT, Microsoft Exchange, Lotus Notes, Domino, cc: Mail, Novell NDS, Bindery, GroupWise, Netscape Directory and MetaDirectory Server, ISOCOR MetaConnect and X.500, various ODBC/SQL databases, and other systems.

As of this writing, MMS is still a relatively new synchronization tool, available only through Microsoft Consulting Services or an MMS partner. Check the Microsoft Web site at *www.microsoft.com* for the most up-to-date information.

More Info For further information on using MMS, read the white paper "Microsoft Metadirectory Services," on the Supplemental Course Materials CD-ROM (\chapt07\metadire).

Design Step: Planning Directory Service Synchronization with Active Directory

The design step for planning directory service synchronization with Active Directory has been divided into two areas:

- Planning Microsoft Exchange Server 5.5 synchronization with Active Directory
- Planning Novell NetWare Bindery or NDS synchronization with Active Directory

Design Step: Planning Microsoft Exchange Server 5.5 Synchronization with Active Directory

To plan Microsoft Exchange Server 5.5 synchronization with Active Directory, you must complete the following tasks:

1. Analyze the current Windows 2000 domain structure and Exchange Server site topology.

2. Map Exchange Server sites and containers to Active Directory domains and OUs.

3. Define objects to be synchronized.

4. Map Exchange Server attributes to Active Directory attributes.

5. Determine the location of Active Directory Connectors.

6. Define the connection agreements needed to synchronize directories.

7. Configure connection agreements.

Analyzing the Current Domain Structure and Exchange Server Site Topology

To synchronize the Exchange Server 5.5 directory service with Windows 2000 Server Active Directory, you must first understand the Exchange Server and Windows 2000 structures that exist in your organization. For Exchange Server, you must determine the number of sites, how the sites are managed, and whether the site will be synchronized with Active Directory. For those Exchange Server sites that will be synchronized, you must also identify the objects to be synchronized and the target container to which the objects will be synchronized.

Mapping Exchange Server Sites and Containers to Active Directory Domains and OUs

By mapping Exchange Server sites and containers to Active Directory domains and OUs, you create a logical path over which objects can travel between the directories. Each connection agreement you create will be based on these paths. An Exchange container can map to multiple Active Directory OUs and an Active Directory OU can map to multiple Exchange containers.

Defining Directory Objects to Be Synchronized

To define the directory objects to be synchronized, identify the objects and containers you want to synchronize. Then determine how the objects will be represented in the target directory.

Mapping Exchange Server Attributes to Active Directory Attributes

You can map Exchange Server attributes to attributes within Active Directory or to new custom attributes. Attribute mapping is controlled by settings on the ADC group policy object in Active Directory. The following object attributes will not synchronize: Advanced Security settings in Exchange and Access Control Lists (ACLs) in both Exchange and Active Directory.

Note A detailed discussion of the ADC group policy is beyond the scope of this training kit. You can find additional information in the *Microsoft Windows 2000 Server Deployment Planning Guide* volume of the *Microsoft Windows 2000 Server Resource Kit* for more information.

Determining the Location of Active Directory Connectors

The minimum requirements for installing ADC are at least one Windows 2000 server; one Active Directory domain; and, at each Exchange Server site, at least one Exchange Server 5.5 with Service Pack 1 or higher. You should also consider the number of ADC servers that will be required to replicate the data. To avoid ADC traffic across the WAN, a separate ADC should be configured for each site in every Active Directory domain that will host synchronized mailbox objects. The ADC server requires direct IP connectivity because it uses LDAP requests and RPC requests when it writes to the Exchange directory.

ADC can be set up on the following servers:

- Active Directory domain controller
- Active Directory domain controller with Exchange Server
- Active Directory global catalog
- Active Directory global catalog with Exchange Server
- Active Directory member server
- Active Directory member server with Exchange Server
- Active Directory member server with Exchange Server on an Active Directory domain controller
- Active Directory member server with Exchange Server on an Active Directory global catalog

Defining Connection Agreements

For optimal performance, you must determine the minimum number of connection agreements. It is not always necessary to create a connection agreement between each Exchange Server site and Windows 2000 Server domain. However, you must have enough connection agreements to handle replication. Consider the following when determining the number of connection agreements for your organization:

- Speed, number of CPUs, and amount of RAM for each Windows 2000 server, Exchange server, and ADC server. If any of these items could impede replication, you should consider additional connection agreements.

- Network bandwidth. If network bandwidth impedes replication, you should consider additional connection agreements.

- Number of Exchange Server mailboxes and Active Directory users, number of Exchange Server mail recipients and Active Directory contacts, and number of Exchange Server distribution lists, Active Directory groups, and Active Directory servers. If there are more than 500 of any of these objects, you should divide them among several connection agreements.

Configuring Connection Agreements

For each connection agreement you must specify the direction of replication, the schedule of replication, the authentication method, the attributes to be replicated, and the manner in which deleted objects will be handled.

To specify the direction of replication, you must determine how your organization manages the information that's being synchronized. You can manage information on security accounts, directory identity, and messaging from Active Directory. However, you can administer mail recipient objects from Exchange Server, Active Directory, or both directory services. The directory service that manages object identity is determined by the direction of replication you set in a connection agreement.

To specify the replication schedule, you must consider the number of users or mailboxes to be replicated, the frequency of the changes, and the replication schedules for other connection agreements.

The authentication method is the type of authentication the connection agreement uses to make a connection, either not encrypted or with SSL encryption. SSL encryption should be used when replicating to a server in another location. Each connection agreement requires you to set up an account that has permission to read from Exchange Server and Active Directory and permission to write to the target directory.

Each connection agreement allows you to specify the attributes to be replicated, which was discussed earlier in the "Defining Directory Objects to Be Synchronized" section.

Each connection object allows you to specify how deleted objects will be handled. If the connection agreement is replicating from Active Directory to Exchange Server, you can select one of the following options for handling deleted objects:

- Delete The Exchange Mailboxes, Custom Recipients And Distribution Lists. If a user account is removed from Active Directory, the user's Exchange Server mailbox is deleted and the user is deleted from mail recipient and distribution lists

- Keep The Exchange Deleted Items And Store The Deletion List In The Temporary .CSV File. The list of deleted objects is placed in a comma separated values (CSV) log file. Information is appended to this file as replication occurs. The log file is located in %SystemRoot%\MSADC*Connection Agreement Name*\ex55.csv.

If the connection agreement is replicating from Exchange Server to Active Directory, you can select one of the following options for handling deleted objects:

- Delete The Windows Users, Contacts And Groups. Deletes from Active Directory any mailbox that was deleted in the Exchange Server directory.

- Keep The Windows Deleted Items And Store The Deletion List In The Temporary .LDF File. Removes any mail attributes on each object in Active Directory whose corresponding mailbox was deleted in the Exchange Server directory. The list of deleted objects is then stored in an LDF file. Information is appended to this file as replication occurs. The log file is located in %SystemRoot%\MSADC*Connection Agreement Name*\win2000.ldf.

Design Step: Planning Novell NetWare Bindery or NDS Synchronization with Active Directory

To plan Novell NetWare Bindery or NDS synchronization with Active Directory, you must complete the following tasks:

1. Analyze the current Novell network.
2. Choose one- or two-way synchronization.
3. Identify the objects to synchronize and plan synchronization sessions.
4. Determine administrative responsibilities.
5. Plan pilot testing and user education.

Analyzing the Current Novell Network

To analyze the current Novell network, you should

- Identify information stored on the Novell network and determine its owners, users, and locations. Identify all types of information stored on your NetWare network, the location in which the information is stored, the persons responsible for the information, the users who have access to the information, and the security requirements for the information.

- Identify all hardware and software in the Novell network, indicating software that runs only on NDS. Diagram the network and all components. Identify file, print, Internet, mail, database, and any other servers. Determine whether NDS-dependent software can be replaced.

- Obtain the hardware and software needed for future requirements. Determine the hardware and software your organization will require in the future to obtain its desired functionality. Purchase server hardware. Purchase Windows 2000 Server (which includes Client Service for NetWare) and Services for NetWare version 5 (which includes MSDSS). Purchase any Active Directory–compliant software required to replace NDS-dependent software. Obtain the latest version of Novell Client Access from the Novell Web site.

- Diagram the current Novell namespace. Determine whether the new Active Directory namespace should be identical to or different from the existing Novell namespace.

- Modify the current Novell or Active Directory namespace. If necessary, use NetWare administrative tools to update NDS containers, and use the Windows 2000 Active Directory Users And Computers administrative tool to create Active Directory OUs.

- Determine how objects will map.

- Determine whether to use direct or remote administration. Determine where you will install MSDSS and Novell Client Access and whether you will remotely administer MSDSS sessions. If you choose remote administration, install MSDSS and Novell Client Access on a computer (a non–domain controller server) running Windows 2000 Server or Windows 2000 Professional.

Choosing One- or Two-Way Synchronization

To determine which type of synchronization to use, consider the following factors:

- Reasons to choose one-way synchronization:
  - To centralize directory administration from Active Directory
  - If your network is Windows-based or if your network is currently NDS-based but you plan to reduce the number of directories over time
  - To administer and update NDS user account passwords to support a single set of logon credentials that let users log on to both a Windows-based and a Novell-based network
  - If you are preparing to migrate your NDS-based directory environment to Active Directory

- Reasons to choose two-way synchronization:
  - If Active Directory and NDS are each administered by a different set of network administrators
  - If your network environment contains NDS as your primary directory and you have no plans to consolidate the number of directory platforms
  - If you are planning to maintain and actively administer both directory environments for an extended period of time

Identifying Objects to Synchronize and Planning Synchronization Sessions

To define the objects to synchronize and plan the synchronization sessions required, you should

- Identify objects to synchronize. Identify the containers you want to synchronize. Identify the Active Directory and NDS or Bindery servers between which you wish to establish a synchronization relationship.

- Determine the number of synchronization sessions. Calculate the number of sessions needed to synchronize the desired NDS or Bindery objects. You can specify only one NDS container or Bindery server per session. All objects within that OU or Bindery server will be synchronized. In general, Microsoft advises customers to configure sessions for containers that hold up to (but not more than) 10,000 total objects. You can have up to 50 simultaneous sessions running on one domain controller, and each session can point to a different NDS or Bindery server source.

Determining Administrative Responsibilities

To determine administrative responsibilities, you should

- Obtain administrator permissions. If you will use one-way synchronization, confirm that you have the required permissions to extend the Active Directory schema. Although MSDSS does this automatically, you must have schema-extending administrative authority. If you will use two-way synchronization, confirm that you have the necessary permissions to extend the NDS schema.

Important To set up a two-way synchronization session, you must have full administrator privileges for the entire NDS container in which you are creating the synchronization session. These privileges must be maintained for the duration of the session, or objects may be deleted from either the NDS directory or Active Directory.

- Decide delegation. When you install MSDSS, a special security group called the MSDSS Admins group is created. The MSDSS Admins group is a domain local security group that is unique to each domain, enabling you to use this group to delegate administrative control to specific users. To decide delegation, you must determine the members of the MSDSS Admins group and to whom MSDSS administrative tasks will be delegated.

Planning Pilot Testing and User Education

To plan pilot testing and user education, you should

- Recruit a pilot group. Recruit and train a group of technically oriented users willing to help test a pilot synchronization and to support other users.

- Educate users. Keep your organization's users informed. Be sure they know what to expect and schedule any necessary training. Explain logon procedures and how passwords will be handled. Because the preferred method for password management is to administer passwords from Active Directory only, clients will be required to log on to Active Directory. Password control can be provided from Active Directory in both one-way and two-way synchronization.

Design Step Example: Planning Directory Service Synchronization with Active Directory

The design step example for planning directory service synchronization with Active Directory has been divided into two areas:

- Microsoft Exchange Server 5.5 synchronization with Active Directory
- Novell NetWare Bindery or NDS synchronization with Active Directory

Design Step Example: Planning Microsoft Exchange Server 5.5 Synchronization with Active Directory

City Power and Light is headquartered in Indianapolis, with two branch offices, located in Gary and Ft. Wayne, and a training facility, located in Evansville. The Indianapolis and Evansville locations are administered by the main IT management department in Indianapolis. The Gary and Ft. Wayne offices each have their own small IT management departments.

The utility is currently running Windows 2000, with a server at each location running Exchange Server 5.5 (Service Pack 1 applied). The branch offices and training facility are connected to Indianapolis by WAN connections, and e-mail is routed there for connectivity to the Internet. The client workstations in Indianapolis are running Windows 2000 Professional, and the branch offices and training facility are running Windows 98–based workstations. The branch offices will continue to use Windows 98 until a decision can be made on whether to upgrade to Windows 2000 Professional or Windows ME. Budget constraints have ruled out the possibility of upgrading to Exchange 2000 Server, so the administrators will use ADC to synchronize Exchange Server directory with Active Directory.

The administrators collectively decided that the Gary and Ft. Wayne branch offices would replicate from their Exchange Server computers to Active Directory so the administration of user accounts could still be handled at the branch offices. In the Indianapolis office and at the Evansville training office, replication would occur from Active Directory to Exchange Server to simplify the administration of user accounts at headquarters.

The administrators performed the following steps to synchronize Exchange Server 5.5 with Active Directory:

1. ADC was installed on one of the Windows 2000 domain controllers.

2. The Exchange Server structure was changed so that its sites and containers could be mapped to Active Directory domains and OUs.

3. Four connection agreements were defined, one between each Exchange Server site and Active Directory.

4. Connection agreements were configured in the following manner:

   - Connections 1 and 4: One-way connection from Active Directory to Exchange Server, replicating user account information, replicating once per day at night, authenticating with SSL encryption, and set as a primary connection agreement to allow new user accounts added to Active Directory to be replicated to Exchange Server automatically.

   - Connections 2 and 3: Two-way connections between Active Directory and Exchange Server, replicating user account information, replicating on a per-event basis, authenticating with SSL encryption.

Figure 7.8 depicts how City Power and Light set up Exchange Server 5.5 synchronization with Active Directory.

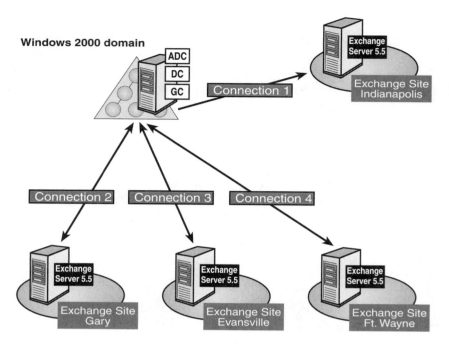

Figure 7.8   Exchange Server 5.5 synchronization with Active Directory

Design Step Example: Planning Novell NetWare Bindery or NDS Synchronization with Active Directory

The following examples outline two ways of synchronizing Novell NetWare Bindery or NDS with Active Directory.

Synchronizing NDS and Active Directory

Company A would like to keep its existing NDS directory and add Active Directory until it is ready to retire NDS. The administrators analyze the Novell network and assess the readiness of the directory for synchronization. They make the necessary adjustments to prepare for synchronization. The one-way directory synchronization option is selected, and the administrators perform an initial reverse synchronization for the entire NDS directory. They determine the information to be synchronized and schedule a forward synchronization session to run from Active Directory to NDS every fifteen minutes. Pilot tests are run to determine whether the system is working correctly. Users are trained to handle the changes. At this point administrators can use Active Directory to manage network objects.

Synchronizing Specific NDS Directory Information with Active Directory

Company B would like to keep only the information stored in its NDS-based human resources application synchronized with Active Directory. No other information will be synchronized. The administrators analyze the Novell network and assess the readiness of the directory for synchronization. They make the necessary adjustments to prepare for synchronization. The two-way directory synchronization option is selected, and the administrators perform an initial reverse synchronization. They specify the objects (Novell container and Active Directory OU) between which to establish a one-to-one relationship. Pilot tests are run to determine whether the system is working correctly. Users are trained to handle the changes. The administrator then configures forward and reverse synchronization sessions for the human resources directory data.

Lesson Summary

In this lesson you learned how to plan Active Directory synchronization with Microsoft Exchange Server 5.5 directory service, Novell NetWare Bindery or NDS, and other LDAP-compliant directory services. To plan Exchange Server 5.5 synchronization with Active Directory, you learned that you must analyze the current Windows 2000 domain structure and Exchange Server site topology, determine which directory service will manage object identity, define objects to be synchronized, map Exchange Server sites and containers to Active Directory domains and OUs, map Exchange Server attributes to Active Directory attributes, determine the location of Active Directory Connectors, define the connection agreements needed to synchronize directories, and configure connection agreements. To plan Novell NetWare Bindery or NDS synchronization with Active Directory, you learned that you must analyze the current Novell network, choose one- or two-way synchronization, identify the objects to synchronize and plan synchronization sessions, determine administrative responsibilities, and plan pilot testing and user education.

Lab 7.1: Planning a Windows NT 4 Directory Services Migration to Windows 2000 Active Directory

Lab Objectives

After completing this lab, you will be able to analyze an organization's Windows NT 4 directory services environment to plan its migration to Windows 2000 Active Directory.

About This Lab

In this lab, you will analyze a medium-sized organization's Windows NT 4 directory services environment to plan its migration to Windows 2000 Active Directory.

Before You Begin

Before you begin this lab, you must be able to

- Identify the factors in an organization's environment that determine its migration strategy
- Indicate the reasons for using the domain upgrade method
- Indicate the reasons for using the domain restructure method
- Explain the steps involved in planning a domain upgrade
- Explain the steps involved in planning a domain restructure
- Explain the steps involved in planning the consolidation of resource domains into organizational units (OUs)

Exercise: Planning a Windows NT 4 Directory Services Migration to Windows 2000 Active Directory

In this exercise, you will analyze a medium-sized organization's Windows NT 4 directory services environment to plan its migration to Windows 2000 Active Directory. Review the scenario; then follow the instructions to plan the Windows NT 4 directory services migration to Windows 2000 Active Directory.

Scenario

Southwest Financial Services is an investment company with locations in Phoenix, Tucson, and Albuquerque. The company is planning to migrate from Windows NT 4 to Windows 2000. The current Windows NT 4 architecture is illustrated in Figure 7.9.

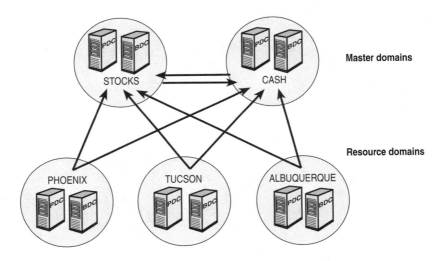

Figure 7.9   Southwest Financial Services Windows NT 4 architecture

Two areas of the business, stock investments and cash investments, are managed by separate IT management organizations. The stock investments area handles only stock investments, while the cash investments area handles only cash investments; the account managers in each area never exchange information. However, management and executive personnel from each area do work together on company reports and trend analysis. Because of the sensitive nature of investments, security is the top concern for Southwest Financial Services.

The infrastructure planners have recently completed the Active Directory implementation plan for the migration. The design provides Southwest Financial Services with the same level of security but reduces the number of domains in the domain structure. The proposed new design is illustrated in Figure 7.10.

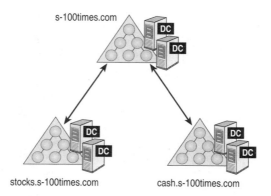

Figure 7.10   Proposed Windows 2000 Active Directory architecture for Southwest Financial Services

The forest root domain is a dedicated domain in which no resources from either the stock or cash investment areas will be placed. Administrators from both IT management organizations will manage the forest root domain together. Both of the master domains are child domains of the root domain. The resource domains are consolidated into organizational units (OUs).

Exercise Questions

1. What migration method(s) will you use to migrate to Windows 2000 Active Directory?

2. List the steps you will take to plan the migration.

Review

The following questions are intended to reinforce key information presented in the chapter. If you are unable to answer a question, review the appropriate lesson and then try the question again. Answers to the questions can be found in Appendix A, "Questions and Answers."

1. You are planning a Windows NT 4 Directory Services migration to Windows 2000 Active Directory. The current production environment cannot withstand any negative effects as a result of the migration process. What migration method should you use?

2. Why should you use the domain restructure method if the production environment cannot withstand any negative effects as a result of the migration process?

3. Your organization has just migrated to Windows 2000 Server and Exchange Server 5.5. You would like to propagate the user information in the Exchange Server directory service to your new Active Directory. What tool should you install to accomplish the synchronization, and where are the tool installation files located?

4. Your organization is running Windows 2000 and has just acquired a small company that uses NDS. You would like to synchronize the directory information with Active Directory. What tool should you install to accomplish the synchronization, and where are the tool installation files located?

APPENDIX   A

Questions and Answers

Page 1

Chapter 1
Introduction to Active Directory

Review Questions

Page 36

1. Your organization would like to include the languages in which each staff member is proficient in the Active Directory database. What action must you take to accomplish this and why?

   If you need to provide information about users not currently defined in the schema, you must extend the schema for the User class. The schema contains a formal definition of the contents and structure of Active Directory, including all attributes, classes, and class properties.

2. How would you arrange two OUs, Orders and Deliveries, so that the Orders OU has administrative control of the Deliveries OU but the Deliveries OU does not have administrative control of the Orders OU?

   By adding OUs to other OUs, or nesting, you can provide administrative control in a hierarchical fashion. By nesting the Deliveries OU within the Orders OU, the Orders OU has administrative control of the Deliveries OU but the Deliveries OU does not have administrative control of the Orders OU.

3. You are considering adding global catalog servers to your network. What are the advantages of such an action? Disadvantages?

   Additional global catalog servers can provide quicker responses to user inquiries, as well as redundancy. However, additional global catalog servers can require more bandwidth for replication traffic.

4. Your client requires all Windows computers in his organization to display the company logo as the background wallpaper. What action should you take?

To create a specific desktop configuration such as background wallpaper for all Windows computers in an organization, you create group policy objects (GPOs) for sites, domains, or OUs. To display the logo on every computer in the organization, you need to apply a global GPO.

5. Your network has a parent domain named stateuniversity.microsoft.com. You want to add a child domain named stateuniversity.expedia.com to form a tree. Can you arrange these domains in a tree? Why or why not?

A tree is a grouping or hierarchical arrangement of one or more Windows 2000 domains that you create by adding one or more child domains to an existing parent domain. Domains in a tree share a contiguous namespace and a hierarchical naming structure. The parent domain stateuniversity.microsoft.com and the domain stateuniversity.expedia.com do not form a contiguous namespace. Therefore, you cannot arrange these domains in a tree.

Page 37

Chapter 2
Introduction to Designing
a Directory Services Infrastructure

Lab 2.1: Analyzing Business Environment

Exercise: Analyzing a Current Business Structure

Business Structures Worksheet

Page 86

1. Diagram the administrative structure of your organization.

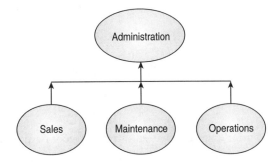

2. List and briefly describe the purpose of each division or department in the administrative structure. Where do these divisions report?

   The Administration department serves as the decision-making unit of the organization and carries out administrative functions. The Maintenance department is responsible for maintaining the company's aircraft. The Operations department is responsible for coordinating the components that keep the aircraft flying, such as scheduling food purveyors, baggage handlers, pilots and flight attendants, and purchasing fuel. The Sales department is responsible for advertising and selling seats on airline flights. The Maintenance, Operations, and Sales departments report to the Administration department.

3. Indicate the number of network users in each division of the administrative structure and the total number of network users in the organization.

   Users in each department: Administration (75), Maintenance (40), Operations (100), Sales (50). Total number of network users: 265.

4. Diagram the geographical structure of your organization.

5. List each administrative division and describe where it is located in the geographical structure.

    Administration: Butte, MT. Maintenance: Salt Lake City, UT. Operations: Reno, NV. Sales: Boise, ID, and Laramie, WY.

6. List the number of network users in each location.

    Butte, MT: 75. Salt Lake City, UT: 40. Reno, NV: 100. Boise, ID: 30. Laramie, WY: 20.

7. Describe how the network users in each department currently use the network.

    The Administration department uses the network for marketing, accounting, training, and IT functions. The Maintenance department uses the network to document their maintenance activities and to maintain parts inventories. The Operations department uses the network to coordinate the scheduling of food purveyors, baggage handlers, pilots and flight attendants, and purchasing fuel. The Sales department uses the system for ticketing and developing advertisements.

8. Add any special operations to your administrative structure diagram.

    There are no special operations at Vigor Airlines.

Review Questions

Page 88

1. You are the manager of your organization's IT department. You assemble a design team that consists of a system administrator, a network administrator, a member of your help desk team, a systems trainer from the training department, and you. What pitfalls might you encounter with your current team?

   Because your team consists of four members of the IT department and only one member from outside the department, it is likely that your team will be unable to provide an accurate analysis of the entire organization. It is also likely that your team will be asked to redo your Active Directory infrastructure design because you have not involved any decision-making managers in your design team. By selecting members of the design team from the entire organization your team will be more effective.

2. You are a design team member and receive a completed business environment analysis document for review. When reviewing the business structure you notice that the diagram shown below is the only diagram included in that part of the analysis. What other diagrams should be included as part of the business structure analysis?

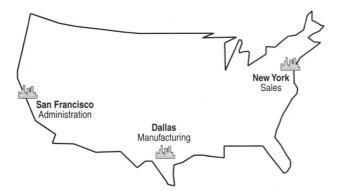

   The diagram included in the business structure analysis shows the geographical structure of the network. A diagram showing the administrative structure must also be included in the analysis. An organization's administrative structure represents the functions, divisions, departments, or positions within an organization and how they are related, including the organization's hierarchy and authority structure.

3. You have inventoried all the hardware devices used in your organization. What's the next step in conducting an analysis of hardware used in your organization?

   Compare your inventory with the list of Windows 2000 Server compatible hardware, available at *http://www.microsoft.com/windows2000/upgrade/ compat/default.asp*.

Page 89

Chapter 3
Creating a Forest Plan

Activity 3.1: Designing a Forest Model

Scenario: Adventure Works

Page 99

1. List the advantages of using a multiple forest model for Adventure Works.

   The advantages of using a multiple forest model are

   - **To allow the retail IT management department to continue managing only the retail operations.**

   - **To allow Adventure Works to keep users in the retail network from accessing corporate resources unless explicit one-way trusts were created.**

2. List the disadvantages of using a multiple forest model for Adventure Works.

   The disadvantages of using a multiple forest model are

   - **Multiple forests require the separate maintenance of corporate and retail network schema, configuration, global catalogs, security, explicit trusts, and domains.**

   - **Multiple forests do not allow for the creation of a single, company-wide schema and global catalog to meet senior management's goal of creating a single view of all products and systems.**

   - **Multiple forests do not provide retail employees with easy access to the corporate intranet and e-mail systems to meet management's goal of cultivating and recruiting employees from the retail stores for operations in the corporate office.**

3. Which model would you choose and why?

   Use a single forest model. The benefits of the single forest model (lower maintenance, meeting senior management goals) easily outweigh allowing the retail IT management department to continue managing only the retail operations.

Lab 3.1: Creating a Forest Model and Schema Modification Plan

Exercise 1: Designing a Forest Model

Exercise Questions

Page 114

1. List the advantages of using a multiple forest model for LitWare, Inc.

   The advantages of using a multiple forest model are

   - **To allow the IT management departments to continue managing LitWare, Inc., and Lucerne Publishing separately.**

   - **To allow LitWare, Inc., to keep its users and users in Lucerne Publishing from accessing each other's resources unless explicit one-way trusts are created.**

2. List the disadvantages of using a multiple forest model for LitWare, Inc.

   The disadvantages of using a multiple forest model are

   - **Multiple forests require the separate maintenance of schema, configuration, global catalogs, security, explicit trusts, and domains.**

   - **Multiple forests do not allow for the creation of a single, company-wide schema and global catalog.**

3. Would you use a single or a multiple forest model for Lit Ware, Inc.? Why?

   Use a multiple forest model. Because there are no initiatives to integrate the two businesses and it is likely that multiple schemas will be required, maintaining the businesses separately seems to be the best choice.

Exercise 2: Designing a Schema Modification Plan

Exercise Questions

Page 115

1. What items should be included in a schema modification plan for LitWare, Inc.?

   The following items should be included in a schema modification plan for LitWare, Inc.: Modification description, modification justification, assessment of impact, complete description of the new schema object class, and written approval to test the modification from the schema modification approval committee.

2. Should the design team design a schema modification plan? Why or why not?

The design team should not design a schema modification plan because it is likely that it is unnecessary. If the new inventory application is directory-enabled, it may automatically modify the schema, providing opportunities to handle the book title and ISBN without manually modifying the schema. You should examine all other alternatives before modifying the schema and you should be sure to test directory-enabled applications that modify the schema before installing them on the network.

Review Questions

Page 116

1. What is the number of forests you should strive for? Why?

Because Windows 2000 domains in a forest share a single schema, configuration container, and global catalog and are linked by two-way transitive trusts, you should strive to have only one forest for your organization.

2. Your organization is considering the implementation of four forests to handle business units that do not wish to work together. The decision makers do not realize the impact of multiple forests on users. What action should you take to assist the users?

You should inform the decision makers how users are affected by multiple forests when logging on and when performing queries. In multiple forest scenarios, when users log on to a computer outside their own forest, they must specify the default UPN, which contains the full domain path for their user account, rather than just their easy-to-remember abstracted UPN. The default UPN is required because the domain controller in the forest will not be able to find the abstracted UPN in its global catalog. The user's abstracted UPN resides only in the global catalog in the user's forest. You should also inform the decision makers that to assist the users with queries, you will have to arrange for user training in making explicit queries across all of an organization's forests because the risk of users making incomplete or incorrect queries can affect how they perform their work.

3. Your organization has implemented two forests. A user in the Accounting domain in Forest 1 needs to access resources located in the Finance domain in Forest 2. However, you must not allow the Finance domain in Forest 2 to access the Accounting domain resources in Forest 1. What must you do to allow access to the resources?

   Domain administrators in both domains must configure an explicit one-way nontransitive trust between the Accounting and Finance domains. If the Finance domain trusts the Accounting domain, users in the Accounting domain can access resources in the Finance domain, but users in the Finance domain cannot access resources in the Accounting domain. Then, either domain administrator, with the correct permissions in both forests, must import the resource object into Forest 1 using the LDIFDE command-line tool. The resource object replicates to Forest 1's global catalog and the user can find the object by querying Forest 1's global catalog. Finally, the user can access the resource in Forest 2.

4. Why should you avoid changing the Active Directory schema?

   You should avoid changing the schema because the Active Directory schema contains hundreds of the most common object classes and attributes that users of a server system require. The need to change the schema is rare.

5. You added a schema class object and a set of schema attribute objects to your organization's schema to represent products made by one of the divisions in the organization. After one year, that organization is spun off and the attributes are no longer needed. What should you do?

   When schema class or attribute objects are added, they cannot be deleted if they are no longer needed. They can only be deactivated. You cannot deactivate the base schema, however; you can deactivate only schema that you have added.

6. Your organization has recently implemented Active Directory and currently has no plans to modify the schema. Why should you familiarize yourself with the base schema class and attribute objects?

   If you know the types of data that Active Directory will hold, you can more effectively determine whether to change the base schema in the future and whom the changes will affect.

Page 119

Chapter 4
Creating a Domain Plan

Activity 4.1: Defining Domains
Scenario 1: Friendship Vineyards

Page 132

1. On the network architecture diagram, use a triangle to indicate the location of the domain(s) you would define for Friendship Vineyards.

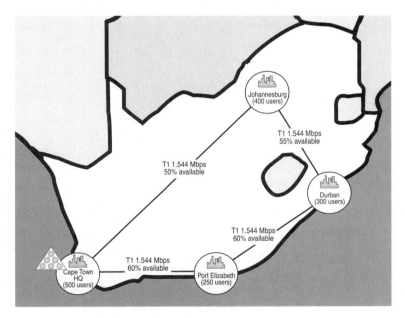

2. Explain your reasoning for defining the domain(s).

   Friendship Vineyards has no security requirements that cannot be handled within one domain. Although the company needs its administrators to apply group policies to the distribution personnel at all locations, the policies involve a user interface requirement, not a special administrative requirement. To satisfy the user interface requirement, administrators can apply policies to the distribution personnel at the OU level. A check of the network architecture diagram shows that all links are sound

**and there is no need to optimize replication. Since there are no require-
ments to preserve the existing Windows NT domains, Friendship Vineyards requires only one domain.**

Scenario 2: Awesome Computers

Page 134

1. On the network architecture diagram, use a triangle to indicate the location of
   the domain(s) you would define for Awesome Computers.

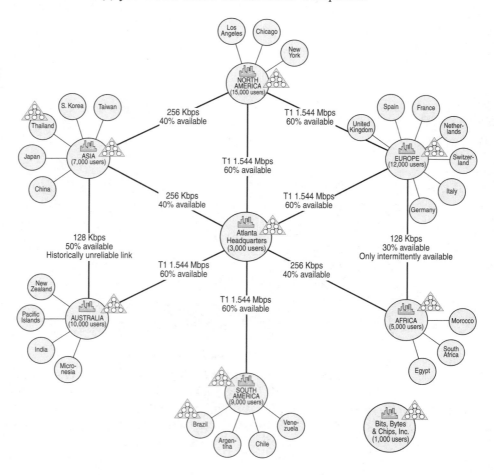

2. Explain your reasoning for defining the domain(s).

   **Awesome Computers has password and account lockout security require-
   ments at each regional office that cannot be handled within a domain.
   Therefore, the company needs to create a domain for each regional office.
   Because language settings are handled by clients in Windows 2000, there
   is no need to define domains based on language settings. Because of the
   legacy applications required in the Brazilian and Thai sales offices, each
   will require its own domain that must remain in mixed mode. Bits, Bytes
   & Chips, Inc., will also require its own domain to retain its presence on
   the Internet. Awesome Computers requires ten domains.**

Activity 4.2: Defining a Root Domain, Defining a Domain Hierarchy, and Naming Domains

Scenario 1: Friendship Vineyards

Page 157

1. On the network architecture diagram, draw a square around the domain you're
   defining as the forest root domain. Explain your reasoning for defining the
   forest root domain.

   **Because the forest for Friendship Vineyards contains only one domain,
   the design team has designated the existing domain as the forest root
   domain.**

2. Complete a domain hierarchy diagram for Friendship Vineyards.

   **Because the forest for Friendship Vineyards contains only one domain,
   there is no domain hierarchy.**

3. Name the forest root domain.

   **Because Friendship Vineyards has a Web presence using the DNS name
   f-100times.com, the forest root domain will need a new DNS name to
   distinguish it from the existing Internet domain. Your design team named
   the forest root domain corp.f-100times.com. Answers may vary.**

Scenario 2: Awesome Computers

Page 160

1. On the network architecture diagram, draw a square around the domain you're
   defining as the forest root domain. Explain your reasoning for defining the
   forest root domain.

The headquarters domain was selected as the forest root domain because it is the most critical to the operation of the organization and because IT decisions that affect the entire organization are handled by the Corporate IT Management department at headquarters. The design team did not feel it was necessary to create a dedicated forest root domain because headquarters is already serving as a separate administrative entity. However, the team realizes that it may still need to designate a dedicated domain and will revisit this issue later in the design process. The diagram below shows the forest root domain defined for Awesome Computers.

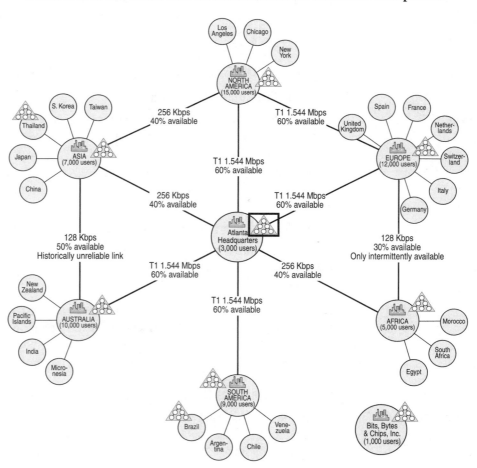

2. Complete a domain hierarchy diagram for Awesome Computers, including the forest root domain, the tree root domains, and the remaining subdomains. Indicate any cross-link trusts that may be necessary by a dotted line.

There are two trees and tree root domains, one for Awesome Computers and one for Bits, Bytes & Chips, Inc. The tree root domain for the Awesome Computers tree is also the forest root domain. To accommodate the regional offices and optimize trust relationships, regional offices will be child domains of the forest root domain, and the sales office domains in Thailand and Brazil will be grandchild domains of their respective regional domains. To accommodate the Brazilian sales office's need to access engineering resources at the European location, a cross-link trust has been established between the two domains. There are no child subdomains for Bits, Bytes & Chips, Inc. The domain hierarchy diagram is shown in the following figure.

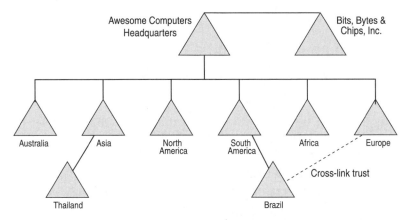

3. Name the domains in the domain hierarchy, including the forest root domain, the tree root domains, and the remaining subdomains.

Because the organization already has an Internet presence using the DNS name a-100times.com, the forest root domain will be named corp.a-100times.com. The forest root domain is also the tree root domain for Awesome Computers. The tree root domain for Bits, Bytes & Chips, Inc., is named corp.b-100times.com. The child subdomains for Awesome Computers are named for each of the regional offices. The remaining

grandchild subdomains are named for the corresponding sales offices. Answers may vary. The following figure shows the domain hierarchy diagram with domain names defined for Awesome Computers.

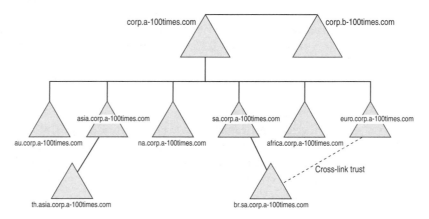

Lab 4.1: Creating a Domain Plan

Exercise: Creating a Domain Plan

Exercise Questions

Page 178

1. On the network architecture diagram, use a triangle to indicate the location of the domain(s) you would define for Parnell Aerospace. Explain your reasoning for defining the domain(s).

    The following figure shows the domains defined for Parnell Aerospace. Answers may vary. Domains were defined for the following reasons:

    - **A domain was defined at the Phoenix location to meet special legal defense contractor requirements for storing product development files.**

    - **A domain was defined at the Tokyo location to meet the special password and account lockout settings requirements.**

    - **A domain was defined at the Berlin location to comply with German administration laws.**

    - **A domain was defined at the Paris location to comply with French law.**

    - **A domain was defined at the Lakes & Sons Seattle location to allow Lakes & Sons to function independently and continue its own Web presence.**

- A domain was defined at the Lakes & Sons Minneapolis location because it can be reached from the Seattle location by SMTP mail only.

- Domains were defined at the New York, London, and Rio de Janeiro locations because various links connected to these locations could not effectively handle replication traffic.

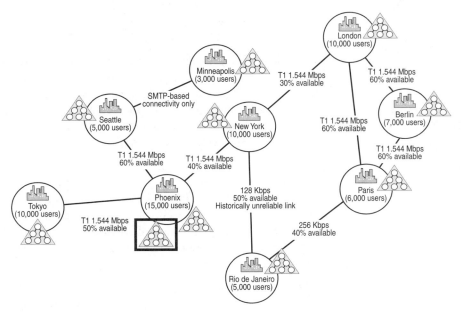

2. On the network architecture diagram, draw a square around the domain you're defining as the forest root domain. Explain your reasoning for defining the forest root domain.

The previous figure shows the forest root domain defined for Parnell Aerospace. At the Phoenix headquarters, two separate departments handle IT management. One department handles IT management for the Phoenix office only, and the other handles IT management for the entire organization. The design team decided to add a dedicated domain as the forest root domain to separate the two IT management departments located in Phoenix and to reap the benefits of using a dedicated forest root domain. Answers may vary.

3. Complete a domain hierarchy diagram for Parnell Aerospace. Name the domains in the domain hierarchy.

Because Parnell Aerospace has registered the DNS name p-100times.com and Lakes & Sons has registered the DNS name l-100times.com, the organization will need two trees in its Active Directory infrastructure. The forest root domain will also serve as the tree root domain for the Parnell Aerospace tree, while the domain at the Seattle location will serve as the tree root domain for the Lakes & Sons tree.

Users at all locations must often access engineering resources at the Phoenix location. Although each regional office domain must then go through the root domain to access resources at the Phoenix headquarters, there is no need to use cross-link trusts in this scenario except for possibly the domain at the Minneapolis location. Your design team must determine whether traffic between Minneapolis and headquarters warrants a cross-link trust.

Because the organization already has an Internet presence using the DNS names p-100times.com and l-100times.com, the Parnell Aerospace tree root and forest root domain will be named corp.p-100times.com. The Lakes & Sons tree root domain will be named corp.l-100times.com. The child subdomains are named for the regional offices using the codes as defined by ISO 3166.

The domain hierarchy diagram and domain names for Parnell Aerospace are shown in the following figure. Answers may vary.

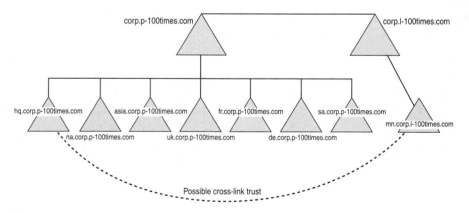

Review Questions

Page 179

1. Your design team is defining domains for an organization. What are the four reasons for defining multiple domains?

   The four reasons for defining multiple domains are to meet security requirements, to meet administrative requirements, to optimize replication traffic, and to retain Windows NT domains.

2. Your design team is defining the forest root domain for an organization. What are the reasons for designating an existing domain as a forest root domain? What are the reasons for designating a dedicated domain as the forest root domain?

   The reasons for designating an existing domain as the forest root domain are

   - **Your forest contains only one domain.**

   - **Your forest contains multiple domains and you can select the domain that is the most critical to the operation of your organization from one of them, but you have no desire to regulate membership in the Enterprise Admins and Schema Admins predefined universal groups in the forest root domain, create a small forest root domain for easier replication, or avoid obsolescence of the root domain name.**

   The reasons for designating a dedicated domain as the forest root domain are

   - **Your forest contains multiple domains and you *cannot* select the domain that is the most critical to the operation of your organization from one of them. The new domain will be dedicated to the operations associated with enterprise management and should not contain any user or many computer accounts.**

   - **Your forest contains multiple domains and you *can* select the domain that is the most critical to the operation of your organization from one of them, but you want to regulate membership in the Enterprise Admins and Schema Admins predefined universal groups in the forest root domain, create a small forest root domain for easier replication, or avoid obsolescence of the root domain name.**

3. Your design team is defining the domain trees for an organization. What is the reason for designating more than one domain tree?

   Your team may need to define more than one domain tree if your organization has more than one DNS name.

4. Your design team is getting ready to create the w-100times.com forest root domain for Wingtip Toys. What should you do before creating the domain?

   You should be sure to register and receive verification for domain names *before* creating your Active Directory domain namespace. After you name your forest root domain you cannot change it and it is difficult to change other domain names.

5. Your design team is determining the existing DNS service used by an organization. What DNS services meet the DNS server requirements to support Active Directory? What DNS service allows you to use Active Directory–integrated zones?

   DNS BIND version 8.1.2 or later and Windows NT 4 DNS meet the DNS server requirements to support Active Directory.

   Although these DNS services are compatible with Active Directory, only the Windows 2000 DNS service allows you to use Active Directory–integrated zones, incremental zone transfer, and secure dynamic updates.

Page 181

Chapter 5
Creating an Organizational Unit Plan

Activity 5.1: Defining OU Structures

Scenario: Arbor Shoes

Page 204

1. Diagram the OU structures needed to delegate administration for the corp.a-100times.com domain. Explain your reasoning for defining each OU.

   Because each of the three locations has a small autonomous IT staff to handle support tasks, OUs were set up for San Francisco, Houston, and Boston. An administrative group at each location will have full control over its top-level OU. Because there are separate administrative groups at each location to handle the basic administration of users, the administration of computers, and the administration of resources, three second-level OUs were set up at each location for each top-level OU.

2. Diagram the OU structures needed to hide objects. Explain your reasoning for defining each OU.

   Arbor Shoes has no requirements for hiding objects.

3. Diagram the OU structures needed to administer group policy. Explain your reasoning for defining each OU.

   A GPO applied to the top-level OU at each location can meet the requirement of providing a specific logon and logoff script for all users at each location, except for users in the Finance department. An additional third-level OU must be defined for the Finance department in each location. Then, a separate GPO must be linked to each Finance department OU in order to provide the separate logon script for users in the Finance department at each location. In addition, Block Policy Inheritance must be set for each Finance department OU so the logoff script set for all users at each location is not inherited by the Finance department.

   The following figure shows the OU structures defined to delegate administration and to administer group policies for Arbor Shoes.

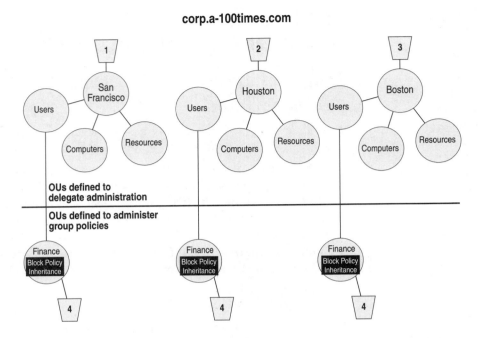

corp.a-100times.com

Activity 5.2: Planning User Accounts

Scenario: Dearing School of Fine Art

Page 226

In the table below, place the new student accounts, by account name, in the appropriate OU.

OU	New student accounts
FTUsers (Fiber Arts)	joberry, mengphua
PTUsers (Fiber Arts)	PT-sarahakh, PT-martawol
FTUsers (Painting)	joshbarn, sherriha, karankha
PTUsers (Painting)	PT-Christin
FTUsers (Drawing)	christob, robyoung
PTUsers (Drawing)	PT-micheald
Computer Art	matthewd, lisajaco

Activity 5.3: Planning Groups

Scenario: The Ski Haus

Page 227

1. Explain how your design team will use security groups to allow the Product Design users in each domain full control of the ski hat design databases in their domains.

   Set up a Denver Product Design global group and add the Denver Product Designer users to the group. Set up a Geneva Product Design global group and add the Geneva Product Designer users to the group. Then add the Denver Product Design global group to a Denver Product Design domain local group and add the Geneva Product Design global group to a Geneva Product Design domain local group. Grant full control permissions for the ski hat design database to each domain local group.

2. Explain how your design team will use security groups to allow the Product Design users in each domain read permission to the Denver and Geneva ski hat design databases.

   Set up a Denver domain local group that has read permission for the ski hat design database. Add the Geneva Product Design global group to the Denver domain local group. Set up a Geneva domain local group that has read permission for the ski hat design database. Then add the Denver Product Design global group to the Geneva domain local group.

3. Explain how your design team will use security groups to allow all Product Design users in both domains change permission to the ski sweater design database in Geneva.

   Set up a universal group. Set up a domain local group in the Geneva domain that has change permission for the ski sweater design database. Add the Geneva Product Design global group and the Denver Product Design global group to the universal group. Add the universal group to a domain local group in Geneva.

Lab 5.1: Defining an OU Structure and Security Groups

Exercise 5.1: Defining an OU Structure

Exercise Questions

Page 229

1. Create an OU structure diagram for Uncle Bob's Root Beer that supports the needs indicated in the scenario.

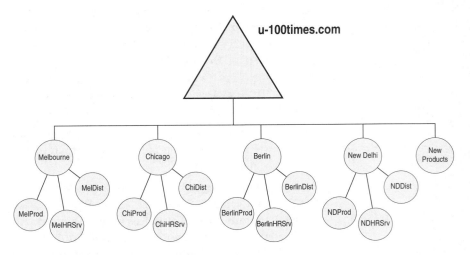

This diagram presents one possible answer. You may have named or planned your OU structure differently.

2. Complete the table below to document each OU in your design, the reason for creating it, and the users and computers that it contains.

OU created	Reason created	Users and computers contained in the OU
Melbourne	**Provides delegation of administration to Melbourne IT management organization.**	**User and computer accounts for Melbourne regional office, except Production servers, HR servers, and Distribution users.**
Chicago	**Provides delegation of administration to Chicago IT management organization.**	**User and computer accounts for Chicago regional office, except Production servers, HR servers, and Distribution users.**

OU created	Reason created	Users and computers contained in the OU
Berlin	Provides delegation of administration to Berlin IT management organization.	User and computer accounts for Berlin regional office, except Production servers, HR servers, and Distribution users.
New Delhi	Provides delegation of administration to New Delhi IT management organization.	User and computer accounts for New Delhi regional office, except Production servers, HR servers, and Distribution users.
New Products	Provides delegation of administration to New Products IT management organization.	User and computer accounts for the New Products department.
MelProd	Provides delegation of administration of server resources to the Melbourne Production department.	Melbourne Production servers.
ChiProd	Provides delegation of administration of server resources to the Chicago Production department.	Chicago Production servers.
BerlinProd	Provides delegation of administration of server resources to the Berlin Production department.	Berlin Production servers.
NDProd	Provides delegation of administration of server resources to the New Delhi Production department.	New Delhi Production servers.
MelHRSrv	Hides Melbourne HR servers.	Melbourne HR servers.
ChiHRSrv	Hides Chicago HR servers.	Chicago HR servers.
BerlinHRSrv	Hides Berlin HR servers	Berlin HR servers.
NDHRSrv	Hides New Delhi HR servers.	New Delhi HR servers.

continued

OU created	Reason created	Users and computers contained in the OU
MelDist	Applies distribution tracking tool using GPO.	Melbourne Distribution users.
ChiDist	Applies distribution tracking tool using GPO.	Chicago Distribution users.
BerlinDist	Applies distribution tracking tool using GPO.	Berlin Distribution users.
NDDist	Applies distribution tracking tool using GPO.	New Delhi Distribution users.

This table presents one possible answer. You may have named or planned your OU structure differently.

Exercise 5.2: Defining Groups

Exercise Questions

Page 232

Complete the table below to document your security group design. Include the name of each security group, the group scope, and the members of the group. Also note whether the members are individuals or list group names if the members are groups.

Group	Scope	Members
Chicago Production Server Administrators	Global	Chicago Production Server Administrators (individuals)
Chicago Production Managers	Global	Chicago Production Managers (individuals)
Chicago Distribution Managers	Global	Chicago Distribution Managers (individuals)
Chicago Production Specialists	Global	Chicago Production Specialists (individuals)
Worldwide Production Managers	Global	Melbourne Production Managers, Chicago Production Managers, Berlin Production Managers, New Delhi Production Managers

Group	Scope	Members
Worldwide Distribution Managers	Global	Melbourne Distribution Managers, Chicago Distribution Managers, Berlin Distribution Managers, New Delhi Distribution Managers
Formulas full	Domain local	Chicago Production Server Administrators
Formulas read	Domain local	Chicago Production Specialists, Worldwide Production Managers
Formulas change	Domain local	Chicago Production Managers
Production and bottling logs full	Domain local	Chicago Production Server Administrators
Production and bottling logs read	Domain local	Chicago Production Specialists, Worldwide Production Managers, Chicago Distribution Managers
Production and bottling logs change	Domain local	Chicago Production Managers
Customer service logs full	Domain local	Chicago Production Server Administrators
Customer service logs read	Domain local	Chicago Production Specialists, Worldwide Production Managers, Worldwide Distribution Managers
Customer service logs change	Domain local	Chicago Production Managers

This table presents one possible answer. You may have named or planned your group structure differently.

Review Questions

Page 233

1. Your design team is getting ready to define OU structures for your organization's Active Directory infrastructure design. What are the three reasons for defining an OU? What is the primary reason?

    The three reasons for defining an OU are: to delegate administration, to hide objects, and to administer group policy. The primary reason for defining an OU is to delegate administration.

2. Your design team has defined an OU to delegate control of user objects. You have diagrammed the desired OU, diagrammed a security group, and listed the administrators who require control of the user object class in the group. You want to allow the OU to set its own membership. Where should the administrator group be placed?

   If the OU is allowed to set its own membership, place the administrator group inside the OU.

3. Your design team has defined a forest, domains, and OUs. Where should user accounts be placed?

   Place the user accounts in the OU administered by the administrative groups and GPOs that apply to the account.

4. Your design team is assigning users to groups. Which group scope is most often used to assign permissions to resources?

   Domain local security groups are most often used to assign permissions to resources.

5. Your organization is running Windows 2000 in native mode. The design team is adding users to groups. Why shouldn't the team add individual users to universal groups?

   You should avoid adding individual users to universal groups because when you update the membership of a universal group, the complete membership of the group is replicated to all global catalog servers in the forest, creating a large amount of network traffic. To ensure minimal impact on replication traffic, you should add global groups, not individual users, to universal groups and change the membership of universal groups as infrequently as possible.

Page 235

Chapter 6
Creating a Site Topology Plan

Activity 6.1: Defining Sites and Placing Domain Controllers in Sites

Scenario: Ramona Publishing

Page 250

1. Diagram the sites needed for Ramona Publishing. Explain your reasoning for defining each site.

   Sites were defined for the following reasons:

   - **Each location has a high-speed backbone that connects a set of 10–100 Kbps LANs.**

   - **The San Juan location is connected to the Miami headquarters only by SMTP mail.**

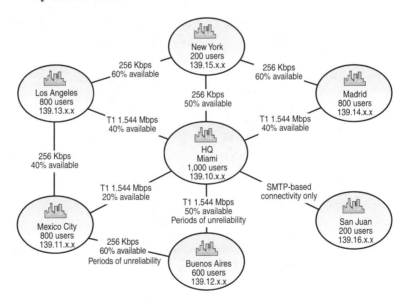

2. Place the domain controllers needed for Ramona Publishing. Explain your reasoning for placing each domain controller.

   The reasons for locating domain controllers in this manner are

   1. There is a one-to-one relationship between the following sites and domains:

   - **Miami—hq.r-100times.com**
   - **Mexico City—mx.r-100times.com**
   - **Buenos Aires—sa.r-100times.com**
   - **San Juan—pr.r-100times.com**
   - **Madrid—eu.r-100times.com**

   Therefore two domain controllers are placed in each of these sites.

   2. The Los Angeles and New York sites are both contained in the us.r-100times.com domain. To meet minimum requirements, one domain controller is placed in each site. To handle the relatively large number of users in the Los Angeles site, an additional domain controller is placed in the Los Angeles site.

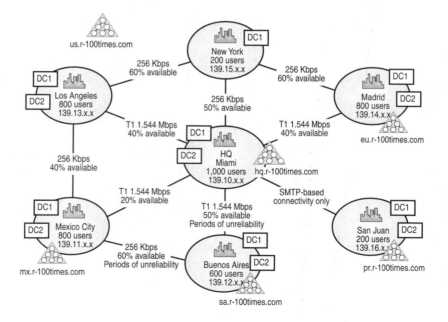

Lab 6.1: Creating a Site Topology Plan

Exercise: Creating a Site Topology Plan

Exercise Questions

Page 279

1. Begin your site topology diagram by indicating the sites needed for Fabrikam, Inc. Explain your reasoning for defining each site.

   Sites were defined for the following reasons:

   - **Each location has a high-speed backbone that connects a set of 10–100 Kbps LANs.**

   - **The Sapporo location is connected to the Tokyo location by SMTP mail only.**

2. Indicate the domain controllers needed for Fabrikam, Inc., on your site topology diagram. Explain your reasoning for placing each domain controller as you did.

   The reasons for locating domain controllers in this manner are

   There is a one-to-one relationship between the following sites and domains:

   - **Sapporo—sp.north.corp.f-100times.com**

   - **Nagoya—hq.corp.f-100times.com**

   - **Fukuoka—fk.south.corp.f-100times.com**

   Therefore two domain controllers are placed in each of these sites.

   The Tokyo, Yokohama, and Kawasaki sites are all contained in the north.corp.f-100times.com domain. To meet minimum requirements, one domain controller is placed in each site. To handle the relatively large number of users in the Tokyo site, an additional domain controller is placed in the Tokyo site.

   The Kyoto and Osaka sites are both contained in the south.corp. f-100times.com domain. To meet minimum requirements, one domain controller is placed in each site.

3. Indicate the site links needed for Fabrikam, Inc., on your site topology diagram. Name each site link by using the first two letters of each connected site name. Indicate the site link configurations for each site link in the table below.

Site Link	Transport	Cost	Frequency	Availability
Na-To	IP	25	15 min	always
Na-Os	IP	25	15 min	always
To-Os	IP	25	15 min	always
To-Yo	IP	50	1 hr	2300 to 0500 daily
To-Ka	IP	50	1 hr	2300 to 0500 daily
Os-Ky	IP	50	1 hr	2300 to 0500 daily
Os-Fu	IP	100	2 hr	2300 to 0500 daily
To-Sa	SMTP	100	2 hr	2300 to 0500 daily

Cost, frequency, and availability answers may vary. However, because there are three different intersite link speeds, your site link table should have at least three costs.

4. Indicate the location of global catalog servers and operations masters for Fabrikam, Inc., on your site topology diagram. Explain your reasoning for placing each global catalog server and operations master.

The reasons for locating global catalog servers in this manner are

- **One global catalog server is placed in all sites to meet minimum requirements.**

- **Because placing more global catalog servers in each site will increase replication traffic, no additional global catalog servers are placed.**

The reasons for locating operations masters in this manner are

- **Because each domain has more than one domain controller, one of the DC1s in each domain was chosen as the operations master domain controller. The standby operations master controller is DC2 in sites where DC2s exist.**

- Because each domain is not very large, both the relative identifier master and PDC emulator roles were assigned to the operations master domain controller.

- Because the infrastructure master role should not be assigned to the domain controller that is hosting the global catalog, it was assigned to a DC2 in each domain.

- Because the schema master and the domain naming master roles should always be assigned to a domain controller designated as the global catalog server, and because their load is very light, the forest-wide roles were assigned to DC1 at hq.corp.f-1000times.com.

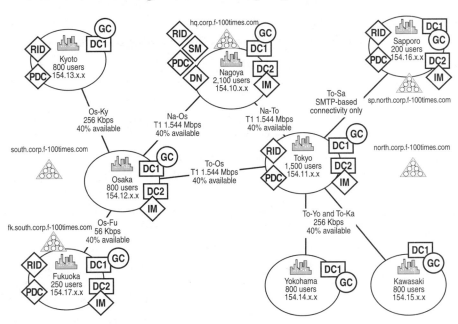

Review Questions

Page 281

1. You are defining sites for an organization that has three sets of LANs, each connected by a T1 line. How many sites should you define?

   You should define a site for each LAN or set of LANs that are connected by a high-speed backbone or for a location that does not have direct connectivity to the rest of the network and is only reachable using SMTP mail. Because a T1 line is not a high-speed backbone, you should define three sites.

2. You have placed the minimum number of domain controllers into sites for your organization. What are the reasons for placing additional domain controllers into sites?

   The reasons for placing additional domain controllers into sites are as follows:

   - **There are a large number of users in the site and the link to the site is slow or near capacity.**

   - **The link to the site is historically unreliable or only intermittently unavailable.**

3. You are configuring site links and you want to set up a site link table for your site topology plan. What configuration information should you include in the table?

   A site link table should include the site link name, method of replication transport, site link cost, replication frequency, and replication availability for each site link.

4. Describe how Active Directory data is replicated between bridgehead servers during intersite replication. Then describe how Active Directory is replicated from the bridgehead server to other domain controllers within a site.

   Polling and pull replication are used between bridgehead servers during intersite replication. Pull replication is the most efficient for intersite replication because the destination domain controller knows which replication data to request. Notification and push replication are used for intrasite replication, when domain controllers are well connected and not restrained by site link schedules.

5. You are assigning the infrastructure master role to a domain controller that has been designated as the global catalog server. Explain why you should do this only under certain conditions and explain those conditions.

   The infrastructure master role should not be assigned to the domain controller that has been designated as the global catalog. If the infrastructure master and global catalog are on the same domain controller, the infrastructure master will not function. The infrastructure master will never find data that is out of date, and so will never replicate any changes to the other domain controllers in the domain. If all of the domain controllers in a domain are also hosting the global catalog, all of the domain controllers will have the current data and it does not matter which domain controller holds the infrastructure master role.

Page 283

Chapter 7
Creating an Active Directory Implementation Plan

Lab 7.1: Planning a Windows NT 4 Directory Services Migration to Windows 2000 Active Directory

Exercise: Planning a Windows NT 4 Directory Services Migration to Windows 2000 Active Directory

Exercise Questions

Page 328

1. What migration method(s) will you use to migrate to Windows 2000 Active Directory?

   Because the current Windows NT domain structure functions fairly well and the scenario mentions no special requirements for keeping the production environment running during the migration process, the domain upgrade method will be used to migrate the domains to Windows 2000.

   A dedicated root domain must be created in the Active Directory forest before the upgrade is performed. After the upgrade is performed, it will be necessary to consolidate the resource domains into OUs in the child domains.

2. List the steps you will take to plan the migration.

   Answers may vary, but should include the following:

   1. A recovery plan will be established.

   2. The domains to be upgraded are listed in order. The dedicated root domain will be established first in the Windows 2000 forest. Then the master domains, STOCKS and CASH, will be upgraded followed by the resource domains, PHOENIX, TUSCON, and ALBUQUERQUE.

   3. List the strategy for upgrading domain controllers in each domain. For each of the STOCKS, CASH, PHOENIX, TUSCON, and ALBUQUERQUE domains in order, the PDC will be upgraded followed by the BDC.

4. **Indicate when you plan to switch to native mode. The switch to native mode will be made when resource domains are consolidated into OUs and when administrators are satisfied with the results of the migration.**

5. **List the present location of resources in Windows NT and the OUs to which the resources will be consolidated. Resources in each of the resource domains will be consolidated into the stocks.s-100times.com and cash.s-100times.com domains as determined by user needs.**

6. **Indicate the trust relationships that must be set up in order for users outside of the forest to access resources when they are consolidated in the target OU. There are no users outside of the forest that need to access resources consolidated into OUs.**

Review Questions

Page 329

1. You are planning a Windows NT 4 Directory Services migration to Windows 2000 Active Directory. The current production environment cannot withstand any negative effects as a result of the migration process. What migration method should you use?

   Use the domain restructure method when the current production environment cannot withstand any negative effects as a result of the migration process.

2. Why should you use the domain restructure method if the production environment cannot withstand any negative effects as a result of the migration process?

   A domain restructure migrates the existing Windows NT environment into a pristine Windows 2000 forest using a nondestructive copy. A pristine forest is an ideal Windows 2000 forest that is isolated from the Windows NT production environment and that operates in native mode. Domain accounts exist in both Windows NT and Windows 2000, and the Windows NT environment is retained until it is ready to be decommissioned.

3. Your organization has just migrated to Windows 2000 Server and Exchange Server 5.5. You would like to propagate the user information in the Exchange Server directory service to your new Active Directory. What tool should you install to accomplish the synchronization, and where are the tool installation files located?

To set up synchronization between Active Directory and Exchange Server 5.5, you must install the Active Directory Connector (ADC). The installation files for ADC are located on the Windows 2000 Server CD in the Valueadd\Msft\Mgmt\ADC folder.

4. Your organization is running Windows 2000 and has just acquired a small company that uses NDS. You would like to synchronize the directory information with Active Directory. What tool should you install to accomplish the synchronization, and where are the tool installation files located?

To enable users of Novell directory services to implement synchronization, Microsoft developed Microsoft Directory Synchronization Services (MSDSS), which is included with Services for NetWare version 5 (SFNW5).

A P P E N D I X   B

Base Schema Class Objects

Schema class objects describe the possible Active Directory objects that can be created, functioning as a template for creating new Active Directory objects. The base schema class objects are the basic set of schema class objects shipped with Windows 2000 Server. If the base schema doesn't meet the needs of your organization, you must consider modifying the schema or creating additional schema class and/or attribute objects; this process is called extending the schema. To determine whether the base schema objects meet the needs of your organization, you must familiarize yourself with the base schema class objects listed in this appendix and the base schema attribute objects listed in Appendix C. If you know the types of data that Active Directory will hold, you can more effectively determine whether you need to change the base schema and whom the changes will impact.

Name	Type	Description
aCSPolicy	Structural	ACS-Policy
aCSResourceLimits	Structural	ACS-Resource-Limits
aCSSubnet	Structural	ACS-Subnet
addressBookContainer	Structural	Address-Book-Container
addressTemplate	Structural	Address-Template
applicationEntity	Structural	Application-Entity
applicationProcess	Structural	Application-Process
applicationSettings	Abstract	Application-Settings

continued

Name	Type	Description
applicationSiteSettings	Abstract	Application-Site-Settings
attributeSchema	Structural	Attribute-Schema
builtinDomain	Structural	Builtin-Domain
categoryRegistration	Structural	Category-Registration
certificationAuthority	Structural	Certification-Authority
classRegistration	Structural	Class-Registration
classSchema	Structural	Class-Schema
classStore	Structural	Class-Store
comConnectionPoint	Structural	Com-Connection-Point
computer	Structural	Computer
configuration	Structural	Configuration
connectionPoint	Abstract	Connection-Point
contact	Structural	Contact
container	Structural	Container
controlAccessRight	Structural	Control-Access-Right
country	Abstract	Country
cRLDistributionPoint	Structural	CRL-Distribution-Point
crossRef	Structural	Cross-Ref
crossRefContainer	Structural	Cross-Ref-Container
device	Abstract	Device
dfsConfiguration	Structural	Dfs-Configuration
dHCPClass	Structural	DHCP-Class
displaySpecifier	Structural	Display-Specifier
displayTemplate	Structural	Display-Template
dMD	Structural	DMD
dnsNode	Structural	Dns-Node
dnsZone	Structural	Dns-Zone
domain	Abstract	Domain
domainDNS	Structural	Domain-DNS

Name	Type	Description
domainPolicy	Structural	Domain-Policy
dSA	Structural	DSA
dSUISettings	Structural	DS-UI-Settings
fileLinkTracking	Structural	File-Link-Tracking
fileLinkTrackingEntry	Structural	File-Link-Tracking-Entry
foreignSecurityPrincipal	Structural	Foreign-Security-Principal
fTDfs	Structural	FT-Dfs
group	Structural	Group
groupOfNames	Abstract	Group-Of-Names
groupPolicyContainer	Structural	Group-Policy-Container
indexServerCatalog	Structural	Index-Server-Catalog
infrastructureUpdate	Structural	Infrastructure-Update
intellimirrorGroup	Structural	Intellimirror-Group
intellimirrorSCP	Structural	Intellimirror-SCP
interSiteTransport	Structural	Inter-Site-Transport
interSiteTransportContainer	Structural	Inter-Site-Transport-Container
ipsecBase	Abstract	Ipsec-Base
ipsecFilter	Structural	Ipsec-Filter
ipsecISAKMPPolicy	Structural	Ipsec-ISAKMP-Policy
ipsecNegotiationPolicy	Structural	Ipsec-Negotiation-Policy
ipsecNFA	Structural	Ipsec-NFA
ipsecPolicy	Structural	Ipsec-Policy
leaf	Abstract	Leaf
licensingSiteSettings	Structural	Licensing-Site-Settings
linkTrackObjectMoveTable	Structural	Link-Track-Object-Move-Table
linkTrackOMTEntry	Structural	Link-Track-OMT-Entry
linkTrackVolEntry	Structural	Link-Track-Vol-Entry
linkTrackVolumeTable	Structural	Link-Track-Volume-Table

continued

Name	Type	Description
locality	Structural	Locality
lostAndFound	Structural	Lost-And-Found
mailRecipient	Auxiliary	Mail-Recipient
meeting	Structural	Meeting
msExchConfigurationContainer	Structural	ms-Exch-Configuration-Container
mSMQConfiguration	Structural	MSMQ-Configuration
mSMQEnterpriseSettings	Structural	MSMQ-Enterprise-Settings
mSMQMigratedUser	Structural	MSMQ-Migrated-User
mSMQQueue	Structural	MSMQ-Queue
mSMQSettings	Structural	MSMQ-Settings
mSMQSiteLink	Structural	MSMQ-Site-Link
mS-SQL-OLAPCube	Structural	MS-SQL-OLAPCube
mS-SQL-OLAPDatabase	Structural	MS-SQL-OLAPDatabase
mS-SQL-OLAPServer	Structural	MS-SQL-OLAPServer
mS-SQL-SQLDatabase	Structural	MS-SQL-SQLDatabase
mS-SQL-SQLPublication	Structural	MS-SQL-SQLPublication
mS-SQL-SQLRepository	Structural	MS-SQL-SQLRepository
mS-SQL-SQLServer	Structural	MS-SQL-SQLServer
nTDSConnection	Structural	NTDS-Connection
nTDSDSA	Structural	NTDS-DSA
nTDSService	Structural	NTDS-Service
nTDSSiteSettings	Structural	NTDS-Site-Settings
nTFRSMember	Structural	NTFRS-Member
nTFRSReplicaSet	Structural	NTFRS-Replica-Set
nTFRSSettings	Structural	NTFRS-Settings
nTFRSSubscriber	Structural	NTFRS-Subscriber
nTFRSSubscriptions	Structural	NTFRS-Subscriptions
organization	Structural	Organization

Name	Type	Description
organizationalPerson	Abstract	Organizational-Person
organizationalRole	Structural	Organizational-Role
organizationalUnit	Structural	Organizational-Unit
packageRegistration	Structural	Package-Registration
person	Abstract	Person
physicalLocation	Structural	Physical-Location
pKICertificateTemplate	Structural	PKI-Certificate-Template
pKIEnrollmentService	Structural	PKI-Enrollment-Service
printQueue	Structural	Print-Queue
queryPolicy	Structural	Query-Policy
remoteMailRecipient	Structural	Remote-Mail-Recipient
remoteStorageServicePoint	Structural	Remote-Storage-Service-Point
residentialPerson	Structural	Residential-Person
rIDManager	Structural	RID-Manager
rIDSet	Structural	RID-Set
rpcContainer	Structural	Rpc-Container
rpcEntry	Abstract	rpc-Entry
rpcGroup	Structural	rpc-Group
rpcProfile	Structural	rpc-Profile
rpcProfileElement	Structural	rpc-Profile-Element
rpcServer	Structural	rpc-Server
rpcServerElement	Structural	rpc-Server-Element
rRASAdministrationConnectionPoint	Structural	RRAS-Administration-Connection-Point
rRASAdministrationDictionary	Structural	RRAS-Administration-Dictionary
samDomain	Auxiliary	Sam-Domain
samDomainBase	Auxiliary	Sam-Domain-Base

continued

Name	Type	Description
samServer	Structural	Sam-Server
secret	Structural	Secret
securityObject	Abstract	Security-Object
securityPrincipal	Auxiliary	Security-Principal
server	Structural	Server
serversContainer	Structural	Servers-Container
serviceAdministrationPoint	Structural	Service-Administration-Point
serviceClass	Structural	Service-Class
serviceConnectionPoint	Structural	Service-Connection-Point
serviceInstance	Structural	Service-Instance
site	Structural	Site
siteLink	Structural	Site-Link
siteLinkBridge	Structural	Site-Link-Bridge
sitesContainer	Structural	Sites-Container
storage	Structural	Storage
subnet	Structural	Subnet
subnetContainer	Structural	Subnet-Container
subSchema	Structural	SubSchema
top	Abstract	Top
trustedDomain	Structural	Trusted-Domain
typeLibrary	Structural	Type-Library
user	Structural	User
volume	Structural	Volume

APPENDIX   C

Base Schema Attribute Objects

Schema attribute objects describe the possible Active Directory objects that can be created, functioning as a template for creating new Active Directory objects. The base schema attribute objects are the basic set of schema attribute objects shipped with Windows 2000 Server. If the base schema doesn't meet the needs of your organization, you must consider modifying the schema or creating additional schema class and/or attribute objects; this process is called extending the schema. To determine whether the base schema objects meet the needs of your organization, you must familiarize yourself with the base schema attribute objects listed in this appendix and the base schema class objects listed in Appendix B. If you know the types of data that Active Directory will hold, you can more effectively determine whether you need to change the base schema and whom the changes will impact.

Name	Syntax	Description
accountExpires	Large Integer	Account-Expires
accountNameHistory	Unicode String	Account-Name-History
aCSAggregateTokenRatePerUser	Large Integer	ACS-Aggregate-Token-Rate-Per-User
aCSAllocableRSVPBandwidth	Large Integer	ACS-Allocable-RSVP-Bandwidth
aCSCacheTimeout	Integer	ACS-Cache-Timeout
aCSDirection	Integer	ACS-Direction
aCSDSBMDeadTime	Integer	ACS-DSBM-DeadTime
aCSDSBMPriority	Integer	ACS-DSBM-Priority
aCSDSBMRefresh	Integer	ACS-DSBM-Refresh
aCSEnableACSService	Boolean	ACS-Enable-ACS-Service

continued

Name	Syntax	Description
aCSEnableRSVPAccounting	Boolean	ACS-Enable-RSVP-Accounting
aCSEnableRSVPMessageLogging	Boolean	ACS-Enable-RSVP-Message-Logging
aCSEventLogLevel	Integer	ACS-Event-Log-Level
aCSIdentityName	Unicode String	ACS-Identity-Name
aCSMaxAggregatePeakRatePerUser	Large Integer	ACS-Max-Aggregate-Peak-Rate-Per-User
aCSMaxDurationPerFlow	Integer	ACS-Max-Duration-Per-Flow
aCSMaximumSDUSize	Large Integer	ACS-Maximum-SDU-Size
aCSMaxNoOfAccountFiles	Integer	ACS-Max-No-Of-Account-Files
aCSMaxNoOfLogFiles	Integer	ACS-Max-No-Of-Log-Files
aCSMaxPeakBandwidth	Large Integer	ACS-Max-Peak-Bandwidth
aCSMaxPeakBandwidthPerFlow	Large Integer	ACS-Max-Peak-Bandwidth-Per-Flow
aCSMaxSizeOfRSVPAccountFile	Integer	ACS-Max-Size-Of-RSVP-Account-File
aCSMaxSizeOfRSVPLogFile	Integer	ACS-Max-Size-Of-RSVP-Log-File
aCSMaxTokenBucketPerFlow	Large Integer	ACS-Max-Token-Bucket-Per-Flow
aCSMaxTokenRatePerFlow	Large Integer	ACS-Max-Token-Rate-Per-Flow
aCSMinimumDelayVariation	Large Integer	ACS-Minimum-Delay-Variation
aCSMinimumLatency	Large Integer	ACS-Minimum-Latency
aCSMinimumPolicedSize	Large Integer	ACS-Minimum-Policed-Size
aCSNonReservedMaxSDUSize	Large Integer	ACS-Non-Reserved-Max-SDU-Size
aCSNonReservedMinPolicedSize	Large Integer	ACS-Non-Reserved-Min-Policed-Size
aCSNonReservedPeakRate	Large Integer	ACS-Non-Reserved-Peak-Rate
aCSNonReservedTokenSize	Large Integer	ACS-Non-Reserved-Token-Size
aCSNonReservedTxLimit	Large Integer	ACS-Non-Reserved-Tx-Limit
aCSNonReservedTxSize	Large Integer	ACS-Non-Reserved-Tx-Size
aCSPermissionBits	Large Integer	ACS-Permission-Bits
aCSPolicyName	Unicode String	ACS-Policy-Name
aCSPriority	Integer	ACS-Priority
aCSRSVPAccountFilesLocation	Unicode String	ACS-RSVP-Account-Files-Location

Name	Syntax	Description
aCSRSVPLogFilesLocation	Unicode String	ACS-RSVP-Log-Files-Location
aCSServerList	Unicode String	ACS-Server-List
aCSServiceType	Integer	ACS-Service-Type
aCSTimeOfDay	Unicode String	ACS-Time-Of-Day
aCSTotalNoOfFlows	Integer	ACS-Total-No-Of-Flows
additionalTrustedServiceNames	Unicode String	Additional-Trusted-Service-Names
addressBookRoots	Distinguished Name	Address-Book-Roots
addressEntryDisplayTable	Octet String	Address-Entry-Display-Table
addressEntryDisplayTableMSDOS	Octet String	Address-Entry-Display-Table-MSDOS
addressSyntax	Octet String	Address-Syntax
addressType	Case Insensitive String	Address-Type
adminContextMenu	Unicode String	Admin-Context-Menu
adminCount	Integer	Admin-Count
adminDescription	Unicode String	Admin-Description
adminDisplayName	Unicode String	Admin-Display-Name
adminPropertyPages	Unicode String	Admin-Property-Pages
allowedAttributes	Object Identifier	Allowed-Attributes
allowedAttributesEffective	Object Identifier	Allowed-Attributes-Effective
allowedChildClasses	Object Identifier	Allowed-Child-Classes
allowedChildClassesEffective	Object Identifier	Allowed-Child-Classes-Effective
altSecurityIdentities	Unicode String	Alt-Security-Identities
aNR	Unicode String	ANR
applicationName	Unicode String	Application-Name
appliesTo	Unicode String	Applies-To
appSchemaVersion	Integer	App-Schema-Version
assetNumber	Unicode String	Asset-Number
assistant	Distinguished Name	Assistant
assocNTAccount	Octet String	Assoc-NT-Account
attributeDisplayNames	Unicode String	Attribute-Display-Names

continued

Name	Syntax	Description
attributeID	Object Identifier	Attribute-ID
attributeSecurityGUID	Octet String	Attribute-Security-GUID
attributeSyntax	Object Identifier	Attribute-Syntax
attributeTypes	Unicode String	Attribute-Types
auditingPolicy	Octet String	Auditing-Policy
authenticationOptions	Integer	Authentication-Options
authorityRevocationList	Octet String	Authority-Revocation-List
auxiliaryClass	Object Identifier	Auxiliary-Class
badPasswordTime	Large Integer	Bad-Password-Time
badPwdCount	Integer	Bad-Pwd-Count
birthLocation	Octet String	Birth-Location
bridgeheadServerListBL	Distinguished Name	Bridgehead-Server-List-BL
bridgeheadTransportList	Distinguished Name	Bridgehead-Transport-List
builtinCreationTime	Large Integer	Builtin-Creation-Time
builtinModifiedCount	Large Integer	Builtin-Modified-Count
businessCategory	Unicode String	Business-Category
bytesPerMinute	Integer	Bytes-Per-Minute
c	Unicode String	Country-Name
cACertificate	Octet String	CA-Certificate
cACertificateDN	Unicode String	CA-Certificate-DN
cAConnect	Unicode String	CA-Connect
canonicalName	Unicode String	Canonical-Name
canUpgradeScript	Unicode String	Can-Upgrade-Script
catalogs	Unicode String	Catalogs
categories	Unicode String	Categories
categoryId	Octet String	Category-Id
cAUsages	Unicode String	CA-Usages
cAWEBURL	Unicode String	CA-WEB-URL
certificateAuthorityObject	Distinguished Name	Certificate-Authority-Object

Name	Syntax	Description
certificateRevocationList	Octet String	Certificate-Revocation-List
certificateTemplates	Unicode String	Certificate-Templates
classDisplayName	Unicode String	Class-Display-Name
cn	Unicode String	Common-Name
co	Unicode String	Text-Country
codePage	Integer	Code-Page
cOMClassID	Unicode String	COM-ClassID
cOMCLSID	Unicode String	COM-CLSID
cOMInterfaceID	Unicode String	COM-InterfaceID
comment	Unicode String	User-Comment
cOMOtherProgId	Unicode String	COM-Other-Prog-Id
company	Unicode String	Company
cOMProgID	Unicode String	COM-ProgID
cOMTreatAsClassId	Unicode String	COM-Treat-As-Class-Id
cOMTypelibId	Unicode String	COM-Typelib-Id
cOMUniqueLIBID	Unicode String	COM-Unique-LIBID
contentIndexingAllowed	Boolean	Content-Indexing-Allowed
contextMenu	Unicode String	Context-Menu
controlAccessRights	Octet String	Control-Access-Rights
cost	Integer	Cost
countryCode	Integer	Country-Code
createDialog	Unicode String	Create-Dialog
createTimeStamp	Generalized Time	Create-Time-Stamp
createWizardExt	Unicode String	Create-Wizard-Ext
creationTime	Large Integer	Creation-Time
creationWizard	Unicode String	Creation-Wizard
creator	Unicode String	Creator
cRLObject	Distinguished Name	CRL-Object
cRLPartitionedRevocationList	Octet String	CRL-Partitioned-Revocation-List

continued

Name	Syntax	Description
crossCertificatePair	Octet String	Cross-Certificate-Pair
currentLocation	Octet String	Current-Location
currentParentCA	Distinguished Name	Current-Parent-CA
currentValue	Octet String	Current-Value
currMachineId	Octet String	Curr-Machine-Id
dBCSPwd	Octet String	DBCS-Pwd
dc	Unicode String	Domain-Component
defaultClassStore	Distinguished Name	Default-Class-Store
defaultGroup	Distinguished Name	Default-Group
defaultHidingValue	Boolean	Default-Hiding-Value
defaultLocalPolicyObject	Distinguished Name	Default-Local-Policy-Object
defaultObjectCategory	Distinguished Name	Default-Object-Category
defaultPriority	Integer	Default-Priority
defaultSecurityDescriptor	Unicode String	Default-Security-Descriptor
deltaRevocationList	Octet String	Delta-Revocation-List
department	Unicode String	Department
description	Unicode String	Description
desktopProfile	Unicode String	Desktop-Profile
destinationIndicator	Print Case String	Destination-Indicator
dhcpClasses	Octet String	dhcp-Classes
dhcpFlags	Large Integer	dhcp-Flags
dhcpIdentification	Unicode String	dhcp-Identification
dhcpMask	Print Case String	dhcp-Mask
dhcpMaxKey	Large Integer	dhcp-MaxKey
dhcpObjDescription	Unicode String	dhcp-Obj-Description
dhcpObjName	Unicode String	dhcp-Obj-Name
dhcpOptions	Octet String	dhcp-Options

Name	Syntax	Description
dhcpProperties	Octet String	dhcp-Properties
dhcpRanges	Print Case String	dhcp-Ranges
dhcpReservations	Print Case String	dhcp-Reservations
dhcpServers	Print Case String	dhcp-Servers
dhcpSites	Print Case String	dhcp-Sites
dhcpState	Print Case String	dhcp-State
dhcpSubnets	Print Case String	dhcp-Subnets
dhcpType	Integer	dhcp-Type
dhcpUniqueKey	Large Integer	dhcp-Unique-Key
dhcpUpdateTime	Large Integer	dhcp-Update-Time
directReports	Distinguished Name	Reports
displayName	Unicode String	Display-Name
displayNamePrintable	Print Case String	Display-Name-Printable
distinguishedName	Distinguished Name	Obj-Dist-Name
dITContentRules	Unicode String	DIT-Content-Rules
division	Unicode String	Division
dMDLocation	Distinguished Name	DMD-Location
dmdName	Unicode String	DMD-Name
dNReferenceUpdate	Distinguished Name	DN-Reference-Update
dnsAllowDynamic	Boolean	Dns-Allow-Dynamic
dnsAllowXFR	Boolean	Dns-Allow-XFR
dNSHostName	Unicode String	DNS-Host-Name
dnsNotifySecondaries	Integer	Dns-Notify-Secondaries
dNSProperty	Octet String	DNS-Property
dnsRecord	Octet String	Dns-Record
dnsRoot	Unicode String	Dns-Root
dnsSecureSecondaries	Integer	Dns-Secure-Secondaries

continued

Name	Syntax	Description
dNSTombstoned	Boolean	DNS-Tombstoned
domainCAs	Distinguished Name	Domain-Certificate-Authorities
domainCrossRef	Distinguished Name	Domain-Cross-Ref
domainID	Distinguished Name	Domain-ID
domainIdentifier	Integer	Domain-Identifier
domainPolicyObject	Distinguished Name	Domain-Policy-Object
domainPolicyReference	Distinguished Name	Domain-Policy-Reference
domainReplica	Unicode String	Domain-Replica
domainWidePolicy	Octet String	Domain-Wide-Policy
driverName	Unicode String	Driver-Name
driverVersion	Integer	Driver-Version
dSASignature	Octet String	DSA-Signature
dSCorePropagationData	Generalized Time	DS-Core-Propagation-Data
dSHeuristics	Unicode String	DS-Heuristics
dSUIAdminMaximum	Integer	DS-UI-Admin-Maximum
dSUIAdminNotification	Unicode String	DS-UI-Admin-Notification
dSUIShellMaximum	Integer	DS-UI-Shell-Maximum
dynamicLDAPServer	Distinguished Name	Dynamic-LDAP-Server
eFSPolicy	Octet String	EFSPolicy
employeeID	Unicode String	Employee-ID
employeeNumber	Unicode String	Employee-Number
employeeType	Unicode String	Employee-Type
Enabled	Boolean	Enabled
enabledConnection	Boolean	Enabled-Connection
enrollmentProviders	Unicode String	Enrollment-Providers
extendedAttributeInfo	Unicode String	Extended-Attribute-Info
extendedCharsAllowed	Boolean	Extended-Chars-Allowed

Name	Syntax	Description
extendedClassInfo	Unicode String	Extended-Class-Info
extensionName	Unicode String	Extension-Name
facsimileTelephoneNumber	Unicode String	Facsimile-Telephone-Number
fileExtPriority	Unicode String	File-Ext-Priority
flags	Integer	Flags
flatName	Unicode String	Flat-Name
forceLogoff	Large Integer	Force-Logoff
foreignIdentifier	Octet String	Foreign-Identifier
friendlyNames	Unicode String	Friendly-Names
fromEntry	Boolean	From-Entry
fromServer	Distinguished Name	From-Server
frsComputerReference	Distinguished Name	Frs-Computer-Reference
frsComputerReferenceBL	Distinguished Name	Frs-Computer-Reference-BL
fRSControlDataCreation	Unicode String	FRS-Control-Data-Creation
fRSControlInboundBacklog	Unicode String	FRS-Control-Inbound-Backlog
fRSControlOutboundBacklog	Unicode String	FRS-Control-Outbound-Backlog
fRSDirectoryFilter	Unicode String	FRS-Directory-Filter
fRSDSPoll	Integer	FRS-DS-Poll
fRSExtensions	Octet String	FRS-Extensions
fRSFaultCondition	Unicode String	FRS-Fault-Condition
fRSFileFilter	Unicode String	FRS-File-Filter
fRSFlags	Integer	FRS-Flags
fRSLevelLimit	Integer	FRS-Level-Limit
fRSMemberReference	Distinguished Name	FRS-Member-Reference
fRSMemberReferenceBL	Distinguished Name	FRS-Member-Reference-BL
fRSPartnerAuthLevel	Integer	FRS-Partner-Auth-Level
fRSPrimaryMember	Distinguished Name	FRS-Primary-Member

continued

Name	Syntax	Description
fRSReplicaSetGUID	Octet String	FRS-Replica-Set-GUID
fRSReplicaSetType	Integer	FRS-Replica-Set-Type
fRSRootPath	Unicode String	FRS-Root-Path
fRSRootSecurity	NT Security Descriptor	FRS-Root-Security
fRSServiceCommand	Unicode String	FRS-Service-Command
fRSServiceCommandStatus	Unicode String	FRS-Service-Command-Status
fRSStagingPath	Unicode String	FRS-Staging-Path
fRSTimeLastCommand	UTC Coded Time	FRS-Time-Last-Command
fRSTimeLastConfigChange	UTC Coded Time	FRS-Time-Last-Config-Change
fRSUpdateTimeout	Integer	FRS-Update-Timeout
fRSVersion	Unicode String	FRS-Version
fRSVersionGUID	Octet String	FRS-Version-GUID
fRSWorkingPath	Unicode String	FRS-Working-Path
fSMORoleOwner	Distinguished Name	FSMO-Role-Owner
garbageCollPeriod	Integer	Garbage-Coll-Period
generatedConnection	Boolean	Generated-Connection
generationQualifier	Unicode String	Generation-Qualifier
givenName	Unicode String	Given-Name
globalAddressList	Distinguished Name	Global-Address-List
governsID	Object Identifier	Governs-ID
gPCFileSysPath	Unicode String	GPC-File-Sys-Path
gPCFunctionalityVersion	Integer	GPC-Functionality-Version
gPCMachineExtensionNames	Unicode String	GPC-Machine-Extension-Names
gPCUserExtensionNames	Unicode String	GPC-User-Extension-Names
gPLink	Unicode String	GP-Link
gPOptions	Integer	GP-Options
groupAttributes	Integer	Group-Attributes

Name	Syntax	Description
groupMembershipSAM	Octet String	Group-Membership-SAM
groupPriority	Unicode String	Group-Priority
groupsToIgnore	Unicode String	Groups-to-Ignore
groupType	Integer	Group-Type
hasMasterNCs	Distinguished Name	Has-Master-NCs
hasPartialReplicaNCs	Distinguished Name	Has-Partial-Replica-NCs
helpData16	Octet String	Help-Data16
helpData32	Octet String	Help-Data32
helpFileName	Unicode String	Help-File-Name
homeDirectory	Unicode String	Home-Directory
homeDrive	Unicode String	Home-Drive
homePhone	Unicode String	Phone-Home-Primary
homePostalAddress	Unicode String	Address-Home
iconPath	Unicode String	Icon-Path
implementedCategories	Octet String	Implemented-Categories
indexedScopes	Unicode String	IndexedScopes
info	Unicode String	Comment
initialAuthIncoming	Unicode String	Initial-Auth-Incoming
initialAuthOutgoing	Unicode String	Initial-Auth-Outgoing
initials	Unicode String	Initials
installUiLevel	Integer	Install-Ui-Level
instanceType	Integer	Instance-Type
internationalISDNNumber	Numerical String	International-ISDN-Number
interSiteTopologyFailover	Integer	Inter-Site-Topology-Failover
interSiteTopologyGenerator	Distinguished Name	Inter-Site-Topology-Generator
interSiteTopologyRenew	Integer	Inter-Site-Topology-Renew
invocationId	Octet String	Invocation-Id

continued

Name	Syntax	Description
ipPhone	Unicode String	Phone-Ip-Primary
ipsecData	Octet String	Ipsec-Data
ipsecDataType	Integer	Ipsec-Data-Type
ipsecFilterReference	Distinguished Name	Ipsec-Filter-Reference
ipsecID	Unicode String	Ipsec-ID
ipsecISAKMPReference	Distinguished Name	Ipsec-ISAKMP-Reference
ipsecName	Unicode String	Ipsec-Name
iPSECNegotiationPolicyAction	Unicode String	IPSEC-Negotiation-Policy-Action
ipsecNegotiationPolicyReference	Distinguished Name	Ipsec-Negotiation-Policy-Reference
iPSECNegotiationPolicyType	Unicode String	IPSEC-Negotiation-Policy-Type
ipsecNFAReference	Distinguished Name	Ipsec-NFA-Reference
ipsecOwnersReference	Distinguished Name	Ipsec-Owners-Reference
ipsecPolicyReference	Distinguished Name	Ipsec-Policy-Reference
isCriticalSystemObject	Boolean	Is-Critical-System-Object
isDefunct	Boolean	Is-Defunct
isDeleted	Boolean	Is-Deleted
isEphemeral	Boolean	Is-Ephemeral
isMemberOfPartialAttributeSet	Boolean	Is-Member-Of-Partial-Attribute-Set
isPrivilegeHolder	Distinguished Name	Is-Privilege-Holder
isSingleValued	Boolean	Is-Single-Valued
keywords	Unicode String	Keywords
knowledgeInformation	Case Insensitive String	Knowledge-Information
l	Unicode String	Locality-Name
lastBackupRestorationTime	Large Integer	Last-Backup-Restoration-Time
lastContentIndexed	Large Integer	Last-Content-Indexed
lastKnownParent	Distinguished Name	Last-Known-Parent
lastLogoff	Large Integer	Last-Logoff

Name	Syntax	Description
lastLogon	Large Integer	Last-Logon
lastSetTime	Large Integer	Last-Set-Time
lastUpdateSequence	Unicode String	Last-Update-Sequence
lDAPAdminLimits	Unicode String	LDAP-Admin-Limits
lDAPDisplayName	Unicode String	LDAP-Display-Name
lDAPIPDenyList	Octet String	LDAP-IPDeny-List
legacyExchangeDN	Case Insensitive String	Legacy-Exchange-DN
linkID	Integer	Link-ID
linkTrackSecret	Octet String	Link-Track-Secret
lmPwdHistory	Octet String	Lm-Pwd-History
localeID	Integer	Locale-ID
localizationDisplayId	Integer	Localization-Display-Id
localizedDescription	Unicode String	Localized-Description
localPolicyFlags	Integer	Local-Policy-Flags
localPolicyReference	Distinguished Name	Local-Policy-Reference
location	Unicode String	Location
lockoutDuration	Large Integer	Lockout-Duration
lockOutObservationWindow	Large Integer	Lock-Out-Observation-Window
lockoutThreshold	Integer	Lockout-Threshold
lockoutTime	Large Integer	Lockout-Time
logonCount	Integer	Logon-Count
logonHours	Octet String	Logon-Hours
logonWorkstation	Octet String	Logon-Workstation
lSACreationTime	Large Integer	LSA-Creation-Time
lSAModifiedCount	Large Integer	LSA-Modified-Count
machineArchitecture	Enumeration	Machine-Architecture
machinePasswordChangeInterval	Large Integer	Machine-Password-Change-Interval

continued

Name	Syntax	Description
machineRole	Enumeration	Machine-Role
machineWidePolicy	Octet String	Machine-Wide-Policy
mail	Unicode String	E-mail-Addresses
mailAddress	Unicode String	SMTP-Mail-Address
managedBy	Distinguished Name	Managed-By
managedObjects	Distinguished Name	Managed-Objects
manager	Distinguished Name	Manager
mAPIID	Integer	MAPI-ID
marshalledInterface	Octet String	Marshalled-Interface
masteredBy	Distinguished Name	Mastered-By
maxPwdAge	Large Integer	Max-Pwd-Age
maxRenewAge	Large Integer	Max-Renew-Age
maxStorage	Large Integer	Max-Storage
maxTicketAge	Large Integer	Max-Ticket-Age
mayContain	Object Identifier	May-Contain
meetingAdvertiseScope	Unicode String	meetingAdvertiseScope
meetingApplication	Unicode String	meetingApplication
meetingBandwidth	Integer	meetingBandwidth
meetingBlob	Octet String	meetingBlob
meetingContactInfo	Unicode String	meetingContactInfo
meetingDescription	Unicode String	meetingDescription
meetingEndTime	UTC Coded Time	meetingEndTime
meetingID	Unicode String	meetingID
meetingIP	Unicode String	meetingIP
meetingIsEncrypted	Unicode String	meetingIsEncrypted
meetingKeyword	Unicode String	meetingKeyword
meetingLanguage	Unicode String	meetingLanguage

Name	Syntax	Description
meetingLocation	Unicode String	meetingLocation
meetingMaxParticipants	Integer	meetingMaxParticipants
meetingName	Unicode String	meetingName
meetingOriginator	Unicode String	meetingOriginator
meetingOwner	Unicode String	meetingOwner
meetingProtocol	Unicode String	meetingProtocol
meetingRating	Unicode String	meetingRating
meetingRecurrence	Unicode String	meetingRecurrence
meetingScope	Unicode String	meetingScope
meetingStartTime	UTC Coded Time	meetingStartTime
meetingType	Unicode String	meetingType
meetingURL	Unicode String	meetingURL
member	Distinguished Name	Member
memberOf	Distinguished Name	Is-Member-Of-DL
mhsORAddress	Unicode String	MHS-OR-Address
middleName	Unicode String	Other-Name
minPwdAge	Large Integer	Min-Pwd-Age
minPwdLength	Integer	Min-Pwd-Length
minTicketAge	Large Integer	Min-Ticket-Age
mobile	Unicode String	Phone-Mobile-Primary
modifiedCount	Large Integer	Modified-Count
modifiedCountAtLastProm	Large Integer	Modified-Count-At-Last-Prom
modifyTimeStamp	Generalized Time	Modify-Time-Stamp
moniker	Octet String	Moniker
monikerDisplayName	Unicode String	Moniker-Display-Name
moveTreeState	Octet String	Move-Tree-State
mscopeId	Print Case String	Mscope-Id

continued

Name	Syntax	Description
mS-DS-ConsistencyChildCount	Integer	MS-DS-Consistency-Child-Count
mS-DS-ConsistencyGuid	Octet String	MS-DS-Consistency-Guid
mS-DS-CreatorSID	SID	MS-DS-Creator-SID
ms-DS-MachineAccountQuota	Integer	MS-DS-Machine-Account-Quota
mS-DS-ReplicatesNCReason	DN Binary	MS-DS-Replicates-NC-Reason
msiFileList	Unicode String	Msi-File-List
msiScript	Octet String	Msi-Script
msiScriptName	Unicode String	Msi-Script-Name
msiScriptPath	Unicode String	Msi-Script-Path
msiScriptSize	Integer	Msi-Script-Size
mSMQAuthenticate	Boolean	MSMQ-Authenticate
mSMQBasePriority	Integer	MSMQ-Base-Priority
mSMQComputerType	Case Insensitive String	MSMQ-Computer-Type
mSMQComputerTypeEx	Unicode String	MSMQ-Computer-Type-Ex
mSMQCost	Integer	MSMQ-Cost
mSMQCSPName	Case Insensitive String	MSMQ-CSP-Name
mSMQDependentClientService	Boolean	MSMQ-Dependent-Client-Service
mSMQDependentClientServices	Boolean	MSMQ-Dependent-Client-Services
mSMQDigests	Octet String	MSMQ-Digests
mSMQDigestsMig	Octet String	MSMQ-Digests-Mig
mSMQDsService	Boolean	MSMQ-Ds-Service
mSMQDsServices	Boolean	MSMQ-Ds-Services
mSMQEncryptKey	Octet String	MSMQ-Encrypt-Key
mSMQForeign	Boolean	MSMQ-Foreign
mSMQInRoutingServers	Distinguished Name	MSMQ-In-Routing-Servers
mSMQInterval1	Integer	MSMQ-Interval1
mSMQInterval2	Integer	MSMQ-Interval2

Name	Syntax	Description
mSMQJournal	Boolean	MSMQ-Journal
mSMQJournalQuota	Integer	MSMQ-Journal-Quota
mSMQLabel	Case Insensitive String	MSMQ-Label
mSMQLabelEx	Unicode String	MSMQ-Label-Ex
mSMQLongLived	Integer	MSMQ-Long-Lived
mSMQMigrated	Boolean	MSMQ-Migrated
mSMQNameStyle	Boolean	MSMQ-Name-Style
mSMQNt4Flags	Integer	MSMQ-Nt4-Flags
mSMQNt4Stub	Integer	MSMQ-Nt4-Stub
mSMQOSType	Integer	MSMQ-OS-Type
mSMQOutRoutingServers	Distinguished Name	MSMQ-Out-Routing-Servers
mSMQOwnerID	Octet String	MSMQ-Owner-ID
mSMQPrevSiteGates	Distinguished Name	MSMQ-Prev-Site-Gates
mSMQPrivacyLevel	Enumeration	MSMQ-Privacy-Level
mSMQQMID	Octet String	MSMQ-QM-ID
mSMQQueueJournalQuota	Integer	MSMQ-Queue-Journal-Quota
mSMQQueueNameExt	Unicode String	MSMQ-Queue-Name-Ext
mSMQQueueQuota	Integer	MSMQ-Queue-Quota
mSMQQueueType	Octet String	MSMQ-Queue-Type
mSMQQuota	Integer	MSMQ-Quota
mSMQRoutingService	Boolean	MSMQ-Routing-Service
mSMQRoutingServices	Boolean	MSMQ-Routing-Services
mSMQServices	Integer	MSMQ-Services
mSMQServiceType	Integer	MSMQ-Service-Type
mSMQSignCertificates	Octet String	MSMQ-Sign-Certificates
mSMQSignCertificatesMig	Octet String	MSMQ-Sign-Certificates-Mig
mSMQSignKey	Octet String	MSMQ-Sign-Key

continued

Name	Syntax	Description
mSMQSite1	Distinguished Name	MSMQ-Site-1
mSMQSite2	Distinguished Name	MSMQ-Site-2
mSMQSiteForeign	Boolean	MSMQ-Site-Foreign
mSMQSiteGates	Distinguished Name	MSMQ-Site-Gates
mSMQSiteGatesMig	Distinguished Name	MSMQ-Site-Gates-Mig
mSMQSiteID	Octet String	MSMQ-Site-ID
mSMQSiteName	Case Insensitive String	MSMQ-Site-Name
mSMQSiteNameEx	Unicode String	MSMQ-Site-Name-Ex
mSMQSites	Octet String	MSMQ-Sites
mSMQTransactional	Boolean	MSMQ-Transactional
mSMQUserSid	Octet String	MSMQ-User-Sid
mSMQVersion	Integer	MSMQ-Version
msNPAllowDialin	Boolean	msNPAllowDialin
msNPCalledStationID	IA5-String	msNPCalledStationID
msNPCallingStationID	IA5-String	msNPCallingStationID
msNPSavedCallingStationID	IA5-String	msNPSavedCallingStationID
msRADIUSCallbackNumber	IA5-String	msRADIUSCallbackNumber
msRADIUSFramedIPAddress	Integer	msRADIUSFramedIPAddress
msRADIUSFramedRoute	IA5-String	msRADIUSFramedRoute
msRADIUSServiceType	Integer	msRADIUSServiceType
msRASSavedCallbackNumber	IA5-String	msRASSavedCallbackNumber
msRASSavedFramedIPAddress	Integer	msRASSavedFramedIPAddress
msRASSavedFramedRoute	IA5-String	msRASSavedFramedRoute
msRRASAttribute	Unicode String	ms-RRAS-Attribute
msRRASVendorAttributeEntry	Unicode String	ms-RRAS-Vendor-Attribute-Entry
mS-SQL-Alias	Unicode String	MS-SQL-Alias
mS-SQL-AllowAnonymousSubscription	Boolean	MS-SQL-AllowAnonymousSubscription

Name	Syntax	Description
mS-SQL-AllowImmediateUpdatingSubscription	Boolean	MS-SQL-AllowImmediateUpdatingSubscription
mS-SQL-AllowKnownPullSubscription	Boolean	MS-SQL-AllowKnownPullSubscription
mS-SQL-AllowQueuedUpdatingSubscription	Boolean	MS-SQL-AllowQueuedUpdatingSubscription
mS-SQL-AllowSnapshotFilesFTPDownloading	Boolean	MS-SQL-AllowSnapshotFilesFTPDownloading
mS-SQL-AppleTalk	Unicode String	MS-SQL-AppleTalk
mS-SQL-Applications	Unicode String	MS-SQL-Applications
mS-SQL-Build	Integer	MS-SQL-Build
mS-SQL-CharacterSet	Integer	MS-SQL-CharacterSet
mS-SQL-Clustered	Boolean	MS-SQL-Clustered
mS-SQL-ConnectionURL	Unicode String	MS-SQL-ConnectionURL
mS-SQL-Contact	Unicode String	MS-SQL-Contact
mS-SQL-CreationDate	Unicode String	MS-SQL-CreationDate
mS-SQL-Database	Unicode String	MS-SQL-Database
mS-SQL-Description	Unicode String	MS-SQL-Description
mS-SQL-GPSHeight	Unicode String	MS-SQL-GPSHeight
mS-SQL-GPSLatitude	Unicode String	MS-SQL-GPSLatitude
mS-SQL-GPSLongitude	Unicode String	MS-SQL-GPSLongitude
mS-SQL-InformationDirectory	Boolean	MS-SQL-InformationDirectory
mS-SQL-InformationURL	Unicode String	MS-SQL-InformationURL
mS-SQL-Keywords	Unicode String	MS-SQL-Keywords
mS-SQL-Language	Unicode String	MS-SQL-Language
mS-SQL-LastBackupDate	Unicode String	MS-SQL-LastBackupDate
mS-SQL-LastDiagnosticDate	Unicode String	MS-SQL-LastDiagnosticDate
mS-SQL-LastUpdatedDate	Unicode String	MS-SQL-LastUpdatedDate
mS-SQL-Location	Unicode String	MS-SQL-Location

continued

Name	Syntax	Description
mS-SQL-Memory	Large Integer	MS-SQL-Memory
mS-SQL-MultiProtocol	Unicode String	MS-SQL-MultiProtocol
mS-SQL-Name	Unicode String	MS-SQL-Name
mS-SQL-NamedPipe	Unicode String	MS-SQL-NamedPipe
mS-SQL-PublicationURL	Unicode String	MS-SQL-PublicationURL
mS-SQL-Publisher	Unicode String	MS-SQL-Publisher
mS-SQL-RegisteredOwner	Unicode String	MS-SQL-RegisteredOwner
mS-SQL-ServiceAccount	Unicode String	MS-SQL-ServiceAccount
mS-SQL-Size	Large Integer	MS-SQL-Size
mS-SQL-SortOrder	Unicode String	MS-SQL-SortOrder
mS-SQL-SPX	Unicode String	MS-SQL-SPX
mS-SQL-Status	Large Integer	MS-SQL-Status
mS-SQL-TCPIP	Unicode String	MS-SQL-TCPIP
mS-SQL-ThirdParty	Boolean	MS-SQL-ThirdParty
mS-SQL-Type	Unicode String	MS-SQL-Type
mS-SQL-UnicodeSortOrder	Integer	MS-SQL-UnicodeSortOrder
mS-SQL-Version	Unicode String	MS-SQL-Version
mS-SQL-Vines	Unicode String	MS-SQL-Vines
mustContain	Object Identifier	Must-Contain
name	Unicode String	RDN
nameServiceFlags	Integer	Name-Service-Flags
nCName	Distinguished Name	NC-Name
nETBIOSName	Unicode String	NETBIOS-Name
netbootAllowNewClients	Boolean	netboot-Allow-New-Clients
netbootAnswerOnlyValidClients	Boolean	netboot-Answer-Only-Valid-Clients
netbootAnswerRequests	Boolean	netboot-Answer-Requests
netbootCurrentClientCount	Integer	netboot-Current-Client-Count

Name	Syntax	Description
netbootGUID	Octet String	Netboot-GUID
netbootInitialization	Unicode String	Netboot-Initialization
netbootIntelliMirrorOSes	Unicode String	netboot-IntelliMirror-OSes
netbootLimitClients	Boolean	netboot-Limit-Clients
netbootLocallyInstalledOSes	Unicode String	netboot-Locally-Installed-OSes
netbootMachineFilePath	Unicode String	Netboot-Machine-File-Path
netbootMaxClients	Integer	netboot-Max-Clients
netbootMirrorDataFile	Unicode String	Netboot-Mirror-Data-File
netbootNewMachineNamingPolicy	Unicode String	netboot-New-Machine-Naming-Policy
netbootNewMachineOU	Distinguished Name	netboot-New-Machine-OU
netbootSCPBL	Distinguished Name	netboot-SCP-BL
netbootServer	Distinguished Name	netboot-Server
netbootSIFFile	Unicode String	Netboot-SIF-File
netbootTools	Unicode String	netboot-Tools
networkAddress	Case Insensitive String	Network-Address
nextLevelStore	Distinguished Name	Next-Level-Store
nextRid	Integer	Next-Rid
nonSecurityMember	Distinguished Name	Non-Security-Member
nonSecurityMemberBL	Distinguished Name	Non-Security-Member-BL
notes	Unicode String	Additional-Information
notificationList	Distinguished Name	Notification-List
nTGroupMembers	Octet String	NT-Group-Members
nTMixedDomain	Integer	NT-Mixed-Domain
ntPwdHistory	Octet String	Nt-Pwd-History
nTSecurityDescriptor	NT Security Descriptor	NT-Security-Descriptor
o	Unicode String	Organization-Name
objectCategory	Distinguished Name	Object-Category

continued

Name	Syntax	Description
objectClass	Object Identifier	Object-Class
objectClassCategory	Enumeration	Object-Class-Category
objectClasses	Unicode String	Object-Classes
objectCount	Integer	Object-Count
objectGUID	Octet String	Object-Guid
objectSid	SID	Object-Sid
objectVersion	Integer	Object-Version
oEMInformation	Unicode String	OEM-Information
oMObjectClass	Octet String	OM-Object-Class
oMSyntax	Integer	OM-Syntax
oMTGuid	Octet String	OMT-Guid
oMTIndxGuid	Octet String	OMT-Indx-Guid
operatingSystem	Unicode String	Operating-System
operatingSystemHotfix	Unicode String	Operating-System-Hotfix
operatingSystemServicePack	Unicode String	Operating-System-Service-Pack
operatingSystemVersion	Unicode String	Operating-System-Version
operatorCount	Integer	Operator-Count
optionDescription	Unicode String	Option-Description
options	Integer	Options
optionsLocation	Print Case String	Options-Location
originalDisplayTable	Octet String	Original-Display-Table
originalDisplayTableMSDOS	Octet String	Original-Display-Table-MSDOS
otherFacsimileTelephoneNumber	Unicode String	Phone-Fax-Other
otherHomePhone	Unicode String	Phone-Home-Other
otherIpPhone	Unicode String	Phone-Ip-Other
otherLoginWorkstations	Unicode String	Other-Login-Workstations
otherMailbox	Unicode String	Other-Mailbox

Name	Syntax	Description
otherMobile	Unicode String	Phone-Mobile-Other
otherPager	Unicode String	Phone-Pager-Other
otherTelephone	Unicode String	Phone-Office-Other
otherWellKnownObjects	DN Binary	Other-Well-Known-Objects
ou	Unicode String	Organizational-Unit-Name
owner	Distinguished Name	Owner
packageFlags	Integer	Package-Flags
packageName	Unicode String	Package-Name
packageType	Integer	Package-Type
pager	Unicode String	Phone-Pager-Primary
parentCA	Distinguished Name	Parent-CA
parentCACertificateChain	Octet String	Parent-CA-Certificate-Chain
parentGUID	Octet String	Parent-GUID
partialAttributeDeletionList	Octet String	Partial-Attribute-Deletion-List
partialAttributeSet	Octet String	Partial-Attribute-Set
pekKeyChangeInterval	Large Integer	Pek-Key-Change-Interval
pekList	Octet String	Pek-List
pendingCACertificates	Octet String	Pending-CA-Certificates
pendingParentCA	Distinguished Name	Pending-Parent-CA
perMsgDialogDisplayTable	Octet String	Per-Msg-Dialog-Display-Table
perRecipDialogDisplayTable	Octet String	Per-Recip-Dialog-Display-Table
personalTitle	Unicode String	Personal-Title
physicalDeliveryOfficeName	Unicode String	Physical-Delivery-Office-Name
physicalLocationObject	Distinguished Name	Physical-Location-Object
pKICriticalExtensions	Unicode String	PKI-Critical-Extensions
pKIDefaultCSPs	Unicode String	PKI-Default-CSPs
pKIDefaultKeySpec	Integer	PKI-Default-Key-Spec

continued

Name	Syntax	Description
pKIEnrollmentAccess	NT Security Descriptor	PKI-Enrollment-Access
pKIExpirationPeriod	Octet String	PKI-Expiration-Period
pKIExtendedKeyUsage	Unicode String	PKI-Extended-Key-Usage
pKIKeyUsage	Octet String	PKI-Key-Usage
pKIMaxIssuingDepth	Integer	PKI-Max-Issuing-Depth
pKIOverlapPeriod	Octet String	PKI-Overlap-Period
pKT	Octet String	PKT
pKTGuid	Octet String	PKT-Guid
policyReplicationFlags	Integer	Policy-Replication-Flags
portName	Unicode String	Port-Name
possibleInferiors	Object Identifier	Possible-Inferiors
possSuperiors	Object Identifier	Poss-Superiors
postalAddress	Unicode String	Postal-Address
postalCode	Unicode String	Postal-Code
postOfficeBox	Unicode String	Post-Office-Box
preferredDeliveryMethod	Enumeration	Preferred-Delivery-Method
preferredOU	Distinguished Name	Preferred-OU
prefixMap	Octet String	Prefix-Map
presentationAddress	Address	Presentation-Address
previousCACertificates	Octet String	Previous-CA-Certificates
previousParentCA	Distinguished Name	Previous-Parent-CA
primaryGroupID	Integer	Primary-Group-ID
primaryGroupToken	Integer	Primary-Group-Token
primaryInternationalISDNNumber	Unicode String	Phone-ISDN-Primary
primaryTelexNumber	Unicode String	Telex-Primary
printAttributes	Integer	Print-Attributes
printBinNames	Unicode String	Print-Bin-Names

Name	Syntax	Description
printCollate	Boolean	Print-Collate
printColor	Boolean	Print-Color
printDuplexSupported	Boolean	Print-Duplex-Supported
printEndTime	Integer	Print-End-Time
printerName	Unicode String	Printer-Name
printFormName	Unicode String	Print-Form-Name
printKeepPrintedJobs	Boolean	Print-Keep-Printed-Jobs
printLanguage	Unicode String	Print-Language
printMACAddress	Unicode String	Print-MAC-Address
printMaxCopies	Integer	Print-Max-Copies
printMaxResolutionSupported	Integer	Print-Max-Resolution-Supported
printMaxXExtent	Integer	Print-Max-X-Extent
printMaxYExtent	Integer	Print-Max-Y-Extent
printMediaReady	Unicode String	Print-Media-Ready
printMediaSupported	Unicode String	Print-Media-Supported
printMemory	Integer	Print-Memory
printMinXExtent	Integer	Print-Min-X-Extent
printMinYExtent	Integer	Print-Min-Y-Extent
printNetworkAddress	Unicode String	Print-Network-Address
printNotify	Unicode String	Print-Notify
printNumberUp	Integer	Print-Number-Up
printOrientationsSupported	Unicode String	Print-Orientations-Supported
printOwner	Unicode String	Print-Owner
printPagesPerMinute	Integer	Print-Pages-Per-Minute
printRate	Integer	Print-Rate
printRateUnit	Unicode String	Print-Rate-Unit
printSeparatorFile	Unicode String	Print-Separator-File

continued

Name	Syntax	Description
printShareName	Unicode String	Print-Share-Name
printSpooling	Unicode String	Print-Spooling
printStaplingSupported	Boolean	Print-Stapling-Supported
printStartTime	Integer	Print-Start-Time
printStatus	Unicode String	Print-Status
priority	Integer	Priority
priorSetTime	Large Integer	Prior-Set-Time
priorValue	Octet String	Prior-Value
privateKey	Octet String	Private-Key
privilegeAttributes	Integer	Privilege-Attributes
privilegeDisplayName	Unicode String	Privilege-Display-Name
privilegeHolder	Distinguished Name	Privilege-Holder
privilegeValue	Large Integer	Privilege-Value
productCode	Octet String	Product-Code
profilePath	Unicode String	Profile-Path
proxiedObjectName	DN Binary	Proxied-Object-Name
proxyAddresses	Unicode String	Proxy-Addresses
proxyGenerationEnabled	Boolean	Proxy-Generation-Enabled
proxyLifetime	Large Integer	Proxy-Lifetime
publicKeyPolicy	Octet String	Public-Key-Policy
purportedSearch	Unicode String	Purported-Search
pwdHistoryLength	Integer	Pwd-History-Length
pwdLastSet	Large Integer	Pwd-Last-Set
pwdProperties	Integer	Pwd-Properties
qualityOfService	Integer	Quality-Of-Service
queryFilter	Unicode String	Query-Filter
queryPoint	Unicode String	QueryPoint

Name	Syntax	Description
queryPolicyBL	Distinguished Name	Query-Policy-BL
queryPolicyObject	Distinguished Name	Query-Policy-Object
rangeLower	Integer	Range-Lower
rangeUpper	Integer	Range-Upper
rDNAttID	Object Identifier	RDN-Att-ID
registeredAddress	Octet String	Registered-Address
remoteServerName	Unicode String	Remote-Server-Name
remoteSource	Unicode String	Remote-Source
remoteSourceType	Integer	Remote-Source-Type
remoteStorageGUID	Unicode String	Remote-Storage-GUID
replicaSource	Unicode String	Replica-Source
replInterval	Integer	Repl-Interval
replPropertyMetaData	Octet String	Repl-Property-Meta-Data
replTopologyStayOfExecution	Integer	Repl-Topology-Stay-Of-Execution
replUpToDateVector	Octet String	Repl-UpToDate-Vector
repsFrom	Replica Link	Reps-From
repsTo	Replica Link	Reps-To
requiredCategories	Octet String	Required-Categories
retiredReplDSASignatures	Octet String	Retired-Repl-DSA-Signatures
revision	Integer	Revision
rid	Integer	Rid
rIDAllocationPool	Large Integer	RID-Allocation-Pool
rIDAvailablePool	Large Integer	RID-Available-Pool
rIDManagerReference	Distinguished Name	RID-Manager-Reference
rIDNextRID	Integer	RID-Next-RID
rIDPreviousAllocationPool	Large Integer	RID-Previous-Allocation-Pool
rIDSetReferences	Distinguished Name	RID-Set-References

continued

Name	Syntax	Description
rIDUsedPool	Large Integer	RID-Used-Pool
rightsGuid	Unicode String	Rights-Guid
roleOccupant	Distinguished Name	Role-Occupant
rootTrust	Distinguished Name	Root-Trust
rpcNsAnnotation	Unicode String	rpc-Ns-Annotation
rpcNsBindings	Unicode String	rpc-Ns-Bindings
rpcNsCodeset	Unicode String	rpc-Ns-Codeset
rpcNsEntryFlags	Integer	rpc-Ns-Entry-Flags
rpcNsGroup	Unicode String	rpc-Ns-Group
rpcNsInterfaceID	Unicode String	rpc-Ns-Interface-ID
rpcNsObjectID	Unicode String	rpc-Ns-Object-ID
rpcNsPriority	Integer	rpc-Ns-Priority
rpcNsProfileEntry	Unicode String	rpc-Ns-Profile-Entry
rpcNsTransferSyntax	Unicode String	rpc-Ns-Transfer-Syntax
sAMAccountName	Unicode String	SAM-Account-Name
sAMAccountType	Integer	SAM-Account-Type
schedule	Octet String	Schedule
schemaFlagsEx	Integer	Schema-Flags-Ex
schemaIDGUID	Octet String	Schema-ID-GUID
schemaInfo	Octet String	Schema-Info
schemaUpdate	Generalized Time	Schema-Update
schemaVersion	Integer	Schema-Version
scopeFlags	Integer	Scope-Flags
scriptPath	Unicode String	Script-Path
sDRightsEffective	Integer	SD-Rights-Effective
searchFlags	Enumeration	Search-Flags
searchGuide	Octet String	Search-Guide

Name	Syntax	Description
securityIdentifier	SID	Security-Identifier
seeAlso	Distinguished Name	See-Also
seqNotification	Integer	Seq-Notification
serialNumber	Print Case String	Serial-Number
serverName	Unicode String	Server-Name
serverReference	Distinguished Name	Server-Reference
serverReferenceBL	Distinguished Name	Server-Reference-BL
serverRole	Integer	Server-Role
serverState	Integer	Server-State
serviceBindingInformation	Unicode String	Service-Binding-Information
serviceClassID	Octet String	Service-Class-ID
serviceClassInfo	Octet String	Service-Class-Info
serviceClassName	Unicode String	Service-Class-Name
serviceDNSName	Unicode String	Service-DNS-Name
serviceDNSNameType	Unicode String	Service-DNS-Name-Type
serviceInstanceVersion	Octet String	Service-Instance-Version
servicePrincipalName	Unicode String	Service-Principal-Name
setupCommand	Unicode String	Setup-Command
shellContextMenu	Unicode String	Shell-Context-Menu
shellPropertyPages	Unicode String	Shell-Property-Pages
shortServerName	Unicode String	Short-Server-Name
showInAddressBook	Distinguished Name	Show-In-Address-Book
showInAdvancedViewOnly	Boolean	Show-In-Advanced-View-Only
sIDHistory	SID	SID-History
signatureAlgorithms	Unicode String	Signature-Algorithms
siteGUID	Octet String	Site-GUID
siteLinkList	Distinguished Name	Site-Link-List

continued

Name	Syntax	Description
siteList	Distinguished Name	Site-List
siteObject	Distinguished Name	Site-Object
siteObjectBL	Distinguished Name	Site-Object-BL
siteServer	Distinguished Name	Site-Server
sn	Unicode String	Surname
sPNMappings	Unicode String	SPN-Mappings
st	Unicode String	State-Or-Province-Name
street	Unicode String	Street-Address
streetAddress	Unicode String	Address
subClassOf	Object Identifier	Sub-Class-Of
subRefs	Distinguished Name	Sub-Refs
subSchemaSubEntry	Distinguished Name	SubSchemaSubEntry
superiorDNSRoot	Unicode String	Superior-DNS-Root
superScopeDescription	Unicode String	Super-Scope-Description
superScopes	Print Case String	Super-Scopes
supplementalCredentials	Octet String	Supplemental-Credentials
supportedApplicationContext	Octet String	Supported-Application-Context
syncAttributes	Integer	Sync-Attributes
syncMembership	Distinguished Name	Sync-Membership
syncWithObject	Distinguished Name	Sync-With-Object
syncWithSID	SID	Sync-With-SID
systemAuxiliaryClass	Object Identifier	System-Auxiliary-Class
systemFlags	Integer	System-Flags
systemMayContain	Object Identifier	System-May-Contain
systemMustContain	Object Identifier	System-Must-Contain
systemOnly	Boolean	System-Only
systemPossSuperiors	Object Identifier	System-Poss-Superiors

Name	Syntax	Description
telephoneNumber	Unicode String	Telephone-Number
teletexTerminalIdentifier	Octet String	Teletex-Terminal-Identifier
telexNumber	Octet String	Telex-Number
templateRoots	Distinguished Name	Template-Roots
terminalServer	Octet String	Terminal-Server
textEncodedORAddress	Unicode String	Text-Encoded-OR-Address
thumbnailLogo	Octet String	Logo
thumbnailPhoto	Octet String	Picture
timeRefresh	Large Integer	Time-Refresh
timeVolChange	Large Integer	Time-Vol-Change
title	Unicode String	Title
tokenGroups	SID	Token-Groups
tokenGroupsGlobalAndUniversal	SID	Token-Groups-Global-And-Universal
tokenGroupsNoGCAcceptable	SID	Token-Groups-No-GC-Acceptable
tombstoneLifetime	Integer	Tombstone-Lifetime
transportAddressAttribute	Object Identifier	Transport-Address-Attribute
transportDLLName	Unicode String	Transport-DLL-Name
transportType	Distinguished Name	Transport-Type
treatAsLeaf	Boolean	Treat-As-Leaf
treeName	Unicode String	Tree-Name
trustAttributes	Integer	Trust-Attributes
trustAuthIncoming	Octet String	Trust-Auth-Incoming
trustAuthOutgoing	Octet String	Trust-Auth-Outgoing
trustDirection	Integer	Trust-Direction
trustParent	Distinguished Name	Trust-Parent
trustPartner	Unicode String	Trust-Partner
trustPosixOffset	Integer	Trust-Posix-Offset

continued

Name	Syntax	Description
trustType	Integer	Trust-Type
uASCompat	Integer	UAS-Compat
uNCName	Unicode String	UNC-Name
unicodePwd	Octet String	Unicode-Pwd
upgradeProductCode	Octet String	Upgrade-Product-Code
uPNSuffixes	Unicode String	UPN-Suffixes
url	Unicode String	WWW-Page-Other
userAccountControl	Integer	User-Account-Control
userCert	Octet String	User-Cert
userCertificate	Octet String	X509-Cert
userParameters	Unicode String	User-Parameters
userPassword	Octet String	User-Password
userPrincipalName	Unicode String	User-Principal-Name
userSharedFolder	Unicode String	User-Shared-Folder
userSharedFolderOther	Unicode String	User-Shared-Folder-Other
userSMIMECertificate	Octet String	User-SMIME-Certificate
userWorkstations	Unicode String	User-Workstations
uSNChanged	Large Integer	USN-Changed
uSNCreated	Large Integer	USN-Created
uSNDSALastObjRemoved	Large Integer	USN-DSA-Last-Obj-Removed
USNIntersite	Integer	USN-Intersite
uSNLastObjRem	Large Integer	USN-Last-Obj-Rem
uSNSource	Large Integer	USN-Source
validAccesses	Integer	Valid-Accesses
vendor	Unicode String	Vendor
versionNumber	Integer	Version-Number
versionNumberHi	Integer	Version-Number-Hi

Name	Syntax	Description
versionNumberLo	Integer	Version-Number-Lo
volTableGUID	Octet String	Vol-Table-GUID
volTableIdxGUID	Octet String	Vol-Table-Idx-GUID
volumeCount	Integer	Volume-Count
wbemPath	Unicode String	Wbem-Path
wellKnownObjects	DN Binary	Well-Known-Objects
whenChanged	Generalized Time	When-Changed
whenCreated	Generalized Time	When-Created
winsockAddresses	Octet String	Winsock-Addresses
wWWHomePage	Unicode String	WWW-Home-Page
x121Address	Numerical String	X121-Address

Glossary

A

abstract class
A type of schema class object used as a template only to form new structural classes. An abstract class cannot have instances in the directory. A new abstract class can be derived from an existing abstract class.

access control entry (ACE)
An entry in an access control list (ACL) containing a security ID (SID) and a set of access rights. A process with a matching security ID is allowed access rights, denied rights, or allowed rights with auditing, depending on the specified access rights.

access control list (ACL)
The mechanism for limiting access to certain items of information or to certain controls based on users' identity and their membership in various predefined groups. An access control list is typically used by system administrators for controlling user access to network resources such as servers, directories, and files and is typically implemented by granting permissions to users and groups for access to specific objects.

ACE
See access control entry.

ACL
See access control list.

Active Directory
The directory service included with Windows 2000 Server. It stores information about objects on a network and makes this information available to users and network administrators. Active Directory gives network users access to resources anywhere on the network using a single logon process, provided the users are permitted to use these resources. It provides network administrators with an intuitive hierarchical view of the network and a single point of administration for all network objects. *See also* directory; directory service.

Active Directory Connector (ADC)
A synchronization agent in Windows 2000 Server, Windows 2000 Advanced Server, and Windows 2000 Datacenter Server that provides an automated way of keeping directory information between the two directories consistent. Without the ADC, you would have to manually enter new data and updates in both directory services.

Active Directory Installation Wizard
A Windows 2000 Server tool that facilitates the following during Setup: installation of Active Directory, creation of trees in a forest, replication of an existing domain, installation of Kerberos authentication software, and promotion of servers to domain controllers.

Active Directory Migration Tool (ADMT)
A tool that enables the migration of existing Windows NT 4 and earlier domains into Windows 2000. It can also be used to consolidate multiple Windows 2000 domains (within the same or within different forests) into a single domain. ADMT allows you to test the migration settings and analyze the migration impact before and after the migration process.

Active Directory Sizer
A tool for estimating the hardware required for deploying Active Directory based on an organization's profile, domain information, and site topology.

ADC
See Active Directory Connector.

administrative structure
A representation of the functions, divisions, departments, or positions within an organization and their relationships, including the organization's hierarchy and authority structure. The administrative structure reflects how an organization is managed and how it conducts administrative operations.

administrator
A person responsible for setting up and managing domain controllers or local computers and their user and group accounts, assigning passwords and permissions, and helping users with networking issues.

ADMT
See Active Directory Migration Tool.

attribute
Information that indicates whether a file is read-only, hidden, ready for archiving (backing up), compressed, or encrypted, and whether the file contents should be indexed for fast file searching.

authentication
The process by which the system validates the user's logon information. A user's name and password are compared against the list of authorized users. If the system detects a match, access is granted to the extent specified in the permissions list for that user. When a user logs on to an account on a computer running Windows 2000 Professional, the authentication is performed by the workstation. When a user logs on to an account on a Windows 2000 Server domain, authentication may be performed by any server in that domain. *See also* server; trust relationship.

auxiliary class
A type of schema class used to group attributes to be applied as a group to a structural class. An auxiliary class cannot have instances in the directory. A new auxiliary class can be derived from an existing auxiliary class.

average available bandwidth
The average amount of bandwidth that is actually available for use after normal network traffic is handled.

AXFR
See full zone transfer.

B

backup domain controller (BDC)
In the environment running Microsoft Windows NT Server 4 or earlier, a computer running Windows NT Server that receives a copy of the domain's directory database (which contains all account and security policy information for the domain). The copy is synchronized periodically and automatically with the master copy on the primary domain controller (PDC). BDCs also authenticate user logon information and can be promoted to function as PDCs as needed. Multiple BDCs can exist in a domain. Windows NT 3.51 and 4 BDCs can participate in a Windows 2000 domain when the domain is configured in mixed mode. *See also* mixed mode; primary domain controller.

bandwidth
The amount of data that can be transmitted across a communications channel in a specific amount of time. In computer networks, greater bandwidth indicates faster data-transfer capability and is expressed in bits per second (bps).

base schema
A basic set of schema classes and attributes shipped with Windows 2000 Server. There are nearly 200 schema class objects and more than 900 schema attribute objects provided in the base schema.

BDC
See backup domain controller.

Berkeley Internet Name Domain (BIND)
An implementation of the Domain Name System (DNS) written and ported to most available versions of the UNIX operating system. The Internet Software Consortium maintains the BIND software.

BIND
See Berkeley Internet Name Domain.

Bindery
A database in Novell NetWare 2.*x* and 3.*x* that contains organizational and security information about users and groups.

bridgehead server
A domain controller in a site, designated automatically by the Knowledge Consistency Checker as the contact point for exchange of directory information between this site and other sites. *See also* preferred bridgehead server.

business environment
The manner in which an organization structures and manages its nontechnical resources.

business environment analysis document
A document that describes the current state of each business environment component. When complete, this document can be distributed to each member of the design team, providing a starting point for discussion and assessing future needs.

business process
A series of steps that must be taken to achieve a desired result within the organization.

business strategy
A long-range plan for defining and achieving the objectives set up by an organization.

Business Strategy Influences Worksheet
A worksheet that can be used to analyze the factors that may influence the business strategy in an organization.

business structure

A representation of the daily operating structure of an organization.

Business Structures Worksheet

A worksheet that can be used to analyze an organization's administrative and geographical structures.

C

catalog service

An information store that contains selected information about every object in every domain in the directory, and which is used for performing searches across an enterprise. The catalog service provided by Active Directory is called the global catalog.

child domain

For DNS, a domain located in the namespace tree directly beneath another domain (the parent domain). For example, "example.microsoft.com" is a child domain of the parent domain, "microsoft.com." A child domain is also called a subdomain.

child object

An object that resides in another object. For example, a file is a child object that resides in a folder, which is the parent object. *See also* parent object; object.

command decisions

Decisions made by one person.

communication flow

The process by which ideas, messages, or information arrive at their destination.

Communication Flow Worksheet

A worksheet that can be used to analyze how ideas, messages, or information arrive at their destination in an organization.

configuration container

A naming context containing the replication topology and related metadata that is replicated to every domain controller in the forest. Directory-aware applications store information in the configuration container that applies to the entire forest.

connection agreement

A configurable section in the Active Directory Connector user interface that holds information such as the server names to contact for synchronization, object classes to synchronize, target containers, and the synchronization schedule.

connection object

An Active Directory object that represents a replication connection from one domain controller to another. The connection object is a child of the replication destination's NTDS Settings object and identifies the replication source server, contains a replication schedule, and specifies a replication transport. Connection objects are created automatically by the Knowledge Consistency Checker, but they can also be created manually. Connections generated automatically must not be modified by the user unless they are first converted into manual connections.

consensus decisions

Decisions reached by agreement from the entire group affected by the decision. Because the matter is not decided until the entire group agrees, this method is time consuming and does not guarantee that an effective decision will be made.

consultative decisions
Decisions made by one person, but only after that person gathers facts, ideas, and opinions from other people. This process involves a variety of people but still hinges on the analysis and judgment of one person.

container object
An object that can logically contain other objects. For example, a folder is a container object. *See also* noncontainer object; object.

contiguous namespace
A namespace where the name of the child object in an object hierarchy always contains the name of the parent domain. A tree is a contiguous namespace.

cross-link trust
A two-way trust relationship that is explicitly created between two Windows 2000 domains that are logically distant from each other in a forest or tree hierarchy. The purpose of a cross-link trust is to optimize the inter-domain authentication process. A cross-link trust can be created only between Windows 2000 domains in the same forest. All cross-link trusts are transitive. A cross-link trust is also known as a shortcut trust. *See also* implicit two-way transitive trust.

D

DACL
See discretionary access control list.

data store (the database file Ntds.dit)
The directory database.

Decision Making Worksheet
A worksheet that can be used to analyze how options are identified and actions are selected in an organization.

decision matrix
A comparison of the criteria used to make a decision with the available options.

delegated decision
Decision that has been pushed down an organization's chain of command. The delegatee must make the decision.

delegation of administration
The ability to assign responsibility for management and administration of a portion of the namespace to another user, group, or organization.

design team
The people in an organization involved in the Active Directory infrastructure design process.

desktop
The on-screen work area on which windows, icons, menus, and dialog boxes appear.

directory
An information source (for example, a telephone directory) that contains information about people, computer files, or other objects. In a file system, a directory stores information about files. In a distributed computing environment (such as a Windows 2000 domain), the directory stores information about objects such as printers, fax servers, applications, databases, and other users.

directory database

The physical storage for each replica of Active Directory. The directory database is also called the store.

directory-enabled application

Software that has the capability to read Active Directory objects (and their attributes) or has the capability to create schema class or attribute objects.

directory service

Both the directory information source and the services that make the information available and usable. A directory service enables the user to find an object given any one of its attributes. *See also* Active Directory; directory.

directory synchronization

The sharing of data between two directory services so that changes made to objects in one directory are propagated automatically to the other directory. When data is synchronized between directory services, system administration is more efficient because there is no longer a need to manage multiple directories.

discretionary access control list (DACL)

The part of an object's security descriptor that grants or denies specific users and groups permission to access the object. Only the owner of an object can change permissions granted or denied in a DACL; thus access to the object is at the owner's discretion. *See also* access control entry; object; system access control list; security descriptor.

disjointed namespace

A namespace in which the names of a parent object and a child of this parent object are based on different DNS root domain names. A forest is a disjointed namespace.

distinguished name (DN)

A name that uniquely identifies an object by using the relative distinguished name for the object, plus the names of container objects and domains that contain the object. The distinguished name identifies the object as well as its location in a tree. Every object in Active Directory has a distinguished name. A typical distinguished name might be CN=MyName, CN=Users,DC=Microsoft,DC=Com. This distinguished name identifies the "MyName" user object in the microsoft.com domain.

distribution group

A group that is used solely for e-mail distribution and is not security enabled. Distribution groups cannot be listed in discretionary access control lists (DACLs) used to define permissions on resources and objects. Distribution groups can be used only with e-mail applications (such as Microsoft Exchange) to send e-mail to collections of users. If you do not need a group for security purposes, create a distribution group instead of a security group.

DN

See distinguished name.

DNS

See Domain Name System.

DNS Environment Worksheet
A worksheet that can be used to analyze an organization's existing DNS environment.

DNS notify list
A list maintained by the primary master for a zone of other Domain Name System (DNS) servers that should be notified when zone changes occur. The notify list is made up of Internet Protocol (IP) addresses for DNS servers configured as secondary masters for the zone. When the listed servers are notified of a change to the zone, they will initiate a zone transfer with another DNS server and update the zone.

DNS server
A computer that runs DNS server programs containing name-to-IP address mappings, IP address-to-name mappings, information about the domain tree structure, and other information. DNS servers also attempt to resolve client queries. A DNS server is also called a DNS name server.

domain
In Windows 2000 and Active Directory, a logical organization of computers and other resources defined by the administrator of a Windows 2000 Server network that share a common directory database. A domain has a unique name and provides access to the centralized user accounts and group accounts maintained by the domain administrator. Each domain has its own security policies and security relationships with other domains and represents a single security boundary of a Windows 2000 computer network. Active Directory is made up of one or more domains, each of which can span more than one physical location. For DNS, a domain is any tree or subtree within the DNS namespace. Although the names for DNS domains often correspond to Active Directory domains, DNS domains should not be confused with Windows 2000 and Active Directory networking domains.

domain consolidation
See domain restructure.

domain controller
In a Windows 2000 Server domain, a computer running Windows 2000 Server that manages user access to a network, which includes logging on, authentication, and access to the directory and shared resources.

domain hierarchy
A tree structure of parent and child domains.

domain local group
A security or distribution group that can contain universal groups, global groups, and accounts from any domain in the domain tree or forest. A domain local group can also contain other domain local groups from its own domain. Rights and permissions can be assigned only at the domain containing the group.

domain name
In Windows 2000 and Active Directory, the name given by an administrator to a logical organization of computers and other resources that share a common directory. For DNS, domain names are specific node names in the DNS namespace tree. DNS domain names use singular node names, joined together by periods (.) that indicate each node level in the namespace. *See also* Domain Name System (DNS); namespace.

domain namespace
The database structure used by the Domain Name System (DNS). *See also* Domain Name System (DNS).

Domain Name System (DNS)
A static, hierarchical name service for TCP/IP hosts. The network administrator configures the DNS with a list of host names and IP addresses, allowing users of workstations configured to query the DNS to specify remote systems by host names rather than IP addresses. DNS domains should not be confused with Windows 2000 networking domains. *See also* domain.

domain naming master
The domain controller assigned to control the addition or removal of domains in the forest. At any time, there can be only one domain naming master in the forest.

domain plan
A group of planning documents that represent the Active Directory domain structure, which includes defining domains, defining the forest root domain, defining a domain hierarchy, naming domains, and planning DNS server deployment.

domain restructure
A migration method that involves the redesign of the Windows NT domain structure, which often results in fewer, consolidated domains. This method of migration allows organizations to redesign and improve the structure to take full advantage of Windows 2000 features. A domain restructure migrates the existing Windows NT environment into a pristine Windows 2000 forest

using a nondestructive copy. A domain restructure is also known as a domain consolidation or simply a restructure.

domain upgrade
The process of installing an existing Windows NT domain structure and its users and groups intact into the Windows 2000 DNS-based domain hierarchy. A domain upgrade is also known as an in-place upgrade or simply an upgrade.

dynamic update
An updated specification to the Domain Name System (DNS) standard that permits hosts that store name information in the DNS to dynamically register and update their records in zones maintained by DNS servers that can accept and process dynamic update messages.

E

explicit one-way nontransitive trust
A type of trust relationship in which only one of the two domains trusts the other domain. For example, domain A trusts domain B, and domain B does not trust domain A. All one-way trusts are nontransitive.

F

fault tolerance
The ability of a computer or operating system to ensure data integrity when a hardware failure occurs.

file
A collection of information that has been given a name and is stored on a disk. This information can be a document or a program.

firewall

A combination of hardware and software that provides a security system, usually to prevent unauthorized access from outside to an internal network or intranet. A firewall prevents direct communication between network and external computers by routing communication through a proxy server outside of the network. The proxy server determines whether it is safe to let a file pass through to the network. A firewall is also called a security-edge gateway.

folder

A grouping of files or other folders, graphically represented by a folder icon, in both Windows 2000 and Macintosh environments. A folder represents a PC's file system directory.

forest

A collection of one or more Windows 2000 domains that share a common schema, configuration, and global catalog and are linked with two-way transitive trusts.

forest model

A representation of the forest structure for an organization.

forest plan

A group of planning documents that represent the Active Directory forest structure, which includes a forest model and a schema modification plan. To design a forest model, you assess an organization's forest needs and determine the number of forests it requires. To design a schema modification plan, you create a schema modification policy, assess an organization's schema needs, and determine whether to modify the schema.

forest root domain

The first domain created in an Active Directory forest. After the forest root domain has been created, you cannot create a new forest root domain, a parent for the existing forest root domain, or rename the forest root domain.

forward lookup

In the Domain Name System (DNS), a query process in which the friendly DNS domain name of a host computer is searched to find its Internet Protocol (IP) address.

FQDN

See fully qualified domain name.

fully qualified domain name (FQDN)

A DNS domain name that has been stated unambiguously so as to indicate with absolute certainty its location in the domain namespace tree. Fully qualified domain names differ from relative names in that they are typically stated with a trailing period (.), for example, "host.example.microsoft.com.", to qualify their position to the root of the namespace.

full zone transfer (AXFR)

The standard query type supported by all Domain Name System (DNS) servers to update and synchronize zone data when the zone has been changed. When a DNS query is made using AXFR as the specified query type, the entire zone is transferred as the response.

G

geographical structure
A representation of the physical locations of the functions, divisions, departments, or positions within an organization. It reflects how an organization is structured geographically—at a regional, national, or international level.

global catalog
A domain controller that contains a partial replica of every domain in Active Directory. A global catalog holds a replica of every object in Active Directory, but with a limited number of each object's attributes. The global catalog stores those attributes most frequently used in search operations (such as a user's first and last names) and those attributes required to locate a full replica of the object. The Active Directory replication system builds the global catalog automatically. The attributes replicated into the global catalog include a base set defined by Microsoft. Administrators can specify additional properties to meet the needs of their installation.

global catalog server
A Windows 2000 domain controller that holds a copy of the global catalog for the forest.

global group
For Windows 2000 Server, a group that can be used in its own domain, in member servers and workstations of the domain, and in trusting domains. In all those places a global group can be granted rights and permissions and can become a member of local groups. However, a global group can contain user accounts only from its own domain. *See also* local group; group.

globally unique identifier (GUID)
A 128-bit number that is guaranteed to be unique. GUIDs are assigned to objects when the objects are created. The GUID never changes, even if you move or rename the object. Applications can store the GUID of an object and use the GUID to retrieve that object regardless of its current DN.

GPO
See group policy object.

group
A collection of users, computers, contacts, and other groups. Groups can be used as a security mechanism or as e-mail distribution collections. Distribution groups are used only for e-mail. Security groups are used both to grant access to resources and as e-mail distribution lists. *See also* domain local group; global group; native mode; universal group.

group policy
The Windows 2000 component that specifies the behavior of users' desktops, security settings, software installation, startup and shutdown scripts, folder redirections, and so on. A group policy object, which an administrator creates using the Group Policy snap-in, is the mechanism for configuring options that control these features.

group policy object (GPO)
A collection of group policy settings. GPOs are essentially the documents created by the Group Policy snap-in. GPOs are stored at the domain level, and they affect users and computers contained in sites, domains, and organizational units. In addition, each Windows 2000 computer has exactly one group of settings stored locally, called the local GPO.

group scopes

A categorization of groups that enables you to use groups in different ways to assign permissions. The scope of a group determines where in the network you are able to use the group to assign permissions to the group. The three group scopes are global, domain local, and universal.

GUID

See globally unique identifier.

H

Hardware and Software Worksheet

A worksheet that can be used to conduct an inventory of an organization's hardware and installed software and to compare the inventory with the list of hardware and software compatible with Windows 2000 Server.

hierarchical namespace

A namespace, such as the DNS namespace and the Active Directory namespace, that is hierarchically structured and provides rules that allow the namespace to be partitioned.

host ID

A number used to identify an interface on a physical network bounded by routers. The host ID should be unique to the network.

host name

The name of a device on a network. For a device on a Windows NT or Windows 2000 network, this can be the same as the computer name, but it may not be. The host name must be in the Hosts file, or it must be known by a DNS server, for that host to be found by another computer attempting to communicate with it.

Host (H) resource record

A resource record used in a forward lookup zone to list the host name–to-IP-address mappings.

I

implicit two-way transitive trust

A type of trust relationship in which both of the domains in the relationship trust each other. In a two-way trust relationship, each domain has established a one-way trust with the other domain. For example, domain A trusts domain B, and domain B trusts domain A. Two-way trusts can be transitive or nontransitive. All two-way trusts between Windows 2000 domains in the same domain tree or forest are transitive.

incremental zone transfer (IXFR)

An alternate query type that can be used by some Domain Name System (DNS) servers to update and synchronize zone data when a zone is changed. When IXFR is supported between DNS servers, servers can keep track of and transfer only the incremental resource record changes between each version of the zone.

information flow

The process by which the data arrives at its destination.

Information Flow Worksheet

A worksheet that can be used to analyze the process by which data arrives at its destination in an organization.

information technology (IT)

The application of technology to the management and processing of information.

infrastructure design

A plan that represents an organization's network infrastructure. This plan is used to determine how to configure Active Directory to store information about objects on an organization's network and make the information available to users and network administrators.

infrastructure designers

The key personnel involved in designing an Active Directory infrastructure.

infrastructure master

The domain controller assigned to update group-to-user references whenever group memberships are changed and to replicate these changes to any other domain controllers in the domain. At any time, there can be only one infrastructure master in a particular domain.

in-place upgrade

See domain upgrade.

Internet Protocol (IP)

The messenger protocol of TCP/IP that is responsible for addressing and sending IP packets over the network. IP provides a best-effort, connectionless delivery system that does not guarantee that packets arrive at their destination or in the sequence in which they were sent.

intersite replication

Replication traffic that occurs between sites.

intrasite replication

Replication traffic that occurs within a site.

IP

See Internet Protocol.

IP address

A 32-bit address used to identify a node on an IP internetwork. Each node on the IP internetwork must be assigned a unique IP address, which is made up of a network identifier and a host identifier. This address is typically represented in dotted-decimal notation, with the decimal value of each octet separated by a period, for example, 192.168.7.27. In Windows 2000, you can configure the IP address statically or dynamically through DHCP.

IT

See information technology.

IT management organization

The entity in an organization that is responsible for the management of the computing environment, usually performed by the IT, IS (information services) or MIS (management information services) department.

IT Management Organization Worksheet

A worksheet that can be used to analyze an organization's IT management organization and the processes it employs.

IXFR

See incremental zone transfer.

K

KCC
See Knowledge Consistency Checker.

Kerberos V5
An Internet standard security protocol for handling authentication of user or system identity. With Kerberos V5, passwords that are sent across network lines are encrypted, not sent as plain text. Kerberos V5 includes other security features as well.

Knowledge Consistency Checker (KCC)
A built-in service that runs on all domain controllers and automatically establishes connections between individual machines in the same site. These are known as Windows 2000 Directory Service connection objects. An administrator may establish additional connection objects or remove connection objects. At any point where replication within a site becomes impossible or has a single point of failure, the KCC will step in and establish as many new connection objects as necessary to resume Active Directory replication.

L

LAN
See local area network.

LDAP
See Lightweight Directory Access Protocol.

Lightweight Directory Access Protocol (LDAP)
The primary access protocol for Active Directory. LDAP version 3 is defined by a set of Proposed Standard documents in Internet Engineering Task Force (IETF) RFC 2251.

local area network (LAN)
A group of computers and other devices dispersed over a relatively limited area and connected by a communications link that allows one device to interact with any other on the network. *See also* wide area network.

local group
For Windows NT Server, a group that can be granted permissions and rights only for the domain controllers of its own domain. However, it can contain user accounts and global groups both from its own domain and from trusted domains.

For Windows 2000 Professional and member servers running Windows 2000 Server, a group that is granted permissions and rights from its own computer to only those resources on its own computer on which the group resides. *See also* global group.

local group policy object
A group policy object (GPO) stored on each computer whether the computer is part of an Active Directory environment or a networked environment. Local GPO settings can be overwritten by nonlocal GPOs and are the least influential if the computer is in an Active Directory environment. In a non-networked environment (or in a networked environment lacking a Windows 2000 domain controller), the local GPO's settings are more important because they are not overwritten by nonlocal GPOs.

M

management representatives panel
Management-level personnel who are responsible for approving business decisions within an organization. The panel should contain a selected group of upper-level business unit managers. Management representatives must have the authority and ability to approve and support design decisions made by infrastructure designers at each stage of the design development process.

master domain
In Windows NT, the domain that is trusted by all other domains on the network and acts as the central administrative unit for user and group accounts. *See also* resource domain.

master server
An authoritative DNS server for a zone. Master servers can vary and will be one of two types (either primary or secondary masters), depending on how the server obtains its zone data.

member server
A computer that runs Microsoft Windows 2000 Server but is not a domain controller of a Windows 2000 domain. A member server participates in a domain, but does not store a copy of the directory database. For a member server, permissions can be set on resources that allow users to connect to the server and use its resources. Resource permissions can be granted for domain global groups and users as well as for local groups and users. *See also* domain controller; global group; local group.

metadata
Information about the properties of data, such as the type of data in a column (numeric, text, and so on) or the length of a column. Information about the structure of data. Information that specifies the design of objects such as cubes or dimensions.

Microsoft Directory Synchronization Services (MSDSS)
A service included with Services for NetWare version 5 (SFNW5) to enable users of Novell directory services to implement synchronization with Windows 2000 Server.

Microsoft File Migration Utility
A utility included with Services for NetWare version 5 (SFNW5) to enable users of Novell Bindery or NDS directory to migrate their file system to the Windows 2000 NTFS version 5 file system (NTFS5).

Microsoft Management Console (MMC)
A framework for hosting administrative tools, called consoles. A console may contain tools, folders or other containers, World Wide Web pages, and other administrative items. These items are displayed in the left pane of the console, called a console tree. A console has one or more windows that can provide views of the console tree. The main MMC window provides commands and tools for authoring consoles. The authoring features of MMC and the console tree itself may be hidden when a console is in User mode.

Microsoft Metadirectory Services (MMS)
Services that handle sophisticated directory management needs, including the need to synchronize more than two directory services, the need for business rule-based processing, or the need for join capabilities. MMS is available through a service engagement with trained providers.

migration
The process of making existing applications and data work on a different computer or operating system

mixed mode
The default domain mode setting on Windows 2000 domain controllers. Mixed mode allows Windows NT and Windows 2000 backup domain controllers to coexist in a domain. Mixed mode does not support the universal and nested group enhancements of Windows 2000. The domain mode setting can be changed to Windows 2000 native mode when all Windows NT domain controllers are upgraded to Windows 2000 Server or removed from a domain. See also native mode.

MMC
See Microsoft Management Console.

MMS
See Microsoft Metadirectory Services.

MSDSS
See Microsoft Directory Synchronization Services.

multimaster replication
A replication model in which any domain controller accepts and replicates directory changes to any other domain controller. This differs from other replication models in which one computer stores the single modifiable copy of the directory and other computers store backup copies. *See also* domain controller; replication.

N

name resolution
The process of translating a name into some object or information that the name represents. A telephone book forms a namespace in which the telephone numbers can be resolved to names of telephone subscribers. The Windows NT file system forms a namespace in which the name of a file can be resolved to the file itself. The Active Directory forms a namespace in which the name of an object in the directory can be resolved to the object itself. *See also* Domain Name System (DNS).

Name Server (NS) resource record
A resource record used in a zone to designate the Domain Name System (DNS) domain names for authoritative DNS servers for the zone.

namespace
A set of unique names for resources or items used in a shared computing environment. For Microsoft Management Console (MMC), the namespace is represented by the console tree, which displays all of the snap-ins and resources that are accessible to a console. For Domain Name System (DNS), namespace is the vertical or hierarchical structure of the domain name tree.

naming context
A contiguous subtree of Active Directory that is
replicated as a unit to other domain controllers
in the forest that contain a replica of the same
subtree. In Active Directory, a single server
always holds at least three naming contexts:
schema (class and attribute definitions for the
directory), configuration (replication topology and
related metadata), and domain (the subtree that
contains the per-domain objects for one domain).
The schema and configuration naming contexts are
replicated to every domain controller in a specified
forest. A domain naming context is replicated only
to domain controllers for that domain. A naming
context is also called a directory partition.

native mode
The condition in which all domain controllers in
the domain have been upgraded to Windows 2000
and an administrator has enabled native-mode
operation (through the Active Directory Users
And Computers administrative tool). *See also*
mixed mode.

nested groups
A Windows 2000 capability available only in
native mode that allows the creation of groups
within groups. *See also* universal group, global
group, domain local group, forest.

nested OUs
The creation of organizational units (OUs) within
OUs.

NetWare
Novell's network operating system.

Network Architecture Worksheet
A worksheet that can be used to portray the physical environment of an organization's network.

network ID
A number used to identify the systems that are
located on the same physical network bounded by
routers. The network ID should be unique to the
internetwork.

noncontainer object
An object that cannot logically contain other
objects. For example, a file is a noncontainer
object. *See also* container object; object.

nonlocal group policy object
GPOs linked to Active Directory objects (sites,
domains, or OUs) that can be applied to either
users or computers. To use nonlocal GPOs, a
Windows 2000 domain controller must be
installed. Following the properties of Active
Directory, nonlocal GPOs are applied hierarchically from the least restrictive group (site) to the
most restrictive group (OU) and are cumulative.

nontransitive trust
See explicit one-way nontransitive trust.

O

object
An entity such as a file, folder, shared folder,
printer, or Active Directory object described by
a distinct, named set of attributes. For example,
the attributes of a File object include its name,
location, and size; the attributes of an Active
Directory User object might include the user's
first name, last name, and e-mail address.
See also attribute, container object, noncontainer
object, parent object, child object.

object attributes
The characteristics of objects in the directory.

object class
A logical grouping of objects.

object identifier
A label that uniquely identifies an object class or attribute. An object identifier is represented as a dotted decimal string (for example, 1.2.3.4). Object identifiers form a hierarchy with the root object identifier issued by the national registration authority responsible for issuing object identifiers. In the United States, this is the American National Standards Institute (ANSI). Organizations or individuals obtain a root object identifier from an issuing authority and use it to allocate additional object identifiers as they develop new classes and attributes. For example, Microsoft has been issued the root object identifier of 1.2.840.113556. Microsoft uses one of the branches from this root object identifier to allocate object identifiers for Active Directory classes and another branch for Active Directory attributes.

operations master role
A domain controller that has been assigned one or more special roles in an Active Directory domain. The domain controllers assigned these roles perform operations that are single master (not permitted to occur at different places on the network at the same time). Examples of these operations include resource identifier allocation, schema modification, primary domain controller (PDC) election, and certain infrastructure changes. The domain controller that controls the particular operation owns the operations master role for that operation. The ownership of these operations master roles can be transferred to other domain controllers.

organizational unit (OU)
An Active Directory container object used within a domain. An organizational unit is a logical container into which you can place users, groups, computers, and other organizational units. It can contain objects only from its parent domain. An organizational unit is the smallest scope to which you can apply a group policy or delegate authority.

organizational unit plan
A group of planning documents that represent the Active Directory organizational unit structure, which includes defining an OU structure and then planning user accounts and groups.

OU
See organizational unit.

P

parent-child trust
An implicit, two-way transitive trust that is created automatically when a domain is added to the hierarchy.

parent domain
For DNS, a domain that is located in the namespace tree directly above another derivative domain name (child domain). For example, "microsoft.com" is the parent domain for "example.microsoft.com," a child domain.

parent object

The object in which another object resides. A parent object implies relation. For example, a folder is a parent object in which a file, or child object, resides. An object can be both a parent and a child object. For example, a subfolder that contains files is both the child of the parent folder and the parent folder of the files. *See also* child object; object.

partition

A portion of a physical disk that functions as though it were a physically separate disk. Partitions can be created only on basic disks.

path

A sequence of directory (or folder) names that specifies the location of a directory, file, or folder within the directory tree. Each directory name and filename within the path (except for the first) must be preceded by a backslash (\).

PDC

See primary domain controller.

PDC emulator master

A domain controller running Windows 2000 Server assigned to act as a Microsoft Windows NT 4 primary domain controller (PDC) to service network clients that do not have Active Directory client software installed and to replicate directory changes to any Windows NT backup domain controllers (BDCs) in the domain. For a Windows 2000 domain operating in native mode, the PDC emulator master receives preferential replication of password changes performed by other domain controllers in the domain and handles any password authentication requests that fail at the local domain controller. At any time, there can be only one PDC emulator in a particular domain.

peer

Any of the devices on a layered communications network that operate on the same protocol level.

permission

A rule associated with an object to regulate which users can gain access to the object and in what manner. *See also* object.

permissions inheritance

A mechanism that allows a given access control entry (ACE) to be copied from the container where it was applied to all children of the container. Inheritance can be combined with delegation to grant administrative rights to a whole subtree of the directory in a single update operation.

Pointer (PTR) resource record

A resource record used in a reverse lookup zone created within the in-addr.arpa domain to designate a reverse mapping of a host Internet Protocol (IP) address to a host Domain Name System (DNS) domain name.

policy

The mechanism by which desktop settings are configured automatically, as defined by the administrator. Depending on context, this can refer to Windows 2000 group policy, Windows NT 4 system policy, or a specific setting in a group policy object.

preferred bridgehead server

A computer with the appropriate bandwidth to transmit and receive information that you specify as a bridgehead server. *See also* bridgehead server.

preferred bridgehead server table
A table used to plan preferred bridgehead servers that includes the names of the domain controllers to be preferred bridgehead servers for each site.

primary DNS server
The authoritative server for a primary zone. A primary zone database file must be administered and maintained on the primary DNS server for the zone.

primary domain controller (PDC)
In a Microsoft Windows NT Server 4 or earlier domain, the computer running Windows NT Server that authenticates domain logons and maintains the directory database for a domain. The PDC tracks changes made to accounts of all computers in a domain. It is the only computer to receive these changes directly. A domain has only one PDC. In Windows 2000, one of the domain controllers in each domain is identified as the PDC for compatibility with Windows NT 4 and earlier versions of Windows NT. *See also* backup domain controller.

primary zone database file
The master zone database file. Changes to a zone, such as adding domains or hosts, are performed on the server that contains the primary zone database file.

pristine forest
An ideal Windows 2000 forest that is isolated from the Windows NT production environment and operates in native mode. *See also* domain restructure.

production environment
An organization's everyday computing environment.

Products and Customers Worksheet
A worksheet that can be used to analyze an organization's products and customers.

Q

query
A request for retrieval, modification, or deletion of specific data.

R

RDN
See relative distinguished name.

relative distinguished name (RDN)
The part of an object's distinguished name that is an attribute of the object itself. For most objects this is the Common Name attribute. For security principals, the default common name is the security principal name, also referred to as the SAM account name. For the distinguished name CN=MyName,CN=Users,DC=Microsoft,DC=Com, the relative distinguished name of the "MyName" user object is "CN= MyName". The relative distinguished name of the parent object is "CN=Users".

relative ID master
The domain controller assigned to allocate sequences of relative IDs to each domain controller in its domain. Whenever a domain controller creates a security principal (user, group, or computer object), the domain controller assigns the object a unique security ID. The security ID consists of a domain security ID that is the same for all security IDs created in a particular domain and a relative ID that is unique for each security ID created in the domain. At any time, there can be only one relative ID master in a particular domain.

replica

In Active Directory replication, a copy of a logical Active Directory partition that is synchronized through replication between domain controllers that hold copies of the same directory partition. "Replica" can also refer to the composite set of directory partitions held by any one domain controller. These are specifically called a directory partition replica and server replica, respectively.

replication

The process of copying data from a data store or file system to multiple computers to synchronize the data. Active Directory provides multimaster replication of the directory between domain controllers within a given domain. The replicas of the directory on each domain controller are writable. This allows updates to be applied to any replica of a given domain. The replication service automatically copies the changes from a given replica to all other replicas.

replication availability

A schedule assigned to the site link that indicates when the link is available for replication.

replication frequency

A value assigned to the site link that indicates the number of minutes Active Directory should wait before using a connection to check for replication updates.

replication topology

A description of the physical connections between replicas and sites.

replication transport

Provides the wire protocols required for data transfer during replication. Two default transports are supported in Windows 2000: Remote Procedure Call (RPC) over TCP/IP (referred to as "IP" in administrative tools) and Simple Mail Transport Protocol (SMTP).

Request for Comments (RFC)

An official document of the Internet Engineering Task Force (IETF) that specifies the details for protocols included in the TCP/IP family.

resource

Any part of a computer system or a network, such as a disk drive, printer, or memory, that can be allotted to a program or a process while it is running or can be shared over a local area network.

resource domain

In Windows NT, a trusting domain that establishes a one-way trust relationship with the master (account) domain, enabling users with accounts in the master domain to use resources in the resource domain. *See also* master domain.

resource record

The standard database record used in a zone to associate Domain Name System (DNS) domain names to related data for a given type of network resource, such as a host Internet Protocol (IP) address. Most of the basic resource record types are defined in RFC 1035, but additional resource record types have been defined in other Requests for Comments (RFCs) and approved for use with DNS.

restructure

See domain restructure.

reverse lookup

In the Domain Name System (DNS), a query process by which the Internet Protocol (IP) address of a host computer is searched to find its friendly DNS domain name.

RFC

See Request for Comments.

root domain

The domain at the top of the hierarchy, represented as a period (.). The Internet root domain is managed by several organizations, including Network Solutions, Inc.

S

SAM

See Security Accounts Manager.

schema

A description of the object classes and attributes stored in Active Directory. For each object class, the schema defines what attributes an object class must have, what additional attributes it may have, and what object class can be its parent. Active Directory schema can be updated dynamically. For example, an application can extend the schema with new attributes and classes and use the extensions immediately. Schema updates are accomplished by creating or modifying the schema objects stored in Active Directory. Like every object in Active Directory, a schema object has an access control list so that only authorized users can alter the schema.

schema attribute object

In Active Directory, a single property of an object. An object is described by the values of its attributes.

schema class object

A distinct, named set of attributes that represents a concrete object, such as a user, a printer, or an application. The attributes hold data describing the item that is identified by the directory object. Attributes of a user might include the user's given name, surname, and e-mail address. The terms *object class* and *class* are used interchangeably. The attributes that can be used to describe an object are determined by the content rules. For each object class, the schema defines what attributes an instance of the class must have and what additional attributes it might have.

schema master

The domain controller assigned to control all updates to the schema within a forest. At any time, there can be only one schema master in the forest.

schema modification plan

A group of planning documents that include a schema modification policy and an assessment of an organization's schema needs.

schema modification policy

A written plan created by an organization to administer schema modifications that affect the entire forest. The schema modification policy outlines who has control of the schema and how modifications are administered and should be created for each forest as part of the forest plan documents.

secondary DNS server
A backup DNS server that receives the primary zone database files from the primary DNS server in a zone transfer.

secondary master
An authoritative DNS server for a zone that is used as a source for replication of the zone to other servers. Secondary masters update their zone data only by transferring zone data from other DNS servers. They do not have the ability to perform zone updates.

secondary zone database file
A read-only replica of an existing standard primary zone database file stored in a standard text file on a secondary DNS server.

second-level domain
Domain name that is rooted hierarchically at the second tier of the domain namespace directly beneath the top-level domain name such as ".com" and ".org." When the DNS is used on the Internet, second-level domains are names, such as "microsoft.com," that are registered and delegated to individual organizations and businesses according to their top-level classification. The organization then assumes further responsibility for parenting management and growth of its name into additional subdomains.

Security Accounts Manager (SAM)
A Microsoft Windows 2000 service used during the logon process. SAM maintains user account information, including the list of groups to which a user belongs.

security group
A group that can be used to administer permissions for users and other domain objects.

security ID
See security identifier.

security identifier (SID)
A unique number that identifies a user, group, or computer account. Every account on your network is issued a unique SID when the account is first created. Internal processes in Windows 2000 refer to an account's SID rather than the account's user or group name. If you create an account, delete it, and then create an account with the same user name, the new account will not have the rights or permissions previously granted to the old account because the accounts have different SID numbers.

server
A computer that provides shared resources to network users.

service
A program, routine, or process that performs a specific system function to support other programs, particularly at a low (close to the hardware) level. When services are provided over a network, they can be published in Active Directory, facilitating service-centric administration and usage. Some examples of Windows 2000 services are Security Accounts Manager service, File Replication service, and Routing and Remote Access service.

Service (SRV) resource record
A resource record used in a zone to register and locate well-known TCP/IP services. The SRV resource record is specified in RFC 2052 and is used in Microsoft Windows 2000 or later to locate domain controllers for Active Directory.

share

To make resources, such as folders and printers, available to others.

shortcut trust

See cross-link trust.

SID

See security identifier.

Simple Mail Transfer Protocol (SMTP)

A protocol used on the Internet to transfer mail reliably and efficiently. SMTP is independent of the particular transmission subsystem and requires only a reliable, ordered, data stream channel.

site

One or more well-connected (highly reliable and fast) TCP/IP subnets. A site allows administrators to configure Active Directory access and replication topology quickly and easily to take advantage of the physical network. When users log on, Active Directory clients locate Active Directory servers in the same site as the user. *See also* subnet; well-connected.

site link

A link between two sites that allows replication to occur. Each site link contains the schedule that determines when replication can occur between the sites that it connects. *See also* site link cost; replication availability; replication frequency; replication transport.

site link bridge

The linking of more than two sites for replication using the same transport. When site links are bridged, they are transitive; that is, all site links for a specific transport implicitly belong to a single site link bridge for that transport. A site link bridge is the equivalent of a disjoint network. All site links within the bridge can route transitively, but they do not route outside of the bridge.

site link bridge table

A table used to plan site link transitivity disabling that includes the name of each site link bridge required and the name of the site links contained in the site link bridge.

site link cost

A value assigned to the site link that indicates the cost of the connection in relation to the speed of the link. Higher costs are used for slow links, and lower costs are used for fast links.

site link table

A table used to plan a site link configuration that includes the site link name, method of replication transport, site link cost, replication frequency, and replication availability for each site link.

site topology

A logical representation of a physical network.

site topology plan

A group of planning documents that represent the Active Directory site topology, which includes defining sites, placing domain controllers, defining a replication strategy, and placing global catalog servers and operations masters within a forest.

smart card

A credit card–sized device that is used with a PIN number to enable certificate-based authentication and single sign-on to the enterprise. Smart cards securely store certificates, public and private keys, passwords, and other types of personal information. A smart card reader attached to the computer reads the smart card. *See also* authentication.

SMTP

See Simple Mail Transfer Protocol.

soft skills

The ability to understand people and to communicate and collaborate with them in a diplomatic fashion.

staff representatives panel

A panel containing an exemplary staff member from each business unit or department within an organization that provides feedback in the design process.

standalone server

A computer that runs Microsoft Windows 2000 Server but does not participate in a domain. A standalone server has only its own database of users, and it processes logon requests by itself. It does not share account information with any other computer and cannot provide access to domain accounts.

Start of Authority (SOA) resource record

A record that indicates the starting point or original point of authority for information stored in a zone. The SOA resource record is the first resource record created when adding a new zone. It also contains several parameters used by other computers that use the Domain Name System (DNS) to determine how long they will use information for the zone and how often updates are required.

structural class

The only type of schema class object that can have instances in the directory. A structural class can be derived from either an abstract class or another structural class.

subdomain

A DNS domain located directly beneath another domain (the parent domain) in the namespace tree. For example, "example.microsoft.com" is a subdomain of the domain "microsoft.com." A subdomain is also called a child domain.

subnet

A portion of a network, which may be a physically independent network segment, that shares a network address with other portions of the network and is distinguished by a subnet number. A subnet is to a network what a network is to an internet.

subnet mask

A 32-bit value expressed as four decimal numbers from 0 to 255, separated by periods (for example, 255.255.0.0.). This number allows TCP/IP to distinguish the network ID portion of the IP address from the host ID portion.

T

technical environment
The manner in which an organization structures and manages its technical resources.

technical environment analysis document
A document that describes the current state of each technical environment component. When complete, this document can be distributed to each member of the design team, providing a starting point for discussion and assessing future needs.

Technical Standards Worksheet
A worksheet that can be used to analyze the conventions currently in place for the technical environment.

test environment
An environment that is a simulation of an organization's production environment and allows for the testing of parts of its Windows 2000 deployment, such as its Active Directory infrastructure design, without risk to the organization's network.

top-level domain
A domain that is rooted hierarchically at the first tier of the domain namespace directly beneath the root (.) of the DNS namespace. On the Internet, top-level domain names such as ".com" and ".org" are used to classify and assign second-level domain names (such as "microsoft.com") to individual organizations and businesses according to their organizational purpose.

topology
In Windows, the relationships among a set of network components. In the context of Active Directory replication, topology refers to the set of connections that domain controllers use to replicate information among themselves. *See also* domain controller; replication.

transitive trust
See implicit two-way transitive trust.

tree
A set of Windows NT domains connected via a two-way transitive trust, sharing a common schema, configuration, and global catalog. The domains must form a contiguous hierarchical namespace such that, for example, a.com is the root of the tree, b.a.com is a child of a.com, c.b.a.com is a child of b.a.com, and so on.

tree root domain
The highest-level domain in a tree.

trust path
A series of trust links from one domain to another, established for the purpose of passing authentication requests.

trust relationship
A logical relationship established between domains to allow pass-through authentication, in which a trusting domain honors the logon authentications of a trusted domain. User accounts and global groups defined in a trusted domain can be given rights and permissions in a trusting domain, even though the user accounts or groups don't exist in the trusting domain's directory. *See also* implicit two-way transitive trust; explicit one-way intransitive trust; authentication; domain.

U

Unicode
A standard encoding scheme used for representing text-based data. Unicode uses 2 bytes (16 bits) to represent each character, which allows 65,536 possible unique characters to be assigned. This number of possible character values enables almost all of the written languages of the world to be represented using a single character set.

universal group
A Windows 2000 group that is available only in native mode and valid anywhere in the forest. A universal group appears in the global catalog but contains primarily global groups from domains in the forest. This is the simplest type of group and can contain other universal groups, global groups, and users from anywhere in the forest. *See also* domain local group; forest; global catalog.

upgrade
See domain upgrade.

UPN
See user principal name.

user account
A record that consists of all the information that defines a user in the Windows 2000 network, including the user name and password required for the user to log on, the groups in which the user account has membership, and the rights and permissions the user has for using the computer and network and accessing their resources. For Windows 2000 Professional and member servers, user accounts are managed with the Local Users And Groups console. For Windows 2000 Server domain controllers, user accounts are managed with the Active Directory Users And Computers console.

user principal name (UPN)
A name consisting of a user account name (sometimes referred to as the user logon name) and a domain name identifying the domain in which the user account is located. This is the standard usage for logging on to a Windows 2000 domain. The format is user@domain.com (as in an e-mail address).

W

WAN
See wide area network.

well-connected
Sufficient connectivity to make your network and Active Directory useful to clients on your network. The precise meaning of *well-connected* is determined by your particular needs. *See also* site.

wide area network (WAN)
The extension of a data network that uses telecommunication links to connect to geographically separated areas. *See also* local area network.

Windows 2000 Advanced Server
A powerful departmental and application server that provides rich network operations system (NOS) and Internet services. Advanced Server supports large physical memories, clustering, and load balancing.

Windows 2000 Professional

A high-performance, secure network client computer and corporate desktop operating system that includes the best features of Microsoft Windows 98, while significantly extending the manageability, reliability, security, and performance of Windows NT Workstation 4. Windows 2000 Professional can be used alone as a desktop operating system, networked in a peer-to-peer workgroup environment, or used as a workstation in a Windows 2000 Server domain environment.

Windows 2000 Server

A file, print, and applications server, as well as a Web server platform that contains all of the features of Windows 2000 Professional plus many server-specific functions. This product is ideal for small to medium–sized enterprise application deployments, Web servers, workgroups, and branch offices.

Windows Internet Naming Service (WINS)

A software service that dynamically maps IP addresses to computer names (NetBIOS names). This allows users to access resources by name instead of requiring them to use IP addresses that are difficult to recognize and remember. WINS servers support clients running Windows NT 4 and earlier versions of Microsoft operating systems. *See also* Domain Name System (DNS).

Windows NT Domain Architecture Worksheet

A worksheet that can be used to analyze the organization's existing Windows NT domain architecture.

WINS

See Windows Internet Naming Service.

workgroup

A simple grouping of computers, intended only to help users find such resources as printers and shared folders within that group. Workgroups in Windows 2000 do not offer the centralized user accounts and authentication offered by domains.

Z

zone

In a DNS database, a zone is a contiguous portion of the DNS tree that is administered as a single separate entity by a DNS server. The zone contains resource records for all the names within the zone. *See also* domain; Domain Name System (DNS); DNS server.

zone database file

The file where name-to-IP-address mappings for a zone are stored.

zone replication

The synchronization of DNS data between DNS servers within a given zone.

zone transfer

The process by which Domain Name System (DNS) servers interact to maintain and synchronize authoritative name data. When a DNS server is configured as a secondary master for a zone, it periodically queries another DNS server configured as its source for the zone. If the version of the zone kept by the source is different, the secondary master server will pull zone data from its source DNS server to synchronize zone data. *See also* full zone transfer; incremental zone transfer; zone.

Index